TAX

David Williams is the Price W
tional Business Taxation in t
he works in the Centre for Commercial Law Studies at
Queen Mary and Westfield College. He is a lawyer who has
specialised in taxation for several years and he has written
several other books on tax, including *Tax for the Self-
employed*, *Trends in International Taxation* and *National
Insurance Contributions, Statutory Sick Pay and Statutory
Maternity Pay*.

TEACH YOURSELF

TAXATION

A GUIDE TO THEORY AND PRACTICE IN THE UK

David W. Williams

Hodder & Stoughton
LONDON SYDNEY AUCKLAND

British Library Cataloguing in Publication Data

Williams, David W.
   Taxation: Guide to Theory, Law and
   Practice in the United Kingdom. – (Teach
   Yourself Series)
   I. Title   II. Series
   336.240941

   ISBN 0-340-56826-7

First published 1992

Typeset by Rowland Phototypesetting Limited,
Bury St Edmunds, Suffolk.
Printed in Great Britain for the educational publishing
division of Hodder & Stoughton Limited, Mill Road, Dunton Green,
Sevenoaks, Kent by Clays Limited, St Ives plc.

CONTENTS

1
THE POLL TAX DISASTER

———————— **Introduction** ————————

One of the most significant government reforms in the late 1980s was the introduction of a new tax affecting every resident in Great Britain – the community charge or, as everyone called it, the poll tax. It was first charged in Scotland in 1989 and in England and Wales in 1990. It involved every British local authority in significant administrative changes, and brought many people not previously liable to local taxes into the tax net.

Yet by the 1992 general election the poll tax had been abandoned by the government that introduced it, and the laws necessary to secure its abolition were already in place. According to some critics, the tax had itself cost about 15 billion pounds to collect a sum not significantly greater than that and it had failed badly. Why did it fail? Why was it suggested? The poll tax was an experiment that provides fascinating evidence about what is good and bad about taxes, and about the ways governments collect taxes. That is the concern of this book. But what is a tax?

What is tax?

Taxation is fundamental to society as you and I know it. It is one of the most important aspects of any organised community throughout history. It is an essential aspect of what we call a 'state'. A government can only govern if it has resources, and nearly all governments find they are compelled to demand money to finance governmental operations. History also shows that sometimes people pay willingly, and sometimes they do not. If they do not, the government faces the choice of either making them pay, or running out of money.

That is what is meant by a tax: what the government makes us pay. Taxes are compulsory levies paid to government other than as payment for some specific service or as a penalty for some specific offence. The payments do not have to be of money – goods or free labour will have a similar effect for some purposes. The key aspect is that there is a legal compulsion to pay or to provide. This is a wide definition and we need to explore it later. But note that the one common element between taxes is that they are imposed by law.

Why tax?

There are only limited alternative ways in which a government can acquire the resources to govern. It can ask for, and receive, gifts. It can borrow, and it can print money. Alternatively, it can sell things or services.

Governments do all this, but a government gets little from genuine voluntary gifts, and there is a limit to how much any government can print or borrow before its economy starts to suffer from inflation. Likewise, it can sell anything it has to sell. In recent years a number of governments, including the British government, have made money by selling state property – privatisation or *destatisation* as it has been called. Equally, a state can lay claim to the natural resources of its territory and sell those – for example, oil in the North Sea has been claimed by, and then sold by, a number of European states. However, a state can only sell what it already owns or can claim as its own, and there are also limits to that. In addition, a government can sell its services – tourist, financial or protective services can all raise money. It can also impose compulsory loans on its citizens.

Only rarely will a state manage to meet its budget for more than a year or two with these sources. Some smaller oil states (such as Brunei) have done it, and so have some small islands which have made themselves tax havens, for example the Cayman Islands.

A complex society like Britain has to use the other means – compulsory contributions. At one time it could do this by demanding service. This was the essence of the feudal society of the early English state, where the king demanded services of his barons in exchange for land grants. Many states still demand that citizens undergo a period of compulsory military or state service. However, while compulsory service may help meet the task of defending a state, it does not meet the full needs of a modern state.

The cost of government

The scale of current public expenditure of the United Kingdom is immense. Recently, it has run at about £3,000 a year for every one of the 56 million or more people of the United Kingdom. Most of that goes on the social budget of the state: pensions, social security payments, education, the national health service, personal social services and public housing. Defence and law and order, the next biggest group of items, takes a little less than a quarter of the total. Then there is a long list of minor costs: roads, planning, support to industry and agriculture, research and development, supervision of industry, foreign relations, Northern Ireland and so on.

That is why taxes – and heavy taxes – are unavoidable, and why most people agree that at least some of the things that they are spent on are good. Few would agree that we should not only abolish the national health service and the state pension scheme but also the police and armed forces. However, unless we abolish all these, we need taxes. Yet taxation is often badly understood and subject to much criticism. There is, most of us would also agree, good taxation and bad taxation, even if we do not agree on what that means. Most people agreed that the poll tax was not good.

The poll tax disaster

The poll tax was one reason why Prime Minister Thatcher lost the support of her party prior to her resignation in 1990, perhaps the main reason. The policy behind the tax was reversed as soon as possible by her successor, and a replacement for the poll tax was put before Parliament within months of the poll tax first taking effect in England. The poll tax lasted only three years, but the political, economic and cultural damage it has caused is enormous.

Poll tax was a local tax, intended to replace another form of local tax, the rates. Rates (the 'general rate' was its proper title) dated back to 1601 as a way of raising money from the local population to provide finance for the poor. Its antiquity is something it has in common with many taxes. The adage that 'an old tax is a good tax' has a lot of truth in it from a political viewpoint. Change can be politically expensive. One leading American expert has estimated that for a tax reform to succeed you need to please four people for every one that you offend, in order not to be overwhelmed by the resistance to change. Many of those who benefit stay silent.

The general rate was a system which had survived so long because it was in essence simple and easy to enforce. The tax was payable by everyone who occupied land and buildings in the area being rated – recently the local district council's area.

What was wrong with rates?

There were many good things about the local rates. One was that there could be no argument about who was entitled to the tax. Either my house was in Blank's area, or it was not. Another was that it was very hard to avoid the tax. The land could not be hidden, and could be valued by independent officials well known to be largely non-corrupt whether the occupier wanted it valued or not. And if the tax was not paid, as a last resort either the occupier could be put in prison or the land could be seized – though that rarely happened. As a result, it was cheap to collect.

There were also a number of problems with the rates. One was that rates were the only form of local taxation. For many years before the introduction of poll tax, local expenditure had been rising steadily. There were several reasons for this. One was said to be (by the Conservatives) the spendthrift policies of left-wing councils. Another was said to be (by Labour councils) the increasing burden of local duties imposed on local councils.

At first, the increased cost locally did not matter because central government paid out heavy subsidies to help meet extra local costs. For example, the Home Office has long paid half the costs of local police forces (which are local costs met by local councils). Similarly, there were grants towards education costs (most of which are local costs).

The cost of local taxes

The Conservative government of the 1980s was elected to cut taxes. In part it tried to do this by cutting support to local government. Yet, the more it cut local support, the higher went the rates. Local government was perceived as getting worse, while local taxation was perceived as getting too heavy. Just how heavy it was in 1988 can be seen by reference to international comparisons. Since 1965 an international organisation based in Paris, the OECD (or Organisation for Economic Cooperation and Development), has kept detailed comparative statistics of the taxes collected by its members, the main developed states of the world, including the United Kingdom. Those statistics, published annually as *OECD Revenue Statistics* will be quoted a number of times in this book, because they give a good idea of how Britain compares with its neighbours.

When it came to the rates, the comparison was devastating. Rates are, in essence, a tax on property. In the league table of taxes on property, the United Kingdom has had the heaviest property taxes for many years past, and they had been getting steadily heavier. In 1988, more than 13 per cent of all United Kingdom taxation (including all social security contributions) was collected through the rates. No other country had taxes on property as high as this. Only two countries came anywhere near the British figures: the United States, which is a federation where property taxes are collected at state level, and Japan whose huge cosmopolitan areas are partly financed through a local property tax. What is more, for some years past all the main political parties had agreed that

— 5 —

rates were a bad thing. It did little to help those who were groaning at their rates bills to be told that politicians agreed that the tax was a bad tax.

Replacing the rates

There had been much discussion for many years about how to replace the rates. Many ideas had been proposed. There were a number of variants designed to replace the rates by what would be seen as a fairer property tax. Instead of imposing a tax on the ratable value, it could be charged on the capital value or some other base. It could reflect the number of residents or other aspects of property.

Alternatively, property tax could be replaced by another sort of tax. Reformers looked for examples elsewhere in the world, and found many other forms of local taxation. In the United States of America, many states have local sales taxes, adding perhaps 5 per cent to prices in the local shops. This could be applied to all goods or just some kinds of goods.

Another idea, still popular with some, was the local income tax. This could arise in two ways. One, as used in Germany, is to impose one income tax, but to share its proceeds in an agreed way between the federal government and the Länder, or regions. In Germany, the sharing procedure is written into the constitution, and is therefore protected. Local income tax is also used in the United States, for example in New York and other big cities. An extra percentage of tax is added to the federal income tax, but paid to the state or city authorities. For this reason, the rate of income tax actually paid by people varies from one state to another. This also happens in Sweden, where most of the income tax is paid locally, and the national rate is low. These ideas were, however, unlikely to be attractive to a government that had established its reputation on cutting income tax, and which would not agree a budget-sharing arrangement with local councils.

———————— The wrong solution ————————

Enter the poll tax (stage right). Once the emotion has gone from the subject, there will be fascinating historical research to be done in deciding just who first supported the idea of the poll tax within public circles, and who sold the idea to whom, when and why. We can say little at the moment, because of the combined effect of political expediency, party loyalty and official secrecy. Who took the decisions does not now matter. *Why* did they do so?

The poll tax, its supporters argued, had several important virtues absent from the rates and from other forms of property tax. It was therefore a 'good' tax where property taxes were bad. What is more, the aspects of the poll tax which made it 'good' were aspects which could be used by the government to reinforce its own policy objectives.

What is a poll tax? It is the simplest of taxes. The word 'poll' is an old word meaning 'head', and the poll tax is a very old form of tax levied on each person present at the time the tax is imposed in the area to be taxed. It was the tax being levied at the time of the birth of Christ, by the Romans, requiring everyone to return to their home areas to be taxed.

In principle, the 'community charge' was as simple as any other poll tax. Everyone over the age of 18 had to pay a poll tax to the district council in whose area the person's only or main home was located. The tax was to be collected on the basis that the person lived in the same place throughout the year.

Reasons for the new tax

A major aim of the poll tax was to ensure that everyone paid local tax. This was to prevent the problem occurring with rates, where, in some areas, only a minority of citizens paid any local tax. For this reason, the social security benefit rules were changed so that the poor only received poll tax relief (known as community charge benefit) for 80 per cent of the poll tax. They were required to pay the other 20 per cent. Similarly, it was made clear that all students and young earners still living at home had to pay. Because of pressure, students and some nurses were allowed to pay only 20 per cent of the standard poll tax.

There was much argument about whether the poll tax should be flat rate or related to income. The government announced that it would be a flat rate tax, despite precedents going back several centuries where the rich paid a higher poll tax than the poor. Arguments that the poll tax should

again reflect wealth were rejected, partly because otherwise the fundamental principle that everyone had to pay might be lost. It was also
because the tax was designed to put pressure on voters so that they
would in turn put pressure on their local councils to keep the poll tax low.
The only concessions made to this principle were for students, nurses,
those receiving social security benefits, and others such as prisoners.
The police and armed forces whose rates had been paid by others now
had to pay direct.

Administrative problems

It was here that the administrative problems of the poll tax started.
There were to be many more taxpayers than ratepayers. The sheer cost
of sending tax notices to everyone required all local councils to invest in
major computer systems. Further, people, unlike houses, tend to move
around to the extent that it could not be assumed that people were living
in the same place throughout the year. So the tax had to be imposed on a
daily basis. This itself required even more bureaucracy, because a sort of
running census had to be maintained of where everyone over the age of
18 was living. This demanded even more computer technology.

Another problem that could be ignored in days gone by was the growth in
two-home families. In some areas as many as one house in ten is owned
by someone whose main home is elsewhere. Those local councils did not
complain, because rates were paid, but were they to lose out under the
poll tax? To prevent them doing so, a 'standard' community charge or
house tax was imposed on second homes. The other side of this problem
was those who had no homes. Where should they pay their poll tax? One
answer was to levy the tax on hostels. The other – almost unenforceable
– is that poll tax was due on a daily basis whenever anyone slept in a
building in the area that night. Only those sleeping out of doors and with
no home escaped.

Through these means answers were found to all the key questions about
imposing the tax. But there were more complications to come. First, the
government tried to use the introduction of the poll tax to cut the subsidy
to local government while at the same time putting the blame on local
councils for the high cost of local expenditure. The aim was to cut local

expenditure, and so cut both the local taxes and central government subsidies. This failed completely as a policy. Local councils in some areas found that the central government subsidy was cut so sharply that they were forced into large increases in the local taxes. In other areas, local councils used the opportunity to put up local taxes for other purposes, while persuading the local electorate that this was the government's fault, not theirs.

Second, many people became exposed to paying local taxes for the first time against a background of complaints about central government imposing the tax. For example, those on social security, students, and people living in someone else's home (parents, children) became liable for tax for the first time. Others, particularly council tenants, who had previously had their rates paid with the rent, now had to pay it separately. And in nearly every area, despite a campaign waged by government to try and keep the tax down, the full poll tax payable was several hundred pounds. Much publicity was given to Wandsworth – a stable and prosperous area of London – because it kept its poll tax down to £140. A few miles away the poll tax was more than £500 a year.

Opposition to the tax

The introduction of the poll tax had been a major political event, but there was considerable opposition to the tax on both political and practical grounds from local councils of all parties, and from the opposition parties in particular. This turned spontaneously into a campaign to 'stop the poll tax'. That took two forms: a campaign aimed at getting local councils not to set a poll tax, and a campaign to stop people paying their poll tax. As the chief way of ensuring that the local council knew who was to pay the tax was the poll tax register, one element in this campaign was to try to stop local councils finding out who should be on the register.

The level of political opposition to the tax was itself damagingly high. At the time councils were introducing the tax, there was a series of well-publicised demonstrations. These reached their peak (or nadir, depending on your point of view) with riots in Trafalgar Square that left severe damage, some injury and a rather battered London being watched with some surprise by other Western governments.

Do not pass 'Go': Do not collect £200

The government had anticipated trouble in enforcing the tax, and the law imposing the tax contained sweeping powers to get the tax enforced and collected. For this reason, there was little chance of a local council not complying with the obligation on it to set a poll tax – although some left it literally until the last minute. But getting individuals to comply was another matter.

By reference to the tax collected, the poll tax was a disaster. No one knows how many people managed to evade the tax by ensuring that their names did not appear on the local poll tax register. Some idea of the extent of evasion can be gained from local electoral registers. Although all sorts of assurances were given that putting your name on the electoral register to vote and putting your name on the poll tax register were two different things, many people have probably disappeared – in the legal sense – by not registering on either.

Go direct to jail

It was estimated in several areas that the number of electors listed had dropped by more than ten per cent, even though the population had gone up. Many others, properly registered, refused to pay their poll tax as a matter of principle – and this was encouraged by some members of parliament refusing to do so even when sent to prison for this. Others again paid only part of their tax, or paid it late, or paid it in irregular amounts so as to confuse the collectors. And others, more than six million, failed to pay until they were subject to a court summons to do so.

The immediate effect of non-payment was severe. The government was forced to lend local authorities large sums of money, and to pay grants early, to stop their running out of funds. From the start the effect cumulated, and the tax started to collapse in on itself. Although there are problems introducing most innovations, things usually quieten down quickly, and the problems are forgotten. This has been true over many interferences with freedom such as compulsory seat belts and crash helmets, parking meters and so much more. But continuing problems with local council finance and the effort in collecting the tax ensured that the row over the poll tax did not go away.

The tax was introduced in England and Wales in 1990. In the same year Mrs

Thatcher, Prime Minister for a decade, was challenged for the leadership of her party. After a tussle in which opponents within her own party made it clear that they did not approve of the poll tax, she resigned her post. It was generally felt at the time that her personal responsibility for securing the adoption of the poll tax was a major reason why she had to go.

Poll tax rejected

Her successor, working with another candidate for her post, rapidly used the change of leadership to announce that the poll tax would be replaced. As a first stage towards alleviating the problems, the government announced, in the 1991 budget, a complete reversal of the previous philosophy. Instead of the poll tax resulting in a reduction of central support, it was dramatically increased by about £140 a person. This was funded by an increase in the rate of VAT from 15 per cent to 17.5 per cent, or so the Chancellor announced.

Secondly, the government announced that the poll tax would be replaced in 1993 by a new local tax – though how was not at that time clear. Indeed, one suspects that the only thing that was decided at the time was that the poll tax had to go.

Although the reduction of poll tax should have helped persuade people to pay, the reverse effect occurred. In some areas, local authorities found that 20 per cent of the new level of poll tax was not worth collecting, so all those brought in by the new rules were quietly let off. For many others, the fact that the government agreed that the poll tax was a bad idea merely reaffirmed their determination not to pay.

And as the poll tax entered its third year in 1992, a further problem emerged. So great was the level of non-payment that councils were having to surcharge poll tax bills to meet the costs of default in previous years. Those who had obeyed the law were now being penalised to cover for those who had refused to pay. The stage was set for a new level of protest – those who were prepared to pay their own taxes, but did not see why they should pay the default costs.

Even at this stage, further complications kept emerging. The courts had been overwhelmed for months with summons and orders to compel poll taxpayers to pay. But, it appeared at the beginning of 1992, the legal process used in most courts for these summonses had been illegal. Courts had relied on computer generated lists of non-payers and had not provided proper evidence of non-payment. Court proceedings stopped throughout England and Wales while the law was checked, only re-starting when provision was made to 'correct' the law.

What went wrong?

At that point, we can leave the story. In due course we will forget the poll tax, but will we be able to repair the damage it has done, and will we forget the lessons? The poll tax was a failure – more than that, it was a disaster. It is difficult to be unemotive about the scale of disruption of local activities that it caused.

For all that, the original idea was thought by many to be a good one, and there were interesting policy arguments in its favour. It was simple to understand and to impose. It involved everyone. It was easy to see who was liable for the tax, and difficult to avoid or evade. It was democratic, and it was local. So, what went wrong? Was the poll tax idea a bad one, however it had been implemented, or was it a good idea that went wrong? The more general questions are those we try to answer in the next chapters, but an initial verdict is simply that it was seen by taxpayers as a 'bad' tax.

2

GOOD AND BAD TAXES

———————— **First principles** ————————

Contemporary discussion of what good and bad taxes are still refers to some axioms laid down by the great economist Adam Smith in his *Wealth of Nations* in 1776. Smith, who has been credited with inventing the income tax even though his main job was collecting customs and excise duties, thought deeply about how taxes should be imposed, and his rules still hold good today. His own versions of the key rules are below.

'The subjects of every state ought to contribute towards the support of the government, as nearly as possible, in proportion to their respective abilities; that is, in proportion to the revenue which they respectively enjoy under the protection of the state.'

'The tax which each individual is bound to pay ought to be certain and not arbitrary.'

'Each tax ought to be levied at the time, or in the manner, it is most likely to be convenient for the contributor to pay it.'

'Every tax ought to be so contrived as both to take out and to keep out of the pockets of the people as little as possible over and above what it brings into the public treasury of the state.'

Each of these rules contains considerable wisdom, and is worth exploring. The first refers to what is often called the *equity* of a tax, or its fairness. Many felt that the poll tax was fair, because everyone paid it. Adam Smith suggests that is not what he meant by fair – it would have been fair if the rich had paid more than the poor.

The second rule is that the tax is *certain and not arbitrary*. This covers several things. First, the tax liability must be clearly laid down, not just made up by an official on a whim. But the rule also means that taxpayers know that everyone is going to pay the tax. The fastest way to ensure that someone does not pay his or her tax is to make it clear that 'everyone else' is not paying. There must be certainty of collection – and here the poll tax also failed despite Draconian powers designed to prevent avoidance. A third element of certainty is that people know what the tax is about. Poll tax is clear, but income tax and, for many people, VAT are not.

Smith's third test refers to *convenience of payment*. Here again, the poll tax failed for many people. Large groups of people had either had their rates paid through their council rents or through social security. Others had it paid by their employers. The policy of making people pay their own poll tax directly was deliberate – the government took the calculated gamble that the inconvenience of payment would cause taxpayers to pressurise their local councils into lowering the amount of tax. It failed. Other taxes show how wise this rule can be – the inheritance tax is the easiest of taxes on this basis because the person who, in effect, pays is the person who has just died!

Smith's fourth test was also failed by the poll tax. He wisely stated that taxes should be as *efficient* as possible. Nowadays we would look to that *efficiency* in two ways. First, the costs of collection should be as low as possible both for tax authorities and taxpayers. In the case of the poll tax, the cost on local authorities has been high because of the need for computers, and because of the need to take court proceedings against so many.

The second, broader aspect of this test is that the tax is economically efficient, that is, it is *neutral* in its effect on people's behaviour. It does not make them do things they would not otherwise do, or stop them doing what they were intending to do, unless that is the intention of the tax. The high tax on spirits has the effect of making us drink less, and the tax on tobacco should help us stop smoking. What of the poll tax? It should have been neutral but the evidence suggests it was not – that is why people stopped registering to vote and, perhaps, also with their local doctors, social security offices and elsewhere.

Equity and efficiency

Of these tests, two involve major issues of principle that any tax design must take into account. They are *equity* and *efficiency*. The principle of equity argues that a tax should be fair. The principle of efficiency argues that it should be economically neutral. In practice, the two principles often clash: fairness suggests that the rich should pay more, and efficiency suggests they should not.

———— When is a tax fair? ————

Both supporters and opponents of the poll tax said that a major reason for their view was that the tax was (or was not) fair. Cynics thinking of this are sometimes reminded of the old rhyme about the fairness of communism:

> A Communist's fair
> For he's always willing
> To give you his sixpence
> And pocket your shilling.

In other words, if he gives you everything he has, and you give him everything you have, that's fair. Needless to say, the wealthier you are, the less likely you are to agree with that sentiment. But, in a more roundabout way, that is how Adam Smith judged fairness. As Marx himself put it: 'from each according to his abilities, to each according to his needs.' Did Marx and Smith really agree on basic tax policy?

In an attempt to get nearer to a clear statement of what is fair, the problem can be divided into two. First, we should examine the position of all those who are at the same level – *horizontal equality*. The proposition is that people in equal positions should both pay equally and benefit equally from the state.

But what is equality? If you and I live next door to each other in identical houses on the same road in the same local authority and have the same number of people of the same age living at home, are we equal? Does it matter that my income is twice your income? (and would your answer be the same if I said instead that your income was twice my income?). Those arguing about the poll tax might say both yes and no.

Those saying yes would argue that we were equal because we were receiving equal services and benefits from the local councils. Fairness means that we should be treated alike in terms of having our dustbins cleared, the availability of local places in the schools, and so forth. If we are not treated alike, that is unfair. Therefore, we should be paying the same taxes towards the cost of our local councils. It is also why, if the rates are higher across the street, that may also be fair, because the council with the higher taxes is providing more services. This is known as the *benefit theory* of taxation, that it is fair that we should pay in accordance with the services we may receive. It is, in Britain, used to justify graduated National Insurance contributions. Those who pay more get bigger state pensions on retirement.

Those saying that we are not equal because one of us earns twice what the other earns are looking not at what we gain, but at what we can afford. This is the *ability to pay theory* of taxation. This is the argument of Marx and of Smith, at least superficially. But even here there are sharp differences in the consequences of the argument. The logic of the Smithian position is that if you earn twice as much as I do, and we are otherwise identical in our positions, then you should pay twice as much as I do.

Second, what if my income is below the poverty line, and I can barely afford to pay anything? Should not you pay more than twice what I pay? This is where we must look at *vertical equity*. We must try to draw some views on how much more, if any, the rich should pay than the poor.

Those who follow the argument of Smith would argue that tax should be *proportional* – indeed, that is the word he uses. But others argue that the tax system should be *progressive* – the more you have, the more relatively you should pay. In practice, different taxes follow different approaches. The income tax has traditionally been regarded as a tax that should be progressive, with increasing rates. At one time, that was taken to extremes: an individual with a high unearned income faced a top tax rate of 98 per cent, while the main rate was below 40 per cent, and lower rates went down to 25 per cent. Currently the rate scales are much flatter, with a main rate of 25 per cent, a top rate of 40 per cent, and no lower rate. National Insurance contributions and VAT are, for most people, proportional. One is imposed at 9 per cent of what they earn beyond a minimum level. The other is imposed at 17.5 per cent of much of what they spend. If you earn, or spend, more, the tax rises evenly with the extra money.

By contrast, the benefit theory of taxation tends to produce a different pattern, that of *regressive taxation* where the poor pay relatively more. The poll tax was regressive insofar as it charged most people the same amount of tax. So is the television licence fee.

Which is better, a progressive or a regressive tax? We can only answer that question if we also can answer two other questions:

(a) why is the tax being imposed?
(b) what other taxes are also being imposed?

—————— Why impose taxes? ——————

The answer is usually assumed to be: to raise money for government. That is the main reason – but it is not the only one. Indeed, some taxes operate very effectively without raising any money at all. For many years, much of the public revenues were derived from customs duties or, as they are sometimes called, protective duties. Some customs duties are low, and are designed as revenue earners. But others are – and always have been – high. They are designed to deter importers. The ideal tax for that purpose would be one that stopped imports, although that would mean no duty!

Nowadays the power to levy customs duties in the European Community belongs not to the member states but to the Community itself. Nevertheless, the Community has power to impose what are called anti-dumping duties. If it is thought that another country is exporting goods to the Community too cheaply, a special customs duty can be imposed on the goods to neutralise the subsidy. This has been done, controversially, on a number of goods from both the United States and from South East Asia.

In days gone by, these taxes could be much sharper, and they could penalise imports to favour home products. The Scotch Whisky Association long alleged that this was true of some foreign taxes on their products, compared with those of foreign rivals.

Using taxes to influence people

The purpose of customs duties is to influence behaviour – to interfere with the behaviour of customers by affecting the price structure of the market.

The idea of using taxes to influence behaviour is an old one. It can be aimed at either people or businesses, depending on the kind of effect desired. In the case of individuals, taxes can be used both to discourage and to encourage people buying certain goods or services. People are, arguably, discouraged by high taxes, and are encouraged by tax subsidies. This is one of the arguments for high taxes on cigarettes and on alcohol. It was the argument used in 1991 when the Chancellor of the Exchequer imposed a tax on mobile telephones. It is also the argument of those proposing environmental taxes.

There is one problem about these examples: they are all goods which are in practice *inelastic*, that is, their sales are not affected very much by price. That is why they can be taxed so heavily. In Britain, the taxes on tobacco raise billions of pounds. If the Chancellor really did believe we would stop smoking just because of the taxes, he would have a lot of tax to find somewhere else!

Tax is used in other ways to influence people's behaviour, and with some success. One example is the creation of PEPs (personal equity plans) designed to encourage people to invest in stocks and shares by giving them tax relief on the income from investments. Considerable amounts of money have been invested in this way, giving a certain stability to personal investment of this form.

But the way we behave may be altered by taxes without this really being the intention. There are two major examples in Britain. The first is the tax exemption (except for local taxes) for our homes. The second is the tax exemption for our pension funds. These are both more generous than equivalent reliefs in other European countries, and it is not surprising to note that we invest more in our homes and our pensions than our neighbours do. That perhaps makes us more cautious and less likely to move than our neighbours. Why are we encouraged to do these things? This is where politics feature again. We vote for the parties that give us these tax reliefs, and against those that take them away. What is wrong with that? Some would say it makes us less competitive than our neighbours, and therefore, as a nation, poorer. They would argue that our taxes should be neutral – that they should be designed not to influence our behaviour. (When the chips are down, politicians near to elections tend not to agree.)

Redistribution of wealth

Another major aim of taxation is to redistribute wealth. In a fair society, it is argued, we should use the tax system to make sure that the poorest receive some help from those who are better off. To that extent, we must ensure that the system is not just proportional, it must be progressive. The poorer we are, the more we should receive. The richer we are, the more we should pay.

Those sentiments are hard to argue with, when stated in the abstract, but they are extremely hard to achieve in practice. This is because of the effect of marginal rates of tax.

Assume you earn £1,000, and the tax rate is 25 per cent. You receive £750 for each £1,000 you earn. You probably grumble, but you are unlikely not to earn another £1,000 just because you will only receive three-quarters of it. But what if the tax rate is 75 per cent? Are you going to bother to earn another £1,000 if you only receive £250? There are two answers to this. First, you may decide that there could be a better way of spending your time. You would rather *substitute* other activities for money earning. Alternatively, you will go out and earn more money – £3,000 – instead of just £1,000 so that you will end up £750 better off. This argument is that the tax has an *additive* effect on your efforts.

In a world of theory, you might do either of these things, but you will probably start by doing one and end up doing the other! Take the argument to its logical extreme. This is the position where, whatever our initial levels of income are, we all end up receiving the same from the state. That may, in the view of some, be completely fair, but it is remarkably inefficient. However, would you bother to go out and work harder, if every penny you earned was removed in tax? I doubt it, unless you are either a workaholic or your job is fun and provides its own satisfaction. Unfortunately, for most of us that is not the case. The net result of applying tax at a marginal rate of 100 per cent is, arguably, that everyone earning more than the average amount would stop work. The logic of that position goes on until everyone is earning the same as everyone else – nothing. Then they will all be equal! Is that fair?

That argument sounds rather far-fetched, because, you may feel, no one gets taxed at anything like those rates. In fact, some do. And those that do are frequently earning less than many of us. They are the ones caught in the *poverty trap*. Put yourself in the position where you are earning £100, but you have several children and are receiving family credit plus other means-tested benefits such as free school dinners for the children, housing benefit and poll tax benefit. If your pay goes up, you will get caught quite heavily because from every pound you earn you may lose tax at 25 per cent and National Insurance contributions at 9 per cent. You also lose benefit which was at the rate of more than half the amount you earn. You will only receive the advantage of, say, £2.50 of your extra £10 – an effective total tax rate of 75 per cent. Are you better off working harder or helping out at home with the children? Pride may make you work harder, but is that fair?

The aim of the system is, inevitably, a compromise. Taking taxes and social security together, the poor, disabled, young and old are helped at a cost to the wealthy, healthy workers. But is that necessarily redistribution?

Looked at more closely, there are two operations that can take place at the same time. The first is that people benefit at certain times of their lives and pay at other times. That is what happens under the National Insurance contributions system. This also happens with the state-provided student loans that are steadily replacing student grants. These make sure that a student pays the cost of his or her time at college, rather than other people.

The other operation is the true redistribution, taking money from those who are relatively better off and transferring it to the poorer members of our society. Inheritance tax does this, as do the stamp duty we pay on buying land and capital gains tax. The poor will never pay any of these taxes, and the rich get no advantage from having to pay them, or so it is argued. Even there, other arguments can be considered. The rich do gain something by the transfer of resources to the poor. For a start, that money goes back into the economy that has most probably been the source of the rich person's wealth. Looked at another way, it increases the security of the life of the rich and, perhaps, their relative feeling of well-being.

Should taxes be used to even out our lifetime patterns of income and expenditure, and should they be used to help the poor? There is no right answer to give here to either of those questions. Different religions and philosophies, different personal histories and characters, different times and places will all lead to different answers. It is part of the richness of our experience that we do not all agree on these things. The current answers provided by the British system are explored in Chapter 7.

At any one time, our system provides not a perfect answer but a practical one, and furnishes a balance between the arguments that taxes should influence behaviour or should be neutral. In most societies, it is not an easy answer, because the tax system itself is complex. For differing reasons of history, politics, culture and ideal, a modern state will raise its tax revenues in many ways, and dispense them in many ways. Its political masters will be seeking to shift the system a bit towards their own ideals (or those of their voters), but will never quite succeed.

For a full flavour of this process, we look in the next chapter at how the British tax system has emerged from centuries of history and clashing ideals, and we will then look at the choice which faces the modern legislator of taxes. Before we do, we must first look at the different kinds of taxes that can be imposed, for even this is not simple. For that purpose, it is helpful to have a simple way of analysing a tax.

———————— Anatomy of a tax ————————

Taxes of all kinds (i.e. any kind of compulsory levy) consist of rules defining three aspects of the tax:

1 the tax base

2 the taxpayer

3 the tax incidence

By *tax base* we mean the thing which is taxed, the *taxpayer* being the person who will have to pay the tax on that thing. The 'thing' may vary from the purchase of a packet of cigarettes to a year's earnings from work.

In the case of the poll tax, uniquely, the tax base **is** the taxpayer! With any other tax, we must identify separately what is taxed and who is to pay. Once we have done that, we need only identify the *incidence* of the tax. This consists of two elements: the rate of tax and the occasion when the tax is payable. In the case of cigarettes, the incidence is a set amount of tax on each packet when it is bought by a consumer. In the case of earnings, it is the income tax paid on each pound of earnings added up over a year, and so on.

Anything can be the subject of taxes – from wigs to slaves, from windows to matches to people. How we tax these different bases will depend on who we define as the taxpayer and how we define the incidence. Broadly, we can tax in two ways: we can impose taxation on the tax base at a set amount regardless of the identity of the taxpayer; or we can take the taxpayer into account.

Income tax, along with capital gains tax, corporation tax and National Insurance contributions, takes into account the identity of the taxpayer. These taxes collect the money direct from the taxpayer on whom the tax is imposed, and take into account, to some extent, the level of earnings to decide the incidence. These taxes are called *direct taxes*.

Other taxes are not aimed directly at taxpayers, although they will end up paying them indirectly. VAT, for example, is legally charged to the shopkeeper, although the customer ends up paying it in most cases. Broadly, we pay the same amount of tax on a telephone bill of the same level, or on a bar of chocolate, however well off we are. Other taxes are flat-rate, such as the tax on a litre of fuel or the cost of a gun licence or a passport, again regardless of who we are. These are *indirect taxes.*

We noted earlier in the discussion that some taxes are progressive, some proportional and some regressive. Broadly, the direct taxes are the progressive ones, while the indirect taxes may be either proportional or regressive. There may be exceptions, such as the luxury tax which is only paid by the rich, or the flat-rate income tax, but these are less usual.

The British tax system is made from a mixture of taxes broadly divided between the direct taxes and the indirect taxes. With three dozen different taxes at work, and for many individuals also several kinds of social security benefit, the picture is very complicated. Two points stand out: first, the general burden of taxation on all of us; second, to what extent that burden is shared evenly, or is brought down more heavily on some groups of taxpayer or beneficiary.

The burden of taxation

It is difficult to say when taxes are 'heavy'. Perhaps it is when the taxpayers take to the streets rather than pay. In practice, that would be a faulty guide because it measures not the intensity of taxation but its unacceptability. A 'light' tax may be unacceptable because of the way it is collected, because of who is collecting it or because of where it is going. When the Patriots in Boston chose to protest against the tea tax imposed from London by the Boston Tea Party in 1773, it was not the weight of tax that they were protesting against – it was only 2.5 per cent, a mere £400 a year to the whole colony. It was the symbolism of the tax which represented the absent ruler from England who incurred Bostonian hatred. When John Hampden earned his place in English history as the person who, when confronted by the full majesty of the law, refused to pay the ship money to King Charles, the amount that went unpaid was a mere 20 shillings.

At the opposite extreme, war taxes (the ship money was allegedly a war tax) imposed for popular wars find willing payers despite absorbing a huge share of the state's efforts. Thankfully, the United Kingdom has not had to resort to a war economy in the second half of the 20th century, and the burdens that encumbered it from the two world wars of the first half of the century have been inherited but not increased.

None the less, the burden of taxation in the United Kingdom has, in the last few years, been at levels only previously seen under conditions of war.

Measuring the weight of taxes

To make a statement such as that in the last paragraph, that we are heavily taxed, we need an independent measure. One that has been widely used in recent years is to compare the proceeds of tax collections with the total economic effort of the state. This can be measured by taking the total tax revenues and comparing them with the total value of the productive capacity of a country over a set period (usually a year).

THE BRITISH TAX BURDEN
(total tax as a percentage share of GDP)

1955	29.8
1960	28.5
1965	30.4
1970	37.0
1975	35.7
1980	35.4
1985	38.0
1989	36.3

(*Source: OECD 1990*)

The measure often used for productive capacity is *GDP – gross domestic product*. It is the total value of all goods and services produced by a country over, say, one year, valued on the basis of the value of all final supplies of consumer goods and services and capital goods, measured by reference to their market value. Income from overseas investments is ignored. (The equivalent measure where it is included, used sometimes for comparison purposes, is the *GNP – gross national product –* which also excludes, as compared with GDP, the income earned in the country being measured which is remitted abroad.) GDP is also used as a means of making comparisons between states.

A standard measure of the burden of taxation has, therefore, become the measure of the total tax revenue from all sources of taxation against total GDP at market prices. This measure is taken annually on an internationally comparative basis by the OECD and other international agencies. The figures in the box above show that the burden of taxation in the United Kingdom has risen markedly during the last 35 years, but that most of the rise occurred in the late 1960s. Since 1975, the total tax burden has neither risen nor fallen sharply.

THE HIGH TAX LEAGUE (as per cent of GDP) 1988

1 Sweden	55	**13 UK**	**37**
2 Denmark	52	14 Italy	37
3 Netherlands	48	15 Greece	36
4 Norway	47	16 Portugal	35
5 Belgium	45	17 Canada	34
6 France	44	18 Spain	33
7 Luxembourg	43	19 Switzerland	33
8 Austria	42	20 Iceland	32
9 Ireland	42	21 Japan	31
10 New Zealand	38	22 Australia	31
11 Finland	38	23 USA	30
12 Germany	37	24 Turkey	23

(*Source: OECD 1990*)

The overall rise in our tax burden should not surprise us, as there have been increases in most other states in the same period. However, the amounts of increases have varied significantly. In the 1960s, when the then government was increasing taxes, the example often quoted was that of Sweden. The Swedes had a tax burden lower than ours in 1955 at 25.5 per cent of GDP (they had minimal war costs to meet). This increased sharply, overtaking ours, between 1960 and 1965, and went on rising until last year. By 1989 this had reached 56.8 per cent of GDP, almost double the burden in 1955. By that time, not only had Sweden succeeded in placing itself firmly at the top of the high tax league in terms of the burden on the GDP but also in terms of actual cash spent per person. But its economy was feeling the strain. Since 1989, even the Swedish government has seen the need to cut taxes.

THE HIGH TAX LEAGUE ($ per person) 1988

(EC states in **bold**)

1	Sweden	11900	**12 Belgium**	**7000**
2	**Denmark**	**10900**	13 Canada	6500
3	Norway	10200	14 USA	5700
4	Switzerland	8958	**15 UK**	**5400**
5	**Luxembourg**	**8700**	**16 Italy**	**5400**
6	Finland	8100	17 Australia	4900
7	**France**	**7500**	18 New Zealand	4800
8	**Netherlands**	**7400**	**19 Ireland**	**3800**
9	Japan	7400	**20 Spain**	**2900**
10	**Germany**	**7300**	**21 Greece**	**1900**
11	Austria	7000	**22 Portugal**	**1500**

(*Source: OECD 1990*)

By contrast, the United States had a tax burden of 23.6 per cent of GDP in 1955, lower than that of the UK, and a little lower than that of Sweden. This rose, by about 1970, to 29 per cent and has stayed there for the last 20 years. In cash terms, the US tax bill per person are higher than this suggests because of the relative growth in the American economy. Many feel that taxes in the USA should be higher than they now are. This is because of the recurring fiscal deficit (that is, excess government expenditure in relation to government income) which has caused the USA to borrow large sums of money just to finance its ongoing levels of government activity. However, political pressures keep taxes down.

A major difference between Sweden and the USA that has emerged during the period from 1955 to 1990 is the strong support for the disadvantaged in Sweden while the disparity in income levels in the USA is very sharp. Figures published in 1992 show that the top one per cent of US residents receive 60 per cent of total income.

The UK position

The other general observation that may be made on a comparative basis is that the United Kingdom keeps itself about half-way, or further down, on the lists of high-taxing states. The two lists in the boxes above show the latest available comparative league tables prepared by the OECD. In the most-often quoted league table, using the comparison with national GDP, the United Kingdom finds itself almost exactly at the half-way mark on the league table of the OECD member states, in 13th place. In 1955, the UK was in 4th place, and it has slowly drifted down to its current more lowly position.

This position looks comfortable when it is noted that the United Kingdom is in much the same position as Germany, with the United States, Switzerland and Japan all below. This does not look quite so soothing when we look at the position of the United Kingdom in another league table that the OECD produces – a comparison of the amount of taxation collected per inhabitant in the OECD states. In this second table, Switzerland and Japan are much higher than the UK, with the USA also firmly ahead. This is because of the greater GDP per person of those economies.

The one state that appears near to the UK in both tables is Italy. By coincidence it was in a similar position in 1955, but some say that this is where the comparison ends. In 1989, its tax burden as part of GDP had risen above that of the United Kingdom. However, it does suggest a pause for thought. During the 1980s the United Kingdom enjoyed a period of 'strong' government. This was regularly contrasted with the weak government of Italy (indeed, on occasions it had no government at all in any effective sense). This was because of the different electoral systems of the two states. Did Britain really benefit, and Italy really suffer, because of those differences in the 35 years from 1955 or over the ten years from 1980? These figures do not clearly suggest it.

It may be that the political systems of states do influence their overall tax pattern. The states which are most heavily taxed are the smaller unitary states such as Sweden, Norway, Denmark and the Netherlands. Federal states, or states that require a consensus between politically divided factions before tax increases, have lower taxes: the USA, Australia, Canada, and Switzerland are all federations or confederations. Japan and the more highly taxed Germany are states which operate by consensus. (Germany is also a federation.) But perhaps these systems of government reflect the peoples of the states, and so the tax systems are also reflecting genuine traditional cultural differences between peoples and states.

In terms of the weight of taxation upon us, the United Kingdom is, according to the reliable surveys of the OECD, in a middling sort of position. The burden of tax is usually measured by reference to the GDP (gross domestic product) or GNP (gross national product) of a state. Without getting too far into the technical territory of the economist, the GDP and GNP are measures of the total output of all kinds in a country, i.e. its total productive effort. One measures the internal effect of the effort, whereas the other takes international transactions into account. As noted, the OECD measures tax burden as a share of GDP.

On that basis a 50 per cent tax burden measured against GDP represents the fact that half of the entire productive effort of the nation is being diverted by taxes to general government use. In some states, that is happening. For example, Sweden is the most taxed of all modern states, and in 1991 the total tax burden came to 54 per cent of GDP. In recent years, the burden on all of us in the United Kingdom has fluctuated between 35 per cent and 40 per cent. Put in general terms, just under two fifths of everything we do gets diverted to government by taxes (including social security contributions). Or, if you like, for every hour you work and get paid, 24 minutes are on behalf of the government.

The burden of taxation has been growing steadily for 25 years or more – and it went on growing during much of the time that Mrs Thatcher was Prime Minister. How it came to be that we thought that taxes were being cut when they were actually being raised is something we will look at later.

The other point of concern is how far individuals find themselves paying more or less than this figure. Do we all work 24 minutes in each hour for the government? Broadly, yes we do or at least we pay between 35 pence to 40 pence in each one pound that we earn, then spend, over to the Treasury in some way or other. A number of studies have shown that the burden on both rich and poor averages out roughly at the same level as the national burden.

The reason for this is that we pay different amounts of the various taxes depending on whether we are living from social security, earnings or savings. The richer we are, the more direct tax we pay. The poorer we are, the more the indirect taxes such as excise duties affect us, and the more benefits we can receive.

Finally, these points and others can be illustrated by a simple example. Carol owns a small clothes shop. Em is employed there full time. Em wants to buy a dress on sale in the shop, but Carol refuses to sell it to her cheaply. The dress costs £100. But that is not what it costs Em, or what Carol gets, if we remember to add in the tax.

First, for Em to pay Carol £100, she has to earn £100 after paying income tax (at 25 per cent) and NI (National Insurance) contributions (at 9 per cent). She must therefore earn enough so that, after losing 34 per cent, she is left with £100. That comes to £147. When Carol pays Em, she pays an employer's NI contribution of 10.4 per cent to the DSS (Department of Social Security), so paying £147 costs her £162.

Second, adult clothes are subject to VAT. Under normal rules, if VAT is not added to the price separately, the seller must pay VAT out of the price at the going rate of 17.5 per cent. So Carol is treated as selling the dress to Em at the price which, when we add VAT at 17.5 per cent, gives £100. This means the price without VAT is £85, and £15 is VAT.

Next, Carol pays tax on the profit she makes on the dress. Let us say that she paid £50 plus VAT for the dress, and that her other costs (including the National Business Rate, another tax) are a further £10. That leaves her with a profit of £25. She will pay income tax on this, let us say, at 40 per cent, or £10, leaving her with a net profit of £15.

For Carol to get her £15 profit from selling the dress to Em, she had to pay Em £162, even though the dress only cost Carol £50 plus VAT. The reason (aside from general overheads) is tax. On this transaction, Em had to pay £37 income tax, £15 VAT and £13 NI contributions. Carol paid £15 in NI contributions and £10 in income tax. The total tax both paid is £90. Remember – the dress only cost Em £85 if you exclude VAT.

You might think this is a silly way of going about things – and it is. Had Carol sold the dress to Em at a reduced price, or given it to her instead of a bonus, or told her to wear it as a uniform or lent it to her as an advertisement for Carol's shop, the two could have paid a lot less tax. We see how this could happen later in the book. This is because tax can often be *avoided*. If there are two ways of doing something, and one costs less in tax than the other, it is usually sensible to do it the way which is cheaper in tax terms or more *tax efficient*. Working out how to do this is *tax planning*. Tax avoidance is entirely legal, if not always popular with government or the tax authorities. It is widely practised. So is *tax evasion*, but this is even less popular because it means reducing tax bills illegally, for example by lying to the taxman or misleading the tax authorities in a criminal manner.

We have to take account, in this book, of tax avoidance and the effect it has had on our taxes because of government attempts to stop the tax loss. Tax evasion is more serious, because it is a breach of the law – usually the criminal law, but not always. Refusing to pay the poll tax is not a criminal offence, nor is managing to stay off the poll tax register without actually misleading anyone (which is just as well, or the poll tax might have turned several million of us into criminals). It has certainly turned several million of us into tax avoiders. The irony is that our history shows that levying the poll tax has been a disaster every time it has been tried. Thankfully, that is not true of most of our taxes, and it goes some way to explaining why we use some taxes in this country but not others. How that came about takes us briefly into the fascinating topic of the history of our taxes.

3

TAXES AND
TAXPAYERS

It is not known when taxation was first invented. The word itself predates the English language. It can be found in the laws of England before they were written in English – but that tells us little even though it takes us back more than 700 years. Nor does the famous summons of Caesar Augustus that all the world be taxed, 2,000 years ago, get us anywhere near the start of our history. Certainly, the Romans were proficient at taxing and, unlike the English, could make people pay poll taxes.

Early fiscal history

For the start of our history, we have to go back to the ancient Egyptians (whose surviving writings give us the earliest recorded example of tax avoidance 4,000 years ago), to the Minoans, and probably much earlier still to the early states' records of cities in the Near East perhaps 5,500 years ago. There we find the earliest tax records which show that tax even predates money!

Separately, in each of the earliest societies from which our social systems have evolved, rulers found the need to compel payment from their citizens to the common cause (or the cause of the king or temple). The evidence remaining to us of those early movements suggests that taxes predate money, and were rendered by service or by a tithe (a *tithe* means a tenth part) or similar proportionate levy of crops and herds. When money started to emerge, 2,500 years ago in what is now called Greece, so did an additional means of collecting resources for use by the leadership.

The history of those periods shows that in taxes, perhaps more than most things, little changes. Then, as now, there were divisions between the direct taxes (which it was at one time a dishonour to pay in ancient Athens because they were regarded as unacceptable taxes) and the indirect taxes and internal and external customs and tolls. Then, as now, the exigencies of war forced states to be both inventive and invasive in their tax-collecting procedures. It was in these times that direct personal taxes came to be paid by all, but in times of peace the direct taxes were to wane again, as they did in Imperial Rome during the height of the Empire. The elite (who were in charge) arranged, if possible, to avoid the full weight of tax which fell on the merchants (who were not), for payment in cash, and on the lower orders, for payment in kind. Then, as now, the concerns about avoidance and evasion ran rife. There is nothing new in the failure of merchants keeping proper records if by doing so they pay less tax.

The Romans, as one might anticipate, organised and imposed taxes from the centre as the empire evolved. Their fiscal policies are well documented, and include taxes such as the *tributum*, a tax on land and other capital assets not much different from the tax we know as *rates*. Those who had no property also paid, by way of a *tributum in capita*, or what Mrs Thatcher called the community charge. However, the Romans did not try collecting taxes in that form in Britannia. As in Gaul and Spain, people were conscripted to the armies as a service, and at first there was not much in terms of wealth to tax. It was long after those times that British fiscal history started, perhaps most notably with the Domesday book.

Taxes in Britain

Fascinating though it is, we will not explore these earlier and remoter corners of fiscal history and prehistory. Our concern is limited to the history of the taxes we now use, and the relationship between taxers and the taxed in our country. That is of itself no mean task because, in some ways, the history of British taxation is the history of the evolution of the constitution of our country and of the liberties of its people.

It is a history which shows that those who rejected the poll tax followed a strong historical tradition, while those who sought to impose it ignored that tradition. The recent history of the poll tax has been argued to suggest that our attitudes to what we think are unfair taxes have not changed much since Wat Tyler led the men of Kent into rebellion against a poll tax in the fourteenth century. Whether or not that is a valid observation, it is fair to observe first that many of our taxes are old taxes, and second that with the evolution of those taxes over the centuries we find woven the history of the society we now know, with its strengths and its weaknesses.

The evolution of British taxes

Our present pattern of taxation dates back to the constitutional settlement following the so-called 'Glorious Revolution' of 1688–89. The events that brought William of Orange and his wife Mary to the throne of England in 1688–9 were the cumulative excesses of the Stuart monarchs.

Taxation under the Stuarts had been a controversial activity. Prior to their rule, the Tudor monarchs had lived from their own resources topped up by a grant from Parliament of *tonnage and poundage*, levies on imports and exports, but, save in times of war, little else. Even then it was clear, in England at least, that these were grants of Parliament, and should not be levied by consent. The additional grants could be by way of *subsidy*, a sort of wealth tax, or by way of general levy on each of the shires and boroughs, the amount that each person paid being sorted out locally. James I (and VI) and Charles I both sought these extra levies from parliaments, and were grudgingly given some. But neither liked parliaments and tried to raise revenues by other means.

Charles resorted at one time to forced loans, but these were resisted by those supposed to lend the money, leading to a number of members of Parliament being locked up for non-payment. When those failed to meet needs, he decided to raise taxes without Parliament's help, through the demand for *ship money* – funds to pay for the renewal of the English fleet. When this also hit problems, Parliament had to be resummoned. A

> ## The Petition of Right 1629
>
> . . . no man hereafter be compelled to make or yield any gift, benevolence tax or such like charge without common consent by Act of Parliament.

political battle between King and Parliament was precipitated when Parliament refused to vote funds to the King until he had first dealt with the redress of their grievances (which included complaints about forced loans). Only when the King had accepted the Petition of Right were taxes granted. That Petition is still part of our constitutional framework. But it took another generation, and a civil war, to assert its principles.

Charles wished in 1634 again to levy ship money. The levy was raised. Another was demanded in 1635. The judges found this not to be a tax. Another was demanded in 1636. It was challenged in the famous trial of *R v Hampden* in 1637, and the judges ruled in favour of the King. Thereafter followed the civil war, and the restoration for a short period of the Stuarts, but ending with the hurried exit of James II (or VII).

The arrival of William of Orange was accompanied by solemn statements in the Declaration of Rights reasserting the right of Parliament to decide on taxes. This at last set the record straight. But it left a new fiscal system to be constructed to replace the mess that had gone before. And the level of taxes was a high one, as William used his new-found territories to relieve his home lands of the need to furnish a fleet. There is perhaps

> ## The Declaration of Right 1688
>
> Levying money for and to the use of the crown, by pretence of prerogative, for other time and in other manner than the same was granted by parliament is illegal.

a little irony here. The rows over ship money were occasioned because the Stuarts felt they needed a fleet, among other things, to keep the Dutch at bay. In resisting these taxes, the English created a new Parliamentary tax machine. Its first use was to raise a fleet to keep the enemies of the Dutch at bay!

> 'To pay our just taxes was once thought too much
> But our extraordinary charity is such
> We bankrupt ourselves for maintaining the Dutch
> Which nobody can deny
>
> If we tax and poll on for a year or two more
> The French I dare say will ne'er touch our shore
> For fear of the charge of maintaining our poor
> Which nobody can deny'

(Extract from contemporary ballad of the 1690s)

When Charles II died, there were three major sources of taxation: customs, excise and a smaller (but hated) hearth tax (or tax on chimneys). These were renewed for the life of James II. They were not enough for William. In 1692, in came a property tax. This replaced the general subsidy which had existed since 1371. It was a tax (in modern parlance) at 20 pence in the pound (£), on the value of land, personal property and offices. It was the start of the tax which, in 1992, was again to return, at least in part, to the rate of 20 pence. In strict terms, the tax continued as the land tax which was abolished finally only in 1960, but in mutated form it, and its administrative processes, were absorbed into the income tax when it was introduced as such in 1799.

In came a Dutch form of taxing – the stamp duty. This was developed into an early form of death duty and lasted in that form until estate duty was replaced by capital transfer tax in 1974. (The inheritance tax, as we now call it, is the same tax as the capital transfer tax but, for reasons of political significance only, it was renamed in 1984). Stamp duties were taxes on documents. These taxes still exist both on transfers of stocks and shares (to be abolished when the documents themselves are abolished) and on transfers of land. In these few years, the change of administration had added to the centuries-old forms of indirect taxes new forms of direct tax which, unlike those of previous governments, worked.

Few major changes took place to this pattern of taxes in the two centuries that followed. The exigencies of war against Napoleon in the 1790s imposed, yet again, pressures of the need for tax to service our armies and fleets, out of which came the income tax. The reason for this creation was a bankruptcy of ideas for extending the burden of the property tax (or assessed taxes as they were then called, a name they could still bear with justification).

The excises were imposed on everything in sight by way of sales taxes or licence fees. Wigs, servants, windows (if not hearths), coffee, training contracts, medicines . . . the list was endless but not long enough. The change came with the adoption of an idea thought up by a former customs officer, Adam Smith, with a general tax on available forms of wealth and income.

In comes income tax

The income tax was first adopted in 1799, but it was not welcomed and in 1803 was replaced by a *contribution on properties, profits and gains* as the 1803 Act called it. Although its name has changed since, that 1803 Act still forms the basis of our income tax. Hidden in the successive re-enactments by Parliament, our 1988 Taxes Act still contains important wording straight from the 1803 original. In carrying forward ideas it also carries forward some of the approaches it lifted from the previous 1692 measure in terms of procedure. It was not an important tax once war receded. Indeed, the income tax was repealed from 1816 to 1842. Since then the tax, introduced as a temporary tax, has been with us every year, although in legal form it is still a temporary tax!

For many years after introduction the income tax was a trivial tax, with percentages of one per cent to ten per cent. State revenues in 1888 were much the same in pattern as in 1688. Excises raised the most revenue (£25 million), followed by customs (£20 million) and then the 'Dutch taxes' – stamp duty, income tax, house tax and land tax – raising together a further £25 million.

The 20th century

It was the demands of more egalitarian governments at the beginning of
the 20th century, followed by the desperate search for finance for the
First World War, that forced the rates to climb to substantial levels.
Pressures caused by avoidance have led to the kinds of income caught by
the tax to grow ever since so that, although the rates of income tax have
come down, it is still a high-yielding tax. The yield was pushed very high
by the demands of the Second World War, and the invention during that
war of PAYE (Pay As You Earn). This collected income tax from
employees as they earned their incomes in an efficient and painless
manner. Tax collected through PAYE now accounts for more than 90 per
cent of all income tax and, through a modified form of the same system,
for more than 90 per cent of social security contributions as well.

Following the Lloyd George budget of 1909 (which caused a row with the
House of Lords, and led to that body being permanently deprived of
powers to interfere with tax laws by the Parliament Act 1911), direct
taxes started rising sharply, through both the income tax and supertax
(as the special tax which imposed higher rates of income tax on higher
levels of income was first called), and through estate duties (see below).
It was not until after the election of the Heath government in 1970 that
surtax (which had replaced supertax) went – although it was replaced by
higher-rate tax – and only during the Thatcher government was the
highest rate of income tax lowered below 50 per cent. Equally, it was only
then that the inheritance tax (which, via capital transfer tax, had replaced
estate duty) rate was also reduced below 50 per cent, and the legacy, in
particular, of the rates imposed by the First World War was finally
removed.

During the last 40 years, the search for the best forms of tax has seen
more changes than for centuries past. Several ancient taxes have gone:
inhabited house duty, land tax, stamp duty on all documents other than
share transfers and land transfers, domestic rates, most forms of excise
duty (the tax on matches, pushed out in 1992, is the last of a long line of
which the main contingent was swept away with the purchase tax in 1972)
and, the daftest tax of all, dog licences. At the time of their repeal, these
licences cost three times as much to collect as the revenue derived from
them! During that period other significant taxes have come and gone:
development land tax, development gains tax, betterment levy, selective

employment tax, national insurance levy, supplementary oil duty, and the community charge.

The main changes have been the most recent. Customs duties (which, as we have seen, were long a mainstay of the royal revenues) have declined to an insignificant level. This is because there are no customs duties between the member states of the European Community. Further, as we discuss in a later chapter, customs officers are, from 1993, unable to control movements of Community nationals for fiscal reasons. Those customs duties that are collected, from goods and passengers coming in from outside the Community, belong to the Community not to the United Kingdom. Excises have similarly been reduced to a short list of taxes: tobacco, alcohol and oil.

Instead of the long list of excises, we now have, since 1973, value added tax. This tax is the success story of the last three decades for tax authorities across the world. In the United Kingdom it has jumped to third place from nowhere in just 20 years. The other tax that has crept up in importance is social security contributions which, in 1973 was changed from the flat-rate 'stamp', first introduced in 1911, to an income tax. From 1975, contributions made by employees were to become entirely earnings-related, as were the contributions by their employers and an earnings-related charge on the self-employed was introduced. These changes were precipitated by a deficit in financing social security benefits. The NI Fund, into which the contributions are paid, now has a comfortable surplus. The price for this was the introduction of our second income tax.

—— The balance of British taxation ——

During the last 40 years, there had been a rough balance between the direct taxes (income tax on individuals, profits tax on companies, estate duties and stamp duty) and the indirect taxes (customs duty, purchase taxes, and the excises). However, through the period there was a slow but steady rise in the proportion of tax collected by the direct taxes. There were a number of reasons for this. Collection of the direct taxes became more effective, as the law itself caught more kinds of income. On the other hand, customs duty fell steadily out of favour under the influence of the GATT talks (GATT = General Agreement on Tariffs and Trade), and later British membership of, first, the European Free Trade

Association and then the European Economic Community, and finally the European Community. Purchase tax proved an inadequate tax to reflect an economy which was shifting slowly towards services and away from goods. And there was a limit to the usefulness of excises.

The breakthrough in adjusting the balance between direct and indirect taxes came with the adoption of VAT in 1973. First introduced at the rate of 8 per cent, it now has a main rate of 17.5 per cent, and a much wider catch than it had 20 years ago. The rise of VAT has rescued successive governments from another problem. If taxes are unpopular, experience shows that direct taxes are more unpopular than indirect taxes. The inability to rely on indirect taxes had forced the burden of direct tax up to levels which proved unacceptable. If not defied, they were avoided, or, alternatively, the income that would give rise to the liability was itself converted into other forms such as, hidden in trusts, companies or out of the jurisdiction. The ability to swap the tax burden across to indirect taxes (which has been used since VAT appeared) made the task of lowering the income tax easier.

Another trend evident in Britain, as elsewhere, over the last 30 years is the rise in social security taxes. This itself reflects the rising cost of state social security systems, even ones with relatively restrictive limits such as that in Britain. The rise in countries with more open-ended systems, such as Sweden, has been much sharper. However, in the British context it has come by transferring some of the costs of social security from general taxation to social security taxation. The NI contributions have gone up, with commensurate cuts in general taxes or, more specifically, in income tax.

A final trend is the one which has caused the greatest problems. Rising local expenditure during earlier years of the second half of the 20th century were largely funded by central government, but also were financed by rates. Central government imposed significant duties on local government, and local government itself accepted these and other re-sponsibilities on behalf of its electors. The result was a steady increase in the cost of local government, and therefore of the tax burden we noted in the first chapter. As we saw there, steps were taken to shift the cost to local taxes, the biggest of which was the poll tax. (We have seen the results!)

The Dutch had some good ideas all those years ago – we seem to have only a few new ones! Income tax was a British idea (more correctly, a Scottish idea), but VAT must be credited primarily to the French, and social security taxes to the Germans under Bismark. None the less, they are the British versions of those taxes, and in their formations they also formed Britain. They did so by shaping the relationships between government and the governed.

──────── **The rights of taxpayers** ────────

We have seen that in 1629 and 1689 Parliament extracted from the monarchs of the day the formal concession that there should be no taxation without Parliamentary approval. Put another way, it was an agreement that there be no taxation without representation. Further, built into the forms of our taxes even today, is the other concession, wrung from executive government under the Stuarts, that there be no taxation without prior redress of grievances.

The other fundamental strand to our fiscal constitution was won in 1911. Ironically, it seems that yet again the reason was ship money. In setting his 1909 budget, Chancellor Lloyd George's task of raising taxes for the new old age pensions was made significantly more difficult by the need to build up the navy to meet the German challenge. This time the ship money was being demanded by the 'people's champion' (as Lloyd George was called) from the establishment, rather than the reverse.

By way of comparison with the work of modern chancellors, it is worth noting the range of the 1909 budget: income tax up from (in modern terms) 5 pence to 6 pence in the pound; estate duty up, with measures to prevent avoidance; stamp duties up; tobacco tax up; excises on spirits up; a new supertax of 2.5 pence in the pound on higher incomes; new land taxes; a new petrol tax of one pence per gallon; a new car tax, and a new liquor licence tax. It was a budget to tax the rich (not too many people had cars in 1909!). In its range and comprehensiveness it has been called the first modern budget. The war to follow made sure that Britain would not return to the calmer days of 5 pence income tax again in the 20th century.

Perhaps because of its modernity, it was this budget that precipitated a dispute, which this account need not follow, between the Houses of Lords and Commons and which ended in victory for the elected chamber. From that time, the House of Lords have not interfered with tax legislation. As a result those commanding the majority of members of the House of Commons command tax revenues. In this way, taxation came totally under the control of the government of the day, whatever the politics of that government.

Income tax as an annual tax

The legislation for the income tax must be renewed every year. If it is not then, at least in theory, the tax cannot be imposed. This result is achieved by section 1 of the Taxes Act 1988 which contains the key words 'where any Act enacts that income tax shall be charged for any year, income tax shall be charged for that year . . .'. If a Finance Act fails to do this, there will be no income tax. Each year therefore, Parliament enacts that 'income tax shall be charged for the year . . .'.

The income tax year is also an historical oddity. It runs from 6 April to 5 April. Why? The reason dates back to the change in the calendar in 1751, when 11 days were left out. Before that time, the start of the legal and financial year had been 25 March.

However, leaving 11 days out of the financial year would have cost too much tax, so they shifted the financial year end in that year to 5 April. And there it has stayed ever since. For more modern taxes, the year end was shifted more tidily to 31 March, when the government's annual accounts close.

That poses another problem. If the year starts on 6 April, and the budget is presented only in March (as has long been the tradition) how do they enact a new law in time? The answer is they do not. A special Act called the Provisional Collection of Taxes Act gives Parliament four months from the budget to pass a new Act, and allows the tax to be collected on a temporary basis meanwhile. A new Finance Act has always been passed within four months.

Protecting taxpayers' rights

Although the long history of wresting taxing power from the executive into the hands of the elected government is now a closed chapter of our history, that is not the whole story. Individual rights of taxpayers also deserve consideration.

By definition, taxation is the exercise of compulsion upon the personal rights of taxpayers. It is the requirement that they hand over some of their property without receiving anything directly in return. The right to tax is the right to override property rights of the person taxed. It follows that any tax law is, of its essence, of a particular and unusual nature compared with the general regime of law, which is established to protect people's rights.

Privacy and fairness

There is a further element to the interference with rights. It arises because of the inherent nature of tax collection, particularly of the direct taxes. Fair assessment of these taxes depends on knowing the full income of each individual or company. In Britain, if not elsewhere, information about the precise income or wealth of an individual is regarded as personal information of a kind which, for cultural if not legal reasons, is not in the public domain. Acquiring this information is an invasion of the privacy of that individual. It is a sensitive question, and that sensitivity increases if the individual believes that protecting the information will reduce the tax to be paid. But the sensitivity may be seen as existing separately from the financial benefit of keeping quiet.

At the same time, there is a strong interest in the tax authorities having access to all relevant information. Leaving aside issues of criminal law (as these depend on how the legislation defines criminal activity in the first place), this access to information is necessary both for the efficient collection of tax and its fairness. Fairness requires that each taxpayer pays the proper amount of tax. But the amount which is proper cannot be determined without access to the required information. Therefore, if one is to be treated fairly, the tax authorities must be able to ensure the others pay the right amount of taxes. If the others pay too little, then one (and/or others) will pay too much. Further, if one becomes aware that the others pay too little, one will think it fair to reduce the amount one pays. If that happens, and taxpayer compliance becomes weak, the tax can only be collected by compulsion.

This clash of privacy and fairness is one that does not exist in the same way with all taxes. Our discussion so far is framed with individuals in mind. In the case of businesses, different issues arise. In the case of a business, commercial secrecy may be at stake. Product information is valuable, as is know-how. So, equally, is information about the profit margins of other businesses in the same sector of the economy. Too much openness by a business might destroy its commercial advantages in the market-place or reveal to its competitors that it has none. This is not a question of rights but of financial advantage. There is therefore an important difference. It can be argued that an invasion of privacy is interference with some kind of primary right which is not a matter of financial value. Damage to a friendship or family relationship is not easy to repair. By contrast, a breach of commercial confidence will result in lost profits. The loss may be major, but it is, in principle, quantifiable and could be compensated if wrongfully caused.

Protection

How can the rights to privacy and confidence best be protected? One answer is that different taxes interfere with rights in different ways. For example, the collection of most indirect taxes will not involve questions of privacy because the levy of tax does not usually involve enquiry into the personal circumstances of the taxpayer. This is particularly so of the excises and customs duties. Concealment in these cases might occasionally be claimed to be on the grounds of commercial confidence, but hardly on the basis of an invasion of personal privacy.

Estate duties avoid the problem of privacy in a different way. The person whose property is being valued is dead, but the property has to be valued anyway, and that value has to be made known to anyone with a claim on the estate of the deceased. It is therefore public knowledge, so little privacy is lost by adding the requirements of the tax authorities to the process.

With social security taxes, different issues arise yet again. These are presented as contributory taxes. It is in the interests of the contributors to ensure that they pay the right number of contributors. If they do not, there may be a loss of benefit. To some extent, the process of gathering information is interactive, rather than, as with income tax, one-way. The contributor will be demanding information from the Department so he or she will be less concerned when the Department demands it from him or her. That, at any rate, is one interpretation of the greater willingness usually evident in contributors to cooperate with social security requirements.

The taxes which traditionally raise the greatest disquiet are those which require personal information or inspection of property. In years gone by, it was taxes such as the hearth tax which occasioned this hostility. The tax could only be assessed if an inspector entered the individual's home. But 'the house of everyone is to him as his castle or fortress' as one of England's greatest lawyers put it 350 years ago. That is why taxes that do not require invasion of the home are better than those that do: hence, in Georgian days, the window tax and, in current times, the broad bands of the council tax.

At some point in collecting any tax there has to be enforcement procedure. Those who evade their taxes have, in the interests not only of the state but of the other taxpayers, to be challenged. For that to happen there have to be information powers. Sometimes the powers can be savage, but at other times they can be straightforward. The tradition in Britain has been for the savage powers to be left to Customs and Excise, as a reflection of their role as the waterguard – the anti-smuggling border police. The tradition of the Inland Revenue is much milder.

Behind this question of balance in every case there is a question of balancing rights. In part, the British answer to the question of invasion of personal and business rights is a rigorous discipline of secrecy in connection with all personal tax details. Officials will not pass them on to ministers, and ministers will not ask for them. Neither will publish them, unless in exceptional cases the law requires this. And, to the great credit of both departments, allegations that information received by a department as part of its tax-collecting activities has been leaked in any unofficial or unauthorised way are extremely rare. 'Snooping' tends to be kept to a minimum, and its results are carefully controlled.

The fear of invasion of privacy has long haunted our relations with our taxing masters. One reason for the shape of our income tax is fear of excessive information falling into the hands of officials. The income tax was, and still is, divided into schedules, following the form adopted in the law of 1803 noted on page 36. One reason for this schedular approach was so that different officials could be made responsible for collecting tax under the different schedules without being allowed to compare their information. Consequently, even though an individual was fully taxed on his income, no one official knew what that income was in total. In that way, it was believed, people would more readily pay their taxes.

Enforcement or compliance

The prize aimed at by tax authorities is voluntary compliance. A tax which, like the poll tax, has to be collected with no less than six million court orders in one year, is a disastrous failure. The best tax is one, like the social security contributions regime, which some avoid to some extent, and some evade to some extent (losing benefit as they do), but where the vast majority of the taxpaying public pay with little protest and little argument.

Increasingly, in Britain as elsewhere, the official attitude to taxpayers, long viewed with hostility or mistrust, is being turned into a more positive approach. Australian tax officials now tend to arrive with a grin and a welcome such as 'I'm your local tax inspector and I'm here to help you.' A similar approach is evident in Britain with, first, a taxpayer's charter published jointly in 1986 by the Revenue and Customs, then a new set of charters published in 1991 separately by each of the tax authorities.

Behind the smiles, revenue authorities can be more efficient than ever before. Computers are part of the answer. In the Netherlands, all information collected from or about taxpayers is kept on a central computer database by the tax authority. A return made by someone for VAT, or employer's payroll tax, can be compared with the income tax return of the same individual or business, or that of the employees, at the press of a button. The officials may be more friendly, and better trained in interpersonal relations. They may be more polite, and there may be ways of complaining about rude officials as well as wrong bills, but the fundamental dilemmas of tax have not receded. Tax only works by interfering with both property rights and privacy. The assumption is that it is in the interests of the state, of society and in the interests of other taxpayers. At what point should the rights of the individual transcend the rights of that individual's society or fellow citizens? How much information or property should be demanded? When can others be required to inform on a taxpayer? What safeguards should there be?

Our history has shown us that these dilemmas are inherent in taxation. The broad answer given in all democratic states is to give the choice of taxes to a properly elected government. Only the people can decide how the people are taxed. There are no magic answers, although there are many alternative approaches. In Britain, it falls to the Chancellor of the Exchequer to exercise the democratic power. In the next chapter we see how it is done.

4

IN THIS YEAR'S BUDGET

Planning expenditure

The government's accounts year runs from April 1 to March 31. Ahead of each *financial year*, as the official government accounts year is known, the government prepares its expenditure plans. Because the government cannot spend money without the authority of Parliament, it presents formal estimates to Parliament of its expenditure plans for approval. The plans for any year are placed before the House of Commons in late autumn each year for the next financial year. These estimates are, with or without amendment, accepted by the House as a 'grant of supply to Her Majesty'. In a well-oiled procedure which attracts little publicity in the media, two Acts are passed annually by Parliament to grant supply: a Consolidated Fund Act, releasing funds from the official state bank account, the *consolidated fund*, to the individual department of state and other public bodies, and an Appropriation Act authorising expenditure by each of those bodies.

The budget process

The Chancellor of the Exchequer, chief minister of the Treasury, lays the plans before the House of Commons for approval. More controversially, he also has to seek authority from the House of Commons for the money to meet this expenditure. Traditionally, the request for money has been made just before the start of the new financial year. That is why in 1992 and every year for many years past, the Chancellor stood up in the House on the second (or third) Tuesday of March and presented his Budget and Financial Statement. This is the government's formal statement of what taxes they wish to raise for the next financial year.

In 1993 this pattern changes. Instead, the government announces its estimates of supply and its budget at the same time in December. The pre-Easter ritual becomes a pre-Christmas one. Why? The answer dates back to the days when government financial planning was a simple affair. We saw in the last chapter that the present system dates back to the 1680s. It was then a simple process, and could take place just before the new fiscal year began. This remained until well into the 20th century. But as government expenditure grew, expenditure plans had to be prepared ahead of the new year, and were published in the autumn. Budgets were also prepared at this time, but were kept secret only to be released, with some drama, just before they took effect.

This practice has been criticised for several reasons. It was felt wrong that tax and expenditure plans were published several months apart without any serious attempt being made to link the two. In some states, the law requires there to be a balance between taxes and expenditure, and the two must be determined together. In Britain, this only occurs with earmarked taxes, of which the only one of significance is the NI system. For this reason the level of contributions required to fund benefits to be paid in the following year have been announced in November, not as part of the budget.

Another reason for criticism is that the present system gives taxpayers (and, for PAYE purposes, employers) little notice of proposed changes. Some changes have to be made without warning. A decision, for example, to increase the price of petrol takes effect at 6pm on the day of the budget. It does so in order to prevent disorderly scenes while motorists queue up to avoid new tax rates. Most changes are now announced well ahead, and often take place only after wide consultation.

The Finance Bill, containing the detail of government proposals, cannot be finalised until after the budget, so is not printed until about a month after it (except in election years). By then, the new financial year has started, so in one sense the whole of the Budget takes effect retrospectively. From the financial year 1994–95, this last minute rush will disappear. The Finance Bill will be published in January and will be given the Royal Assent that turns it into law during May. This gives a slightly calmer pace to changes, and will probably also tempt Chancellors not to play games with taxes for electoral or other purposes. Thankfully, budgets after 1993 are likely to be less like the conjuring show where Chancellors pull rabbits out of hats that has been the rule in recent years.

Why is a budget needed?

You saw, in the last chapter, how Parliament gained the upper hand on the Crown over long years of conflict, and how it insisted in having a full say in taxation. This say was maintained by ensuring that at least some taxes were temporary, including income tax. For that reason alone, each year there must be a new tax law. Strictly, income tax could be made a permanent tax by a short amendment to the main Taxes Act. That is, however, unlikely to happen. The annual tax ritual is at the root of the working of the House of Commons and the modern running of the state. It is the beginning of the once yearly review of tax law.

Annual Finance Bills

Leaving aside election years, recent governments have found it necessary every year to introduce lengthy annual laws to revise our ever-growing tax laws. For instance, the Finance Act 1991 had 124 sections and 19 schedules. The Finance Act itself is therefore part of the annual ritual. There has been at least one every year since 1894. This annual Act is the only law passed by Parliament in which the general tax laws of the Kingdom – income tax and the other direct taxes, value added tax and the excises – can be changed. This is because Parliament has special procedures for passing financial legislation which have the effect of preventing any other bill (or draft) containing a taxing provision. Proper procedure must be followed, starting with the Budget Resolutions – formal resolutions giving notice of proposed legislation on tax matters. These resolutions are tabled immediately after the Chancellor sits down having made his budget, and are passed by the House without a vote shortly thereafter.

THE TAX ACTS

Legislation for the main direct taxes is contained in a series of Acts known as *consolidation Acts* – collections of the current law into one Act from the original annual Finance Acts.

The current Acts are:

INCOME AND CORPORATION TAXES ACT 1988

(Called the Taxes Act): As enacted in 1988 this had 844 sections and 31 schedules, which brought together provisions from the previous consolidation in 1970 and 61 other Acts. It has already been amended very heavily.

CAPITAL ALLOWANCES ACT 1990

Another 165 sections and 2 schedules bringing together the previous 1968 consolidation with amendments from 33 other Acts – and already further amended.

TAXATION OF CHARGEABLE GAINS [ACT]*

This brings together all the provisions on CGT and the corporation tax charge on gains into *** sections and ** schedules.

TAXES MANAGEMENT ACT 1970

The oldest and shortest of the laws, it started life with 120 sections.

The fact that there is only one Finance Act each year does not of itself explain the length of recent Acts. That is because of another element of Parliamentary procedure or tradition. By longstanding practice, tax legislation, at least for the main direct taxes, is never delegated to others. This is why the laws enacting the income and corporation taxes, and the charges on capital gains and inheritance tax, are so long and complicated. Only minor (and largely procedural) provisions are allowed into regulations. This contrasts sharply with much modern legislation, which usually contains wide powers allowing government departments to impose rules by means of regulations.

The approach to other taxes is more relaxed. Much social security contribution legislation (not regarded by the Commons as a tax) is in regulations known as the Contributions Regulations. The law – in the Social Security Contributions and Benefits Act 1992, as amended – is contained in 19 sections and two schedules of the Act. The value added tax primary legislation, in the Value Added Tax Act 1983, is longer, but again much of the detailed legislation is in regulations. There are short separate Acts for the other indirect taxes.

Rushing in the new law

Nor has the pressure finished once the Budget has been announced and the process of enacting the Finance Bill started. As we have seen, the government announces its plans for taxes shortly before the start of each new financial year. However, the authority to raise annual taxes runs out on April 5. The problem is that Parliament did not get round to passing the Finance Act necessary to authorise the new year's annual taxes until several months of that year have passed. Strictly, therefore, the annual income tax has no legal basis on which the authorities can demand it from April 6 until the new Finance Act was enacted.

For many years, no one bothered with this irregularity, and the tax was collected as if legal authority existed. However, this did not suit an independently minded backbench MP called Roger Bowles. He challenged the practice in the courts in the case of *Bowles v Bank of England* in 1913. In that case the court ruled that the practice was illegal, and that there was no authority to collect income tax after April 6 until the new Finance Act passed into law, perhaps in July.

The resulting chaos was staunched only by emergency legislation – the *Provisional Collection of Taxes Act*. Re-enacted in 1968, this provides an expedient but formal procedure to get round the problem that Bowles exposed. What must now happen is that, on or before April 6, the House of Commons passes a series of *Budget resolutions.* If the resolutions themselves require it, the 1968 Act gives the resolutions immediate effect as if they were enacted in a Finance Act for a period of precisely four months.

WAYS AND MEANS RESOLUTION NO 23 TO BE MOVED BY THE CHANCELLOR OF THE EXCHEQUER 10 MARCH 1992

That —

1 *Income tax shall be charged for the year 1992–93, and for that year —*
(a) the lower rate shall be 20 per cent.,
(b) the basic rate shall be 25 per cent., and
(c) the higher rate shall be 40 per cent . . .

And it is hereby declared that it is expedient in the public interest that this Resolution should have statutory effect under the provisions of the Provisional Collection of Taxes Act 1968.

{This is the key text of the budget resolution passed by the House of Commons on 10 March 1992 authorising the Inland Revenue to go on collecting income tax after April 6, 1992, notwithstanding that the Finance Act is not enacted. In fact, the 1992 general election changed the timetable, and the Finance Act was, for the first time for many years enacted before the new year started. This resolution therefore never took effect.}

If, within the four month period, a Finance Act approving the Budget resolutions is passed, the resolutions immediately lapse and are super-seded by the new law. If a new Finance Act containing those provisions is not on the statute book by August 6, the government is in trouble. This is because the Budget resolutions not only cease to have effect, but they are to be regarded as never having had effect. This would mean that any tax collected under the authority of a Budget resolution has to be repaid in full. This has never happened!

From 1994, this race against time is easier, because the Finance Bill will be published each January, and the intention will be to give it the Royal

Assent in May. Even so, the enactment process is unlikely to be completed in any year before April 6, so the provisional collection procedure is to be kept in place.

Budget secrecy

The great importance that everyone attaches to paying taxes has ensured that, over the years, the Budget has come to be regarded as an important day in the political calendar. This is added to by rituals such as the red dispatch case in which Chancellors take the Budget speech to the House.

The most important part of the ritual is Budget secrecy. If any Minister, including the Prime Minister, is asked about forthcoming tax plans, they say they cannot speak for the Chancellor, or prejudge the Budget. The Chancellor himself refuses to disclose plans for any year until the Budget speech. Normally, even Cabinet colleagues only find out the details at a Cabinet meeting a few hours before. And the Chancellor, his colleagues who are the Treasury ministers, and their officials keep the details of the Budget a closely guarded secret. So careful are they of details that the key officials are not allowed to talk to anyone at all for three months before Budget day.

The trouble with budget secrecy is that it not only applies to key political and economic decisions such as the rate of income tax, it applies to just about every aspect of the Budget and Finance Bill however technical and non-political. This means that when, a few weeks after the Budget, the new Finance Bill is published, it will be the first occasion for those who will have to pay the new taxes, and their professional advisers, to find out what surprises are in store. In addition, the lack of consultation means that, in the view of some, there will be both economic and legal mistakes, if not political ones, in the draft legislation.

———— The lobbying process ————

The tight timetabling of the Budget and Finance Bills ensure that the three months between Budget and Finance Act are the occasion for hectic activity by many more people than the Chancellor and his officials. Each year, anyone who wants changes made to the tax laws has an opportunity to attempt to gain his wish by seeking the appropriate change in the Finance Bill. Obviously, this involves the efforts of the opposition political parties. It also involves representatives of business and the professions, and, indeed, any special interest group which feels it has a good cause. If the cause is good enough, or the lobbying is strong enough, they may succeed in bullying, embarrassing or genuinely persuading the government into agreeing a change. Of course, if the government proposes a change in tax laws that an interest group does not like, its pressure to block the change will be all the stronger. And all sides know just how short is the timetable. If the pressure is sufficient, the government will be forced to climb down.

Although much of the work of lobbyists and pressure groups takes place outside Parliament, and does not make newspaper headlines, their influence and importance has been growing steadily, and it has now become another part of the Budget ritual. For many groups, this starts with the presentation of *Budget representations*. Many professional bodies and commercial groups make these representations every year: for example, accountants and lawyers, bankers and the CBI. These proposals include desired policy and technical changes. Recently, the practice has grown up of the leading professional bodies concerned with tax (the accountants, the law societies and the Institute of Taxation) putting in joint representations identifying major problems. These are themselves useful documents because they identify in detail problems and injustices in the existing law.

Consultation and committees

In some cases the government adopts a *consultative process* for a proposed change, inviting lobby and special interest groups to express opinions on the change. In such cases, the practice is for the relevant government department (usually the Inland Revenue) to publish a consultative document and invite comments by a given date. Such invitations are taken seriously by the relevant pressure groups who usually present detailed, considered responses. Sometimes the pressure groups get together and consider if a common position can be found, in which case a joint reply may be submitted.

Although both lobbying and consultation occurs increasingly, there is no formal standing arrangement for consultation between government and representatives of taxpayers. A number of arrangements exist for officials to exchange views with taxpayers. There has, for many years, been a joint committee of officials of HM Customs and Excise and those in the import business, and recently a similar Joint Value Added Tax Consultative Committee was set up between VAT officials and VAT taxpayers and their advisers. Other informal but regular meetings exist between officials of the Inland Revenue and professional advisers and pressure groups. One of these is an informal tax law consultative committee representing major interest groups which has been in existence for a few years, known as the Group of Nine (because it consists of representatives of nine major pressure groups).

Human error and compromise

Compared with many of our rivals, the British system is unusual in having so little consultation before new taxes are imposed, with little attempt to reach consensus and a high degree of secrecy. Although this means that a determined government can find it easier to impose new laws in the United Kingdom than in other advanced states, it also means that there is a risk of faulty laws and inadequately thought-out proposals.

Although political compromise is rarely necessary in the United Kingdom, perhaps paradoxically, our system seems to differ from two major deficiencies. First, some of our tax laws are very old and have never properly been brought up to date. That is true of our income tax, as we shall consider later. The second deficiency relates to the technical aspects of our taxes. Because we cannot change taxes by regulation, and our judges are not very good at it either (and have very little scope for action in any event), even the most trifling technical mistake can only be corrected through the annual Finance Bill. Here each proposal has to compete with all others for space, with only a few of the many changes demanded actually becoming law in any year.

In an attempt to get away from the present situation many, including some past Chancellors of the Exchequer, have advocated a procedure in which we have two Finance Bills each year. One would be the 'political' bill, with the tax rates and allowances, plus any political reforms. That would follow the usual timetable. The other would be a 'technical' bill, with the changes which were not politically sensitive and which could proceed at a more leisurely pace with less secrecy and more open consultation. The fact that this has been strongly advocated, but never adopted, may be due to one problem that is not so easy to solve – sorting out what is 'political' and what is 'technical'. Experience shows that anything to do with taxes can at any time become highly political. Could our political parties reach agreement to leave such a technical bill alone?

What the Budget must do

The Budget presents the government's plans for all income and expenditure passing through the *Consolidated Fund* for the next financial year. This is, as we have seen, only part of the real story of government finance. There are several important taxes omitted, including:

(a) the *National Insurance Fund*, into which all social security contributions are paid, and out of which retirement pensions and other contributory social security benefits are paid;

(b) local income and expenditure. This is why the rates and poll tax have not formed any part of the Budget statement;

(c) taxes controlled by the European Communities, not by Parliament. Customs duties are now set at European, not national level, as are agricultural levies (or farm taxes).

The changes in 1994 aim to compensate these omissions by bringing into the Budget the *National Insurance Fund* revenue and expenditure, including all contributions. However, a totally new procedure would be needed if we were to get the whole picture, and if we were to look at the results in Britain of any changes caused by the Community legislation taking direct internal effect and, therefore, not requiring legislation in the United Kingdom. No such procedure is suggested, but if we do not have one, where else will the budget effect of these taxes be reviewed?

The British tax machine

Picture a large factory with a variety of different machines running in it. Some are large, some small – some extremely noisy, but others working very efficiently. Some are ancient, and seem to be tied together with sticking plaster and bits of string. Others are glossy and new. Yet all have to be kept going at the correct rate to produce the goods. That's the sort of equipment with which the Treasury and revenue departments work in gathering our taxes. The collection of about three dozen taxes, used by British government to raise money from us, has to be under constant review to see if the taxes are working effectively in, what the government perceives to be, the nation's interests.

To get an idea of the extent and range of this machine, we shall review the decisions that confront a Chancellor and his officials as they prepare themselves for a new Budget. How does the Chancellor set about asking for the taxes he needs? He has first to undertake what is sometimes called the Budget arithmetic, calculating how much expenditure the government can afford and how the funds are going to be raised. Money can be raised from privatisation proceeds, from fees and charges, from profits and royalties, and of course from borrowing, but the major share must come from taxes. The Budget arithmetic will suggest that either more or less tax has to be raised compared with the previous year, or maybe the aim is a neutral budget – the same level of taxes as the previous year.

Budget arithmetic

The starting point is the predicted value of taxes for last year and, on that basis, for the next year too. In the last chapter, we looked at a summary of those figures for one year, in ranking order of amount of tax collected. The budget arithmetic is concerned partly with this, but partly also with the effect of rolling a tax forward from one year to the next without any change in the rates and rules. It must therefore follow the effects of business activities on each of the taxes.

A complication is caused, in this arithmetic, by inflation. Even if inflation is only, say, five per cent, it will still distort our tax system quite sharply between one year and the next. This causes what is called *fiscal drag*, that is, the changes to our tax system caused by inflation. Each year the effect of inflation is to make fixed rates of tax (for example, on a bottle of whisky) lower in real terms, while making income tax and some other direct taxes higher in real terms (because the value of the personal allowance goes down if it is not adjusted, while in most years earnings rise faster than inflation and therefore cause more income tax to be paid). This means that a decision not to change things in the Budget will itself cause changes. In other words, the Budget arithmetic must take into account the fact that as the law is currently worded we need a Budget each year just to stay in the same place.

There are also complications, for example, because of a sharp rise or drop in the levels of employment, or earnings, or company profits, or sales of cigarettes or claims for tax allowances for pensions that were not foreseen last year.

GUESSING TAX LEVELS

The table below shows how far out the official Budget guesses on tax collections were for 1990–91 and 1991–92 as shown in the Red Book. Figures in £M. + → underestimate; − → overestimate.

Tax	90–1 error	91–2 error
Income tax	+ 500	−1600
Corporation tax	+ 900	−1100
PRT	− 200	− 200
CGT	− 200	− 200
IHT	+ 100	0
Stamp duties	− 200	− 400
VAT	−1300	− 200
Petrol	− 100	0
Tobacco	+ 200	0
Alcohol	0	− 200
Social security	− 500	− 400
Poll tax	− 800	− 500
Rates	0	0

Governments often seem little better than anyone else at guessing future tax levels, and they may find that they end a year with more, or less, tax than planned, and that they need to make adjustments for the next year to compensate. The box shows two recent examples of the level of official error, namely those made at the beginning of the 1990–91 and 1991–92 tax years, as compared with the official figures at the end of the year. The 1990–91 figures show a number of errors, to some extent, cancelling each other out. The full figures show a total overestimate of government revenue of £2 billion. In 1991–92 the errors were all one way, and the overestimate was £4.4 billion. This shows the Treasury misjudging the deep recession that the British economy suffered at that time.

After those problems come the deliberate changes. These may be for political reasons – to encourage or discourage some kind of behaviour – or for technical reasons – a tax allowance does not work properly. Or they may be for international reasons, for example our government has agreed to a change internationally, or is forced to respond to a change in another state's tax laws in order to remain competitive.

The taxes to be reviewed

Although the order in which a Chancellor announces things in his Budget is a political decision, with brinkmanship being a tempting tactic, the changes to be reviewed are usually set out in the Finance Bill in a well-established order as follows:

Excise duties

Taxes on drinks, petrol and other specific taxes are mainly flat-rate. They need uprating each year to keep pace with inflation. This applies to spirits, beer, wine and cider; tobacco products; hydrocarbon oil duty (or petrol tax); vehicle excise duty (the car 'disc' fee); betting and gaming duties. But the Chancellor has an awkward decision: if he puts up excise duties, up goes inflation too. This is because the average household expenditure on which the inflation figures recorded in the RPI (Retail Prices Index) includes each of these items. Even so, this is always headline material. Car tax, though separate, may be added to this list.

Value added tax

Rates and taxable items are reviewed, and technical changes made – not too many, because the main VAT rules are laid down throughout Europe. Any major change needs permission from Brussels, and if the Chancellor does not get it the result could be embarrassing.

Income tax

The rate for the new tax year must be set, plus the levels of personal allowances, mortgage relief, and all other reliefs requiring adjustment. These changes make the biggest headlines. If changes are not made, some occur automatically, on an inflation-linked basis, while others will not be altered, and therefore decrease in real terms. There are then a number of technical changes: anti-avoidance provisions, new reliefs for policy or other reasons.

Corporation tax

This is the income tax on companies, and again its rate for the year, plus allowances, must be set each year, with any changes to the law. Important to business, but not for the headline writers.

Capital gains tax

This tax on profits made on the sale of capital items also needs to have its rates reviewed and any technical or policy changes made.

Oil taxation

The special tax on North Sea oil, the petroleum revenue tax, is not an annual tax, but there will usually be technical changes needed.

Inheritance tax

In most years, the special tax on property left on death, and on large gifts, will require adjustment, although the tax and its rates are permanent.

Stamp duties

These old taxes, literally stamped on documents, are now only important for the deeds by which land is transferred or leased.

Other changes

Other taxes, such as the gas levy, may have to be altered. There will be a few announcements about national savings, and other items of government income or profits.

We have seen the relative importance of the taxes, and the scope for error in a budget. To put that information in context, some idea of the value of tax allowances and reliefs under the control of the Chancellor at Budget time is useful.

ALLOWANCE	AMOUNT (£billion)
Income tax allowances	32.4
Pensions and contributions	10.7
Tax reliefs on homes:	11.5
mortgate relief	6.1
no CGT on homes	2.0
no VAT on homes	3.4
Capital investments	12.2
No VAT on food	7.0
Overseas tax relief	2.3
No VAT on private fuel	2.5

The table shows the main tax allowances for 1992: those in that year worth more than £1 billion for the year.

Tax expenditures

Allowances have been termed *tax expenditures* by tax economists. This reflects the thinking that tax allowances have the same effect on government revenues as direct expenditure. The practice in many OECD states, including the United Kingdom, has been to attempt estimates of the annual cost of each allowance, so that they can be made a positive part of government thinking on expenditure.

For example, the figures for the United Kingdom for 1991–92 in the table above show that the mortgage interest relief on income tax had the same effect as a cash subsidy to homeowners of £6 billion, with a further £2 billion relief for not taxing the gains on sales of taxpayers' main homes, and another £3.4 billion paid out by way of subsidy on new homes (the VAT relief to builders and their customers by way of zero-rating new homes rather than making them liable to standard rate VAT). To put these figures in some context, the planned public expenditure on housing, by way of direct expenditure on public authority building programmes and grants, was about £6 billion. The pattern of housing ownership showed that more than 65 per cent of homes were owner-occupied, the mortgage relief being paid to owner-occupiers of 40 per cent of all homes (compared with 30 per cent ten years before). Mortgage interest relief therefore gets paid, over a lifetime, to most homeowners, and to a majority of all households.

Put another way, the total value of income tax allowances averages £2,500 a year of tax saved for a family of four, with tax savings on pensions of about a further £1,000 for a family and tax relief on the family's house of a further £1,500. These figures show that the 'gaps' in taxes, or allowances, can be even more important than the taxes themselves. For instance, £1.2 billion was collected under the capital gains tax on, for example, the sale of shares. Had capital gains tax applied to people's private houses, that tax would have collected £3.2 billion, or almost three times as much.

One thing politicians have been doing over the last few years is trying to weed out these gaps, because they can involve huge sums. For instance, putting VAT on food would raise as much money as putting the VAT rate on everything else up by 4 per cent (even though VAT *is already* charged on food served in canteens, bars and so forth, and on hot takeaway meals and things such as chocolate and ice-cream). Were that to be done, an average of £250 could, for example, be taken off the poll tax. That would remove the poll tax charge completely from large parts of the country. But who would be better off it that happened? And who would be worse off?

Why these taxes?

The idea of replacing a smaller tax by adjustments to a larger tax is one that has tempted several past Chancellors. Critics regularly argue for the abolition of some of our taxes because they are not needed. For example, we could abolish inheritance tax and increase income tax by the appropriate amount. We could abolish NI contributions and increase income tax by the appropriate amount. We could replace the poll tax by a local share of income tax. We could abolish the vehicle excise duty and compensate by raising the tax on petrol by a little. We could abolish car tax and compensate by raising the tax on petrol a little. Each of those arguments has been heard (some advocated by significant political groupings) recently. Each has the advantage of being *revenue neutral,* that is, they are reforms which leave the Treasury with the same net tax intake. Each has the apparent advantage of simplicity, with the linked advantage of taking tax off some desirable activity or group of people. Each also emphasises how little is the tax yield from some of our taxes. Why do we not do this?

If we count excise duties on oil, tobacco, and alcohol as one tax (there are legally several separate taxes, but the key issues are the same, with considerable areas of common legislation), most of the revenues are raised by six taxes:

1	Income tax	**4**	Excises
2	NI contributions	**5**	Corporation tax
3	VAT	**6**	Business rates

These taxes each raise £15 billion or more. No other tax individually raises much more than £3 billion (save the poll tax, which no longer exists). Together in 1991–92 they raised £185 billion of the state's total revenues of £222 billion. If we abolished some of the main tax expenditures noted earlier in this chapter, for instance income tax allowances, tax relief for pensions, capital allowances, and the main VAT zero rates, we could abolish all the taxes save these six, and still afford to cut tax rates. Why do we not do it?

The base-rate tradeoff

The argument in the last paragraph employs an idea which conveniently can be called the base-rate tradeoff. The rates of a tax can be reduced on a revenue neutral basis if some of the tax expenditures within the tax are abolished. It is a tactic which has been pursued with success in a number of countries, including most western European countries and the USA, in the last decade.

One spectacular example of a base-rate tradeoff was introduced for corporation tax. Before the reform, the main rate of corporation tax was 52 per cent, a rate at which it had been levied for a decade. After it, the rate was 35 per cent (since reduced to 33 per cent), but the Treasury received *more tax* not less from the same taxpayers. This trick was performed by removing from the tax base of the tax, two major forms of allowance: 100 per cent capital allowances for plant and machinery, and other kinds of capital expenditure, and inflation relief for stock (or inventory) values. Result: the taxable profits of the companies had been increased to such an extent that, taxed at 35 per cent, they produced more revenue than the previous, smaller, total of profits taxed at 52 per cent.

The base-rate tradeoff can be performed on any tax, but it is particularly attractive as a revenue-neutral way of reforming a major tax. There are three reasons for this:

(a) any allowance in a tax is a tax expenditure, but it is less obvious than a grant. It is better, for open discussion, to have no tax expenditures, but to adjust the position of taxpayers to the same extent if desired through grants financed from the tax;

(b) a tax without expenditures is simpler: less distorting in an economic sense, less difficult to administer, less tempting to the tax planner looking for *tax shelters* (ways of sheltering income or transactions from tax, that is, ways of arranging activities so that they pay no or less tax);

(c) the attraction of lower tax rates for themselves.

—— Is there a 'best' rate for a tax? ——

It is possible to levy any tax at any rate. The rate could be over 100 per cent. It could be a negative figure. Normally, we expect a tax to be at a rate between one per cent and 99 per cent, if we intend it as a money-raiser for more than one year. The rate we choose will reflect our need for money from that source, and our social judgments about the level at which taxpayers should pay. Those social judgments meant that the British income tax in 1977–78 had a rate table which looked like this:

INCOME TAX RATES 1977–78

On the first	£6,000 of taxable income	34%
On the next	£1,000	40%
On the next	£1,000	45%
On the next	£1,000	50%
On the next	£1,000	55%
On the next	£2,000	60%
On the next	£2,000	65%
On the next	£2,000	70%
On the next	£5,000	75%
On the balance		83%

On so much of the investment income, included in the above as exceeded £1,500:

On the first £500 an additional 10 per cent;
On the balance an additional 15 per cent.

Those used to the income tax rates of the last few years may wince at this (as those who paid those higher rates in 1977–78 probably will!). If we read that budget, we find corporation tax at 52 per cent and similarly high rates of inheritance tax. Yet the Budget that introduced these new rates was a reforming, rate-cutting budget! With the benefit of hindsight, we can see that these very high top rates did little to change the overall balance of the Budget. The total tax revenues of the state that year were less than those after the top tax rate of every tax had been cut to 40 per cent. One reason, it was argued, was that the rates were too high, and defeated their own purpose. No one would go out of his way to invest for an income return of ordinary levels, if 98 per cent of that return were taken away for tax. Few would be prepared to exert themselves if 83 per cent of the results of their exertions were enjoyed by others.

The argument could be stated simply. At the rate of zero per cent, a tax raises no revenue. At the rate of 100 per cent, it will raise no revenue because no one will undertake activities taxed at that rate. They will either avoid the tax, or evade it, or simply stop work. A rate of, say, 50 per cent, will raise tax. Therefore, there must be some point between zero per cent and 100 per cent where there is an optimal rate of tax, that is, the rate which raises the most revenue from that particular kind of tax. If the rate is higher than the optimal rate, the tax will yield less revenue. If it is lower, it will also yield less revenue, though it will do so with less distortion. This idea could be presented in graph form as a simple curve, which was named after its originator as a *Laffer curve*. Each point on the curve represents the tax yield resulting from a particular rate of tax.

A Laffer curve identifying the best tax rate

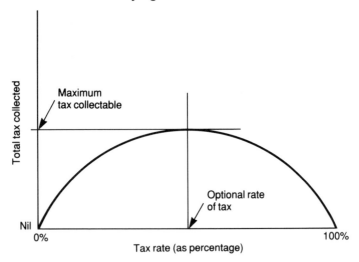

Note: this graph is purely representational. The 'optional rate of tax' is the rate at which maximum tax revenues are collectable. Individual views put this between 15 and 50 per cent.

The Laffer curve is a seductively attractive idea, particularly for those arguing that the present rates are too high up the curve. Cut the rates, and we pay more tax more happily! Commentators since the promulgation of this idea have challenged its theory and also its practical application. How, in real life, can you decide where the points are on the graph? Is it one curve or a twisted, distorted line? Is it affected by factors such as the popularity of the political party imposing it or the purposes of the taxes?

Whether or not it is justified, the idea worked as an approach to taxation because of its simple message: cut tax rates, and you will receive more tax! This was used as a justification for cutting tax rates in the 1980s. It was, in Britain, put to a severe test in the 1992 general election where 'the tax burden' was subject to considerable discussion. One party proposed to decrease the basic rate of income tax, one to increase it a little at the basic rate and rather more at higher rates and one to maintain the basic rate while increasing the effective higher rates sharply. Minor parties added more radical alternatives. The political debate during the campaign returned frequently to the question of tax. The result was that the party promising 'tax cuts' (by which it meant income tax cuts) won a clear victory over all other parties. Was that surprising?

The political judgment

The ideal tax from an economic standpoint still has to be acceptable. The poll tax made that point. Budgets have to be a balance between what is economically sensible and what is politically acceptable.

What makes a tax politically acceptable? Undoubtedly, it is in part a sense of 'fairness'. The 1992 election campaign illustrates several variants of this. First, and unusually, there is the sense of fairness in which tax-payers feel they are not paying enough. That was why one political party felt able to approach the 1992 election on a policy of raising the basic rate of income tax. Second, there is the rather different question of fairness, or equity, between taxpayers. 'He ought to pay as much as me.' Finally, there is the vertical equity aspect of fairness: the rich ought to pay more (see page 16). This, put simply, was the political message of another of the political parties in the 1992 election.

It is from varying concepts of fairness that minor taxes have been evolved. It explains the creation of the capital gains tax, as a way of catching additions to wealth of – typically – wealthier individuals that do not get taxed for income tax. It explains the introduction and maintenance of the estate duty and then the inheritance tax. It provided one reason for the taxes from which our excise duties evolved.

Another political influence is the innate conservatism of many towards taxation. 'An old tax is a good tax.' It may not be 'good', but it is usually better than a new tax. There is a heavy onus of proof, in practice, on anyone wishing to replace an old tax with a new one. It is better to stick with what has been tried and tested, even if it is itself imperfect. As a result, taxes tend to evolve rather than be radically overhauled.

The reluctance to change explains much of our present pattern of direct taxes. The income tax is effectively a very different tax from that which was introduced in 1806, but its legal framework is still much the same, and its name and key structure have not been changed in the last century. New ideas have been fitted into the old framework.

Administrative pressures

There are two further factors which are strong influences on a Chancellor. One is the administrative aspect of any reform, and the other is the international repercussions of a particular choice.

The administrative aspect is a significant, but often understated, influence. Each simplification removes the need for tax officials and, equally, expert advisers. Additional complications mean additional cost in compliance and enforcement. For example, the introduction of a lower rate band of 20 per cent income tax on the first £2,000, proposed by the government in the 1992 March Budget, demanded an extra 800 tax officials to supervise it, as well as extra work for employers in calculating the tax to be deducted. By contrast, the sharp increase in personal income tax allowances which were offered in the 1992 opposition March budget would have taken considerable numbers of people outside the tax net and would, therefore, have cut both official and employer workloads, at least for that year.

Complex rules required skilled and highly trained individuals who may be hard to recruit at public service pay rates, and who, once trained, can easily be 'poached' to the private sector with offers of increased remuneration. It may be difficult to deal with such rules without skilled personnel. In other countries, but thankfully not in the United Kingdom, the question of official corruption also has to be considered when designing a tax. The narrower the scope for official discretion, the narrower the scope for corruption. It helps if taxes are official-proof!

Any reform may impose heavy permanent or temporary burdens on officials. The separate taxation of husband and wife was not introduced until 1990 (even though the need for it had become politically inevitable many years before) because the taxing of the extra three million tax-payers, which the new system involved, required either many more officials or the development of a complex computer system. As the officials could not be recruited, separate taxation had to wait until computers were available.

International aspects

A major limit on recent budgets is one that Chancellors are reluctant to stress: taxes, and the economic effects of those taxes, have to be integrated into an increasingly interlocked world system. There are two pressures at play: one is the need for our pattern of taxation to mesh into the internationally accepted forms of taxation; the other, and opposite, pressure, is that of international competition between states.

The pressure of conformity arises because of the increasing amount of crossborder activity, often run through companies based in both the countries involved. For example, a company which trades in the United Kingdom and in the United States is liable to corporate income tax in both countries on its profits. This form of double taxation is reduced by a bilateral treaty, the United Kingdom–United States Double Tax Treaty. The treaty only works if both the UK and the USA rely on direct corporate taxes. It does not cover, for example, VAT. The conformity is particularly important in the European Community, which is why this is discussed in a later chapter.

The pressures of competition with the Community are at their strongest. If, for example, a business can establish itself anywhere in the Community, one of the factors the business will take into account is the levels of tax in each country. It can do this because there are now no customs duties within the Community, nor does VAT present any problem. Increasingly, any changes in the United Kingdom are reviewed in terms of their international effects as well as their effects in this country.

Compare that with the first 'modern' budget of Lloyd George noted above, where mention of other countries and what they were doing was largely irrelevant except in military terms. Perhaps we are now into the generation of post-modern budgets, where actions of one country cannot be separated from the world economy or what happens in other states. How far, in all this, does the United Kingdom Chancellor have genuine choices? How far do the British people have genuine choices? Is this year's budget becoming so predictable that it is losing its importance? Is that the reason for the budgetary reforms indicated in 1992?

5

TAXING THE WORKERS

—— **Today's taxable employees** ——

When income tax was introduced in 1799 it was not – as it is largely now – a tax on people's earnings from their work. It was a tax on the wealthy, and few paid it. The rules were altered in 1803 to stop some avoidance, but the levy was confined to the privileged few. Now nearly all the income tax collected comes from earnings of employees. Curiously, the rules under which the tax is paid are still, at basis, those of 1803 even though the scope of the tax has changed completely.

In recent years this tax has not proved enough. Most employees have been liable, since 1975, to pay a second income tax – NI contributions. Contributions have to be paid both by employees and employers. The amount payable is worked out separately from income tax under different rules.

The combined rate of these taxes is 34 per cent on a worker receiving the average weekly level of earnings and up to 10.4 per cent on the employer, a composite rate of 44 per cent. Against that, the top rate of income tax is 40 per cent, with no NI contributions on top earnings of the employee and the same 10.4 per cent on the employer, a composite rate of 50 per cent. In other words, the privileged now pay little more than the rest of us. In fact, because of perks, they may pay quite a lot less than this on some of their earnings – but so may the rest of us!

In this chapter, we examine income tax on earnings and the NI contribution system as it applies to employees. But first, who is an employee?

Who is an employee?

The income tax rules operating on employees come under the quaint name of Schedule E. The precise charge is still – in words coming directly from 1803 – on 'offices or employments'. With the typical thoroughness of our tax laws, we are told nothing else about who is, or is not, the holder of an office or employment. It is left to revenue officials and the courts to decide.

The judges decided that, in the absence of any special rules, the decision about who was an employee, self-employed or not employed, was to be taken on the same basis as in general law, for example trade union law. The same rules also apply for NI contributions and social security benefits, and in deciding who is liable to collect VAT.

Despite the importance of the distinction between employees and others, the rules made by the judges are imprecise and difficult to state concisely. The general idea is to distinguish between those at work on their own account, and those who work under a contract for someone else. Applying the rules in practice is more difficult because of the importance of the distinction. It is generally felt that employees pay more tax than the self-employed, partly because of the rules and partly because the self-employed find it easier to fiddle the system. For this reason many people who are in reality employees have tried to allege they are self-employed.

Both employed and self-employed?

You cannot be an employee for one purpose and self-employed for another in connection with the same job. In a case a few years ago two employees arranged to be treated as self-employed for both tax and NI purposes. When they were sacked from their work they claimed they were employees and were unfairly dismissed. The judges agreed that they were employees, and that they had been unfairly dismissed, and were entitled to compensation. However, the judges added that the claimants would probably gain little from this as the effect of the decision would be that both Inland Revenue and social security officials would need to revise the amount of tax and NI contributions payable while the claimants had their jobs. The excess tax due would probably exceed the compensation!

To deal with problem cases, revenue and social security officers have questionnaires to help them sort out what is happening. These ask questions like: Do you work for one person or several? Do you work at your own place of work or someone else's? Do you use your own vehicle or tools? Are you paid by the hour, the week or the job? What happens about sick pay or holidays?

In recent years, the Inland Revenue in particular has examined closely several areas of activity and decided that many who thought they were self-employed are actually employees. This has happened in theatre, television and the film industry, to teachers and to musicians. In many cases, informal agreements have been reached with trade unions or employer groups as to the way in which a person should be treated. It has not solved all the problems, and it has left many more people taxed as employees.

What complicates the rule in the case of those in their own business is the ease with which they can turn themselves into employees. They can do it simply by setting up a company and getting the company to run the business. From that point, the company is the 'person' running its own business, and the individual, if he or she works in the business, is treated as an employee of the company, even if also managing director and only shareholder. This is because directors of companies are office-holders and, as such, are treated in the same way as employees. This also applies to other office-holders such as local councillors, MPs, trustees, bishops or judges.

Another complication is that individuals can be both employed and self-employed at the same time. The fact that they are paying tax in one capacity does not remove liability to pay income tax in the other capacity, although it may prevent a second charge to NI contributions. In cases where someone has both kinds of earnings, each kind of earnings is taxed separately.

Pensions and social security

The Schedule E rules about employment earnings also apply to occupational and private pensions. These forms of pension, whether paid for by the employer or the employee, were tax-privileged before payment and are regarded as delayed earnings. Most forms of state retirement pension and some forms of social security benefit are also taxable as earnings. Those benefits payable to those of working age and usually able to work are taxable, including unemployment benefit, income support, statutory sick pay and statutory maternity pay. Benefits for children, including child benefit, and for the long term disabled, such as the disabled living allowance, are not taxed. One reason for taxing workers' benefits is to reduce the effect of the unemployment and poverty traps. In particular, when unemployment benefit was non-taxable, someone becoming unemployed could receive a large tax rebate as an unintended addition to unemployment support. More controversially, as strikes were regarded as a form of unemployment until recent law changes, strikers could receive an unintended form of state assistance through the tax rebates due.

Income tax on earnings

Most earnings from employment present no problems from a tax point of view except for ensuring that the tax is paid in the right amounts on the right date. Cash earnings are taxed under a well-tried mechanism known as PAYE (Pay As You Earn) both to income tax and to NI contributions. The PAYE system is well crafted and usually ensures that the right amount of both tax and NI contributions are paid by the employee for a tax year. The tax and NI rules, and PAYE, cover all cash payments including overtime and bonuses, holiday and sick pay, and irregular and lump sum payments. Problems arise in two areas: in dealing with payments other than cash and in deciding whether payments do, or do not, come from the job.

Taxing non-cash payments

The trouble in taxing non-cash payments comes from the law itself. Using words lifted straight from 1803, an employee has to pay tax in respect of her or his job on the '*emoluments therefrom*'. If that is meaningless to you, do not worry. The term 'emolument' is obsolete, though it apparently came from the Latin word meaning to 'grind out' so it may still be regarded as entirely appropriate. To counter this obscurity, the law gives us the further guidance that the tax covers '*all salaries, fees, wages, perquisites and profits whatsoever*'. Perquisites is also a word from the past – but perks is not!

It might be thought, given the sweeping terms of this definition, that everything anyone earns from a job, whether in cash or kind, will be subject to income tax. But over a century ago, judges ruled that tax could only be imposed on non-cash benefits to the extent that they could be turned into cash. For example, if my employer gives me free meals in the staff canteen, I cannot, in reality, go out and sell them, and, therefore, I cannot be taxed on them. Two developments led from this narrow reading of the law: schemes to turn pay into non-cash forms by vouchers of various forms, and the perks business. Both kinds of scheme are now affected by anti-avoidance rules, with two important exceptions: profit-related pay and employee share schemes.

Profit-related pay

PRP is not a non-cash scheme, but it is not a normal pay scheme either, though the Conservative government that introduced PRP wished it to become so. The aim of PRP is to use a tax carrot to encourage people to receive part of their pay in the form of a profit-related bonus. The tax carrot is generous – no income tax at all. The limit is also generous for most employees: up to 20 per cent of total earnings or £4,000, whichever is lower in any year. There is some bureaucracy attached, including a bar on any public sector employee receiving a bonus in this form, and a registration scheme. PRP also depends on the employer earning profits after tax – easier said than done in a recession.

Employee share schemes

It has been the aim of several Conservative governments to encourage private share ownership. A major aspect of this policy has been to encourage employees to become shareholders in their own employers. As with PRP, one way of doing this is a tax carrot. The first of the present tax carrots was introduced by the Lib-Lab Pact in 1978.

Another element of share-based schemes has entered the corporate scene from the USA: executive share schemes. These are schemes, aimed at senior members of a company, which are designed to give them significant shareholdings in the company based on the market value of the company's shares. The results sometimes can be spectacular: one corporate boss received $78 million in 1990 from his company (Time Warner) this way! Neither Germany nor Japan see the need for this form of remuneration.

Profit sharing scheme

There are a number of forms of share-related schemes. The one introduced by the Lib-Labs is the *profit sharing scheme* in which a company can pay a bonus to its employees each year from its profits in the form of shares. If the scheme follows the required form, the shares are transferred to a trust and held by the trust for the employee for five years. After that period, the shares are transferred to the employee, who receives them free of any income tax on the original value of the shares and free of any capital gains tax on any increase in market value of the shares while in the trust. This allows an employee to acquire a valuable shareholding in the company over time. The maximum permissible benefit in this scheme is 10 per cent of salary up to a maximum of £8,000. These schemes are widely used by major British companies.

Savings-related share option scheme

Another widely used scheme is a *savings–related share option scheme.* This uses the tax carrot hidden in the SAYE scheme (Save As You Earn) in which the saver enters a 5-year or 7-year contractual savings scheme, receiving a special tax bonus. This is linked to another tax carrot, a tax-free share option scheme. The idea is that I agree to take out an option on the shares of my employer to buy them at not less than 85 per cent of present market value five or seven years from now. I also enter an SAYE contract and start saving on a monthly basis. At the end of five years, I should have saved in tax-efficient form enough to buy the shares on which I have the option. Unless my company is doing badly, the shares will then be worth a lot more than when I acquire the option, so I can buy the shares at a discount to market price, and make a further profit. If the scheme meets Inland Revenue requirements, the profit will be tax free. If the shares are worth less than the option price, I do not buy them, but pocket the savings. The effect is that significant gains can be made, but no losses arise.

Both profit sharing schemes and option schemes are designed to apply to employees generally. A company can add to this executive schemes in which selected individuals are given options to acquire blocks of stock at present prices (with a maximum discount of 15 per cent). These again can be tax free if certain conditions are met. The idea is that the employee will be keen to ensure maximum appreciation of the market value of the employer's shares, so as to benefit most from the option scheme. These schemes can also be twisted to form, what are sometimes termed, 'golden handcuffs' – schemes which prevent senior executives' leaving. For example, the scheme could provide that an executive who leaves loses all entitlement of the scheme.

PRP and employee share schemes are examples of tax being used for social engineering purposes. The aims only apply to one sector of employment, the private sector, and might seem to fail the 'fairness' test of tax, but their objective is to improve industrial and commercial profitability and effectiveness, so that the schemes assist efficiency. It is, as always, a political judgment as to which should prevail.

Paying by voucher

Vouchers are examples of tax engineering – the use of schemes to minimise tax to the advantage only of the taxpayers. They arise from the weakness in the law in catching non-cash payments. An example shows how: Em has to travel to work by train. The cheapest way of doing this is to buy a season ticket, but that costs a lot. Em's employer is prepared to help. How should it do so? It could give Em a grant of the amount of the ticket, although this would be a substantial pay rise. Further, Em would be taxed on the amount paid. Instead, therefore, the employer could arrange, direct with British Rail, for a season ticket to be supplied to Em. This would cost the employer the same, but Em would not be taxed on the ticket. Why? Because season tickets are not transferable, and so the ticket has no cash value in Em's hands.

It is the season ticket 'dodge', and many like it are the targets of the 'voucher' rules. Other forms of 'voucher' include credit cards issued to employees where the employer pays the repayments, schemes where employees are given certificates or vouchers towards the cost of a holiday which the employer pays for, and so forth.

Most voucher schemes do not now work because anti-avoidance tax provisions bring the value of the voucher into tax as if it were cash. To stop the provisions double taxing, they work by treating the employee as earning an amount equal to the cost of the employer in providing the voucher, but ignoring the item or amount that the employee receives by cashing in the voucher. The same effect occurs if the employer provides the employee with a credit card or other means of buying items on the employer's credit.

There are limited exceptions to these provisions, the main ones are: to prevent a charge to tax on travel provided by transport companies such as British Rail to their employees; to prevent tax being imposed on car parking spaces provided at or near work; and to prevent tax on entertainment provided by someone other than the employer (such as an invitation to a party and cabaret run by a client or supplier). If there is no voucher, document, token or stamp of any kind, these anti-avoidance sections do not work. There must be some kind of tangible evidence of the scheme for them to take effect. They could catch faxes, but not telephone calls!

The perks business

From the narrowness of the law grew the perks business. This has led to something of a running battle between tax officials and lobby groups, with various Chancellors of the Exchequer in the middle. The principle of equity, or fairness, in taxation argues that two people earning the same amount from a job should pay the same amount of tax. That is easy if both are being paid in cash, but how do you decide on the amount that an employee receives if he or she is given a benefit in kind? The rule about the cash value to the employee does not work because it is easy to ensure that a perk has no cash value. Nor do the answers provided by the voucher provisions, as they only operate if there are documents of some kind or other which identify particular transactions. A number of possible answers is available. Tax could be levied on the cost to the employee of buying or receiving the asset. For example, if I lose £10 a week in exchange for the company car, that is the value of the car to me. Judges decided that this rule could be applied some years ago, but it merely stopped employers providing benefits in exchange for reduced earnings. Another value would be the cost saved to the employee in connection with the benefit. For example, if I go out and order a new coat, but my employer gives me a cheque with which to pay the bill, then I can be taxed on the value of the cheque. Again, it can be avoided in a very simple way. I choose the coat, but it is the employer who pays the bill direct. That will be caught if the employer gives me a voucher with which to collect my coat, but that, too, can be avoided.

The difficulty in finding a workable general rule has forced governments to seek special legislation dealing with these benefits. However, only a few of these special provisions were aimed at taxpayers generally, the widest ones being the voucher provisions. Others are discussed below. The main provisions were introduced on a selective basis, targetted at the high earners who most abused (in the government's views) the weaknesses of the general law. The targeting was done by setting a cash limit, and catching all those whose total earnings from an employment came above that limit. In 1978, the limit was raised to £8,500, and there it has stayed. Since then average earnings have risen so that even those earning less than average full-time earnings now get caught in the 'special' rules. The old, general rules and the few special rules of general application only now apply to low earners, or those with part-time jobs.

The anti-perk rules

There are two main anti-perk rules. The first captures all sums paid on expense accounts and treats them as cash earnings. This means that the employee is taxed in full on them unless he or she can claim a deduction (as explained below). The second provides that, subject only to specific rules, any benefit provided to an employee or to any member of the employee's family or household, resulting from the employee's employment is treated as taxable earnings.

There are only limited exceptions to this general rule. The main ones are:

- car-parking space at, or near, work,
- accommodation and supplies provided solely for use at work,
- pensions and other payments on death or retirement, and pension contributions to approved pension schemes,
- meals in the staff canteen,
- staff Christmas parties, or equivalent, costing less than £50 a person,
- medical insurance and treatment when travelling abroad on business,
- entertainment provided by an outside body and not in connection with any particular work or service,
- child-care facilities at work,
- services such as free medical or financial advice provided at work, at no extra cost to the employer,
- in limited cases, job-related accommodation (such as police houses or a warden's flat).

Both rules work by the P11D procedure. The employer must complete a form (P11D) detailing all expenses and perks received by an employee, and the Inland Revenue collect the tax by adjusting the tax code used for PAYE. How much must the employer enter on the form as the value of a perk?

Company cars

Aside from pensions (which are not subject to tax under these provisions), the most common perk is an employer-provided car. The value of a car is decided by a tariff laid down each year and which sets the sum of money treated as being received where an employee has a car made available. The amount depends on the age of the car, its value, its engine size and the number of miles driven on business that year. The only exception is for pooled cars, where cars are available to a number of employees.

There is also a separate charge if petrol is provided free of charge by the employer. This charge is also based on the engine size of the car. Taken together, the two charges could amount to a substantial charge to tax. The extent of the provision of cars with jobs suggests, rightly, that for many years the tax charge was much less than the economic value of the car. There were several reasons for this. One is the fact that an employer, particularly a larger one, can buy a car at a big discount, and can therefore buy the car much more cheaply than the employee, and similarly can maintain it more cheaply.

For many years there was a deliberate decision not to tax cars too heavily. The reason was that fleet purchases by employers were traditionally of British-built cars. One of the sources of these cars was the firm variously known as Austin Morris, British Leyland and latterly Rover. It was, of course, a government-owned company. Too high a rate of tax on company cars might stop companies buying such cars, that is, might stop companies buying government-built cars. The price of a 'fair' level of tax on cars might have been a bankrupt state-owned car company.

In the late eighties, there were two important changes to this: the government sold off its car companies, and the environmental lobby gained strength. Recently the tax charge on a company car has risen substantially ahead of inflation – in 1991 by 20 per cent. The tax cost of a car may now in some cases be greater than the tax on a level of cash earnings needed to pay for a car. This is often true where the company gives an executive a second company car. It may be true for low-mileage cars. The hidden bonus remains the company's buying power, but that could be passed on to the executive in other ways, for example a salary deduction scheme. It will be interesting to see if the 'must have a car' culture survives the tax advantages of that attitude.

Rules for other benefits

There are special rules for mobile telephones (charged as a benefit of £200 a year if available for private use), benefits obtained from employee shareholdings (unless in approved schemes as discussed above), expenses connected with accommodation provided by the employer (for instance, free heating), schemes under which the employer pays a director's tax (the tax will itself be taxed), and scholarships (usually made to the employee's children).

Where special rules do not apply, the approach is to charge tax on the cost to the employer of providing the benefit, less any amount that the employee pays. This is inappropriate where the benefit consists of lending property to the employee or family (for example, a holiday cottage for a fortnight). Here the rule is that the employee is charged, on an annual basis, the full rental value of any land, or 20 per cent of the market value at the time of any other item, plus any direct additional expenses. In the example, the employee would be assumed to be receiving a benefit equal to the rent not paid on the holiday cottage (plus a charge on its contents).

Beneficial loans

The final group of anti-perk provisions are designed to deal with another benefit widely enjoyed, particularly in the banking and finance industries – the cheap loan. Typically, the employer allows the employee to borrow money on beneficial terms for set purposes. One is for the purchase of a house on taking up the job. Others, on a smaller scale, may be for the purchase of a car, the purchase of a season ticket, or perhaps a loan to tide an employee over a particular difficulty. The loans are often paid back by deduction from each salary payment at an agreed rate, but the advantage comes in the waiving or reduction of interest on the loan.

An interest-free loan may allow the employee to borrow at a low rate. This is a considerable advantage which, under the normal rules, also saves tax because, again, there is no cash value. Tax law therefore creates a tax value by imposing an official interest rate (most recently, 12.25 per cent), and assuming that all employees ought to pay at this rate. If they do not then they have a beneficial loan, and they will be charged tax on the amount by which the interest they pay is less than the interest they should be paying at this official rate.

To that rule there are two main exceptions. The first, home loans (on which tax relief is allowed in any case) do not get caught, and the second, there will not be a tax charge unless the amount of interest saved is at least £300. This rule allows employers to lend sums of up to £2,500, or so, in season ticket schemes without difficulty, and the first rule allows the cheap mortgages traditionally provided by banks and others at interest rates significantly below commercial rates to continue.

Taxing directors

Directors are, in principle, treated the same as employees because they are office holders. But they present the Inland Revenue with extra problems because they are the select few in charge of their company and so can make special arrangements for themselves. The boards of smaller companies present other problems. These may be the companies set up so that the business is not owned by the individual who, in practice, runs it entirely as his or her own. They can pay themselves in any way they like, including loans ahead of the declaration of dividends and generous benefits in kind. Other members of the family can be made directors and remunerated well for their important advisory duties to the managing director! Tax authorities face problems in taxing directors because the arrangements they make with their companies may seem generous, but may be thoroughly deserved. Equally, there are no national or usual terms of remuneration to reward, for example, the inventor whose invention is being exploited by her or his company to produce huge profits.

Is there anything which does not get caught? As always with British tax law, the rules are not all-embracing. In practice, few areas have escaped the legislators' eyes, except for the issue of overseas earnings and expenses, where another set of special rules has to apply. Items which remain tax-free, apart from specific exceptions such as car parking, are items or services provided by an employer at no marginal cost. It is difficult to identify many goods that can be supplied in that way, but if a member of staff gives advice (medical, legal, financial,) to another member of staff as part of his duties to his employer, it will be difficult to identify how it costs the employer more.

Taxing the lower paid

The rules just described provide an armoury of rules for taxing directors and most employees, but they do not apply to those earning less than £8,500 including the value of perks. They are still subject to the old rules, backed up by the voucher rules. These people are not caught by the car and loan rules. Among employees in this range, the one major benefit historically has, instead, been the provision of free or subsidised accommodation. Many groups have benefited in this way: farm and estate workers; hotel, hostel and hospital staff; the police; members of the armed forces; domestic staff and nannies.

Accommodation and moving costs

In these cases, there may be different reasons for providing the accommodation: because the employee needs to live on or near the job, or because it is a cheap way for the employer to pay the employee. In both cases there is a benefit, sometimes of considerable value, to the employee, but should it be taxed? The answer of our tax laws is to identify three groups of people who should not be taxed, and to tax the rest.

The groups not taxed are those who are provided with their accommodation by reason of their employment because:

1 it is necessary that the employee lives in the accommodation to do the job properly (e. g. a lighthouse keeper);

2 the employee is working in the kind of employment where the provision of accommodation is usual, and where he or she is offered accommodation so that the job can be done better (e. g. farm workers);

3 the employee lives in the accommodation as part of special security arrangements (e. g. some Northern Ireland employees).

Employees within these groups are also exempt from the tax charges on their accommodation that apply to those earning more than £8,500. However, free or subsidised provision of accommodation usually involves the provision of such things as free heating, lighting and maintenance, and perhaps also furniture, which can add up to substantial benefits. Those earning more than £8,500 have to pay tax on those extra benefits – up to a value equal to ten per cent of their pay other than these benefits.

Another major living cost, associated with work, is the cost of moving either to take up a job or at the demand or request of the employer. Moving may cost the employee several thousands of pounds, but strictly this is personal and not work expenditure. None the less, most employers

– including the Inland Revenue itself – provide expenses for employees moving to or during their employment. These expenses may include special allowances because the employee is, for example, moving from one part of the country to a more expensive part, or to cover the costs of having to move at a time when it is difficult to sell the employee's present house.

Strict application of the law, particularly to those earning more than £8,500 in their employment, will make most of such payments taxable as earnings or perks, at least in the cases where the employee is moving without changing employer. If that were done, the employee would still end up out of pocket on the allowances. To avoid this effect, the Inland Revenue has issued an extra-statutory concession, A67, which, while not the law, stops tax on payments that are no higher than those allowed to civil servants required to move because of their employment.

Is it paid for work reasons?

The question of taxing removal expenses of someone given a grant towards taking up a new job raises another question of principle. Is the payment by the future employer a payment in respect of work for the employer? To be taxable as income, the receipt must come *from* the job, rather than from some other reason. For example, if I give one of my staff a present for Christmas, is that a taxable perk?

The rules say that anything given because of the job arises from the work, but gifts given for personal reasons are not job-related and are therefore not taxable. This is why tax inspectors tax the tips received traditionally by taxi-drivers, restaurant staff and hairdressers. It is only if a special tip is given, for example at Christmas, that it can be regarded as a personal gift.

The same rule applies to prizes and bonuses. When Bobby Moore and his team won the World Cup for England in 1966, they all received generous bonuses. The taxman had the cheek to suggest these were taxable, but the judge threw this suggestion out. The team received the bonus only because of winning the Cup. Further, they had no expectation of the bonus, which they were only told about afterwards, and they had no right to it. It was not for future work, but a gratuitous present for past excellence. By contrast, incentive schemes and awards for future effort are taxable, even if the employer pays the tax as well as the award.

Removal expenses illustrate another problem, that of payments made before or after a job. In each case, the general principle is the same: does the payment relate to the job, or is it for some other reason? Normally, removal expenses will be for the job, but they might be paid because of some special factor. This is true also of payments made for people to give up one job in order to take on another.

Payments at the end of a job can be more complicated. In principle, all such payments are taxable, whether made under a contract or as a gift to the employee. But payments made on retirement under a pension scheme, or because of early retirement for ill-health, are tax-free. So is the first £30,000 of any lump sum payment, whatever the reason for the job ending. So also is a statutory redundancy payment made by an employer. The golden handshake, given to someone so that they leave, is often a mixture of different payments, including pay in lieu of notice, advance holiday and so forth. It has to be broken into its constituent parts on the basis that only those parts specifically exempted from tax will escape an income tax charge.

Deductions for employment expenses

Many employees incur expense in connection with their jobs. They buy smart clothes or protective clothes. They commute to work. They buy journals to keep up to date. They buy pictures for the office wall to liven it up. They buy tools to assist because the employer does not provide the ones best for the job. They join a trade union or professional association. When imposing income tax, should allowance be made for these expenses? If I spend £1,000 a year getting to work, and you walk to work to do the same job for the same pay, then in reality I earn £1,000 less than you. The reverse argument is that I have chosen to live a long way from my job, perhaps because it is nicer or the housing is cheaper there. This is a personal factor, not a job-related one, and therefore not relevant to what is fair.

Aside from pension contributions, the law's answer in the UK is a strict one – much stricter than in the USA and other developed countries.

Expenditure is only deductible if it is necessarily incurred because of the job. The precise terms of the legal provision are worth quoting, just to show how out of date they are:

Taxes Act 1988, section 198:

'If the holder of an office or employment is necessarily obliged to incur and defray out of the emoluments of that office or employment the expenses of travelling in the performance of the duties of the office or employment, or of keeping a horse to enable him to perform those duties, or otherwise to expend money wholly, exclusively and necessarily in the performance of those duties, there may be deducted from the emoluments to be assessed the expenses so necessarily incurred and defrayed.'

These rules might be of some use to the occasional hill shepherd, but, for most of us, this set of rules – introduced in the present form in 1842 – is less than generous. One judge summed it up by saying that the rule was 'notoriously rigid, narrow and restricted.' Under the rule we can only deduct travel costs if we are travelling **at**, rather than **to**, work, and then only if it is necessary. This is why commuters receive no tax relief for their travel costs.

In the case of other expenses, little is allowable under a strict application of the rules. First, the cost has to be shown as necessary. This means that it must be an expenditure that anyone undertaking the job must incur to do the job properly. It has been ruled that it is not necessary to buy books for a job or to study for professional or trade examinations. Second, the expense must be both wholly for the job and exclusively for it. If the expense is used both for the job and for private purposes, none of the expense is allowable. If you are required to keep a telephone at home, perhaps to answer emergency calls, but you also use the telephone for family calls, none of the cost of the telephone, apart from the individual work calls that are necessary, is allowable. To claim a full deduction, the employee would have to show that there was one telephone for business calls and another for private calls. The cost of smart clothes for work is never deductible, because the clothes are bought not only for work but also for warmth and decency. Likewise, you do not buy food at work to eat just for work, you buy it to eat to stay alive.

Thankfully, many tax inspectors apply a more practical approach. For example, in the case of a telephone bill, they might allow a sensible apportionment between allowable business cost and private cost. They are encouraged in this reasonable approach by a series of extra-statutory concessions and announced practices. The most important is Concession A1 under which many kinds of workers are allowed a flat-rate deduction for clothes and tools without question. For example, a uniformed police constable is allowed £45 a year, a carpenter £90 a year. There are other concessions covering jobs such as members of Parliament and clergymen. There are a few rules dealing with specific expenditures. The most important allows deduction of the cost of joining a professional body or learned society: for example, the fee paid annually by a pharmacist to stay on the official register.

The only allowable expense that is not necessary in any sense is a deduction for Payroll Giving. This is a new scheme in which an employee can agree to give up to £600 a year by way of deduction from pay to an agreed charity or charities. This is an alternative way of giving to the covenant scheme we look at later.

Why is the law so ungenerous with deductions? One reason is that the rules are designed to be objective on the grounds that this is fairer. By 'objective' they mean that the law applies in the same way to everyone, so that an expense is only deductible if everyone has to incur it. Another reason is that if expenditure for work reasons is really needed the employer will meet the cost. Also, by being mean, the rule is easy to administer. The disadvantage is that it discourages people spending money on doing their job better, for example, by attending evening classes. Whether travel to work should be deductible is another matter. After all, this is often done in company cars which are tax-privileged. Many others travel to work in subsidised rail and bus services. Would it be better to cut the subsidies and to use the money saved to allow more tax relief?

Pensions and pension contributions

Although the law prevents many work expenses being deducted from pay for tax purposes, pension contributions are usually deductible in full. The philosophy behind pension schemes is that they are a way to get people to save for their old age, when they will receive their pensions as deferred pay. To do this, tax relief is provided to both the employee's contribution and the employer's contribution (so that the employee is taxed on her or his income after excluding pension contributions) and to the income of the pension fund (so that no income tax is paid on the pension fund income). It is only when the pension is paid that it is taxed, on the same basis as if it had been earned.

Most public sector employees belong to occupational pension schemes which benefit from these tax privileges as do many of those working for larger companies. The introduction of private pensions was a recent reform based partly on the fairness argument. These schemes allow individuals who cannot, or do not wish to, be members of occupational pension schemes to take out their own schemes commercially, but to get the same tax privileges on their contributions and on the funds that are earned by occupational funds. At the level of the individual contributor and beneficiary, it may be hard to argue with the reasoning that leads to this advantageous tax treatment, especially as it is open to everyone. However, the system has its critics because it involves the Treasury surrendering very considerable amounts of tax revenue. How considerable becomes apparent when the total effect of pension fund investment is considered.

Pension funds are now the largest holders of the shares of companies in Britain. Some of Britain's largest companies now have a majority of their shares held by pension funds. Pension funds are exempt from tax, so this means that a majority of the payments of dividends from these companies will not pay tax in the hands of the shareholders. The significance of this will be explored when we discuss company taxation.

Another criticism of the present position is that the system is excessively generous both compared with other forms of saving (so encouraging people to save in this way rather than other ways) and compared with the state pension scheme. This is because contributions to the state pension scheme are not deductible for income tax purposes. Should this be so? To answer that we must examine Britain's other income tax, NI Contributions.

—— Social security contributions ——

Before we go further, we must discuss names. The title of this section is 'social security contributions', but this tax does not have a proper name and the title used is not the official one. The law imposing these contributions refers clumsily to 'contributions payable to the Secretary of State by earners, employers and others'. As this suggests, the law carefully avoids giving the tax a name other than **contributions**, and the law refrains from taking sides in the argument about whether these contributions are, or are not, taxes. Because of this, it is left for others to name names. The usual name is National Insurance Contributions, or NICs for short (until 1975, the law imposing the previous equivalents of these contributions was called the National Insurance Act) and because the use of this name is so widespread, even though wrong, that is what we will call them here. Why do we need them? Income tax is a vote loser. The electorate does not like it. People have made it clear that in elections they will support anyone who is prepared to cut the rate of tax, and, when it was cut, they did so. For the last 20 years, income tax rates have been reduced by staggering amounts: from a top rate of 83 per cent on earnings to 40 per cent, and from a standard rate that once was 35 per cent to the present rate of 25 per cent, with promises from some of more.

Yet most individuals are paying just as much income tax after these cuts as they were before. How could this happen? The answer lies with our system of NICs, and the changes made to it since 1973 by a series of governments. As income tax went down, so NICs went up. Indeed, some have argued that the famous cut in the basic rate of income tax from 27 per cent to 25 per cent in 1987, which contributed to the Thatcher government staying in office in the general election of that year, was financed by a rise in NICs of an amount much the same as the fall in income tax, and that the cut was paid for by just the same people who received the income tax cuts – so leaving them no better off. How was it that the electorate was fooled so effectively?

The chief reason seems to be that NICs are regarded as far more acceptable to the public than income tax. People seem not to mind paying NICs in anything like the same way as paying tax to the Inland Revenue. Why? Traditionally, little attention is paid by anyone to contribution liability, and so its operation is largely invisible. It is not mentioned in the Budget, and attracts little press and media attention.

The contribution myth

This lack of attention is part of a myth related to the idea that the contributions are not taxes but insurance premiums, and that they are not paid into government funds but into some separate fund which is not part of the finances of the state. The contributions go towards pensions, and those pensions are contributory, that is, you cannot receive the pension without paying the right amount of contributions – just as in an occupational pension scheme. The myth is continued by the government, because payments from NICs – as we saw in the last chapter – are largely paid into a special state fund, the National Insurance Fund.

Pay as you go pensions

NICs are, for employees, employers and the self-employed, a compulsory levy. Furthermore, there is little direct relationship between the amount of contributions paid and the amount of pension received. At the extreme, we shall see below that class 1A and class 4 contributions, and the class 1 contributions made by employers, give rise to no direct benefits. Although the benefits (chiefly the retirement pension) are said to be 'contributory', there is now no clear relationship between the amount paid and the amount received. The NI Fund is a misleading name, because it is not a fund in the same way as most pension funds. It would be more accurate to compare it to a bank account, or rather a current account backed up by a short-term savings account. At any one time, the NI Fund rarely has enough in it for more than three or four months' pension payments. This is because the scheme is 'pay as you go'. Today's contributors are paying today's pensions in the hope that when they retire, tomorrow's contributors will pay for it. Maybe they will, but there is a problem. People are living longer and they are, therefore, drawing more pension. But there are fewer people being born and coming into the working population. In Britain, as in every other developed state, sometime in the next 30 years there are going to be major imbalances between contributors and pensioners. The key ratio is the number of contributors paying for each pensioner. The more contributors (or people in work) for each pensioner, the higher the pensions. This ratio is dropping.

The year 2025

This is starting to happen in Britain, though the problem is not as bad as in some other countries. It is the reason why social security pension levels, for those who retire in ten or more years time, will be lower than those now in payment, and the contributions will then be higher. But the crunch comes in about 2025, when today's 30-year-olds retire. After that, on present predictions, the problems get serious. For the next few years, however, provided that contributions are allowed to rise slowly in real terms (as they have been doing since 1975) things will not be too serious.

This is because in Britain we have a double social security system. We pay NICs towards some of the social security benefits: chiefly retirement pensions, but also unemployment benefit and a few others. Other benefits, chiefly those for children and the long-term ill or disabled, are paid out of the consolidated fund and, therefore, from general taxes.

Very roughly we pay the same amount of money into NICs for one sort of social security benefit as we pay into general taxes for the other sorts (including the NHS). Countries differ widely on what is the right thing to do. Australia and Denmark, for example, do not have any NICs or any equivalent. All social security benefits are paid from general taxes. They therefore have higher rates of income tax than we do. By contrast, in France and the Netherlands, the social security funds meet all social security costs including the health services. Very little comes from income taxes. Consequently, income tax matters a lot less there. Should we make our income tax higher, or lower? Who is right: Denmark, France or Britain? All face the same problem of 'the greying population'. The likely answer in Britain is that we shift more towards the French solution, unless we decide to cut our social security benefits sharply.

How do NICs work?

NICs are imposed in the same clumsy way as income tax: a series of separate charges to tax (or, in reality, a series of separate taxes with the same name). They are mutually exclusive, and only cover some forms of income. Currently, there are five classes of contribution, as set out in the table.

THE CLASSES OF NIC

Class 1 *Primary* contributions paid by an employee on earnings from an employment:
secondary contributions paid by the employee's employer.

Class 1A Contributions paid by an employer who provides an employee for whom class 1 contributions are paid with a company car.

Class 2 Contributions paid by those who are ordinarily self-employed.

Class 3 Contributions paid by those not paying class 1 or class 2 contributions. These contributions are voluntary, unlike all other classes.

Class 4 Contributions paid by the self-employed on taxed earnings from their businesses, in addition to class 2 contributions.

Class 1 contributions

Class 1 NICs are a levy on both employee and employer in respect of the earnings of each employment. The main rate paid by an employee is 9 per cent. The rate paid by the employer depends on the total earnings of the employee, up to 10.4 per cent.

The contribution paid by the employer is payable on the whole of the earnings of the employee, but the employee's contribution is payable only on earnings up to a ceiling. Once the earnings of the employee have exceeded that ceiling, no further contribution is payable. The justification for this ceiling is that earnings above the level of the ceiling are ignored in calculating the earnings-related pension entitlement of the individual. The extra levy on employers finances a reduction in real terms of the contribution on the lowest part of earnings where the contribution is at a lower rate. NICs are payable on each separate payment of earnings by the employer to the employee, not on an annual basis like income tax. This is one of several differences between NICs' liability and income tax liability on the employee.

A major difference between the two taxes is that there are no personal allowances or reliefs or deductions for expenses to offset against total earnings for NIC liability. What you earn is what they tax, once the weekly rate of earnings crosses the minimum figure, currently about £50. By contrast, employees often pay no income tax until their weekly earnings are considerably higher than this, because of personal allowances, deductible work expenses and pension contributions.

Another major difference is that class 1 contributions are based on cash earnings, and are not levied on benefits in kind. Since 1991, a separate levy has been imposed on company cars under class 1A, but otherwise contributions cannot be charged on benefits not paid or payable in cash. There are anti-avoidance provisions of limited scope preventing payments being made by means of encashable bonds or unit trust payments, but payments such as loans of equipment or provision of season tickets do not incur contribution liability. The result is that benefits in kind, other than cars, still retain a significant tax privilege.

Exceptions

There are few exceptions to the liability of an employee or employer to pay full class 1 NICs. The most important are:

- children under 16 (no contributions payable);
- people who have been in Britain for fewer than 52 weeks (no contributions payable);
- employees over pensionable age (men 65, women 60) (no contributions from employees, but employers must pay as usual);
- married women who claimed to pay at a reduced rate before 1977 (they pay at a reduced rate, but employers pay at the full rate).

Contribution liability is imposed on both employees and employers in respect of each employment separately. If you have two jobs, you must pay contributions separately on each job. There is an annual ceiling on contributions, preventing an employee paying more contributions as a result of having two or more jobs than would be the case if all the earnings came from one case. Each employer pays fully in respect of each employment.

Compared with income tax, class 1 NICs are 'rough and ready'. One reason for this is the traditional attitude of not taxing benefits in kind. This was ended with regard to one particular kind of perk, the company car, in 1991, but it was done by adding a new class of contribution, class 1A.

NICs on company cars and free fuel

Any systematic removal of the tax privilege of the company car had to take account of the rules for NICs, even when the tariffs applying for income tax had reached levels where any tax advantage was neutralised. A start was made on neutralising NIC advantages in 1991 with the creation of a new class 1A contribution. These contributions apply to employers only. Due to the ceiling on NICs for employees, most employees with substantial benefits in kind, such as cars, would not pay contribution even if the value of the benefits were subject to contribution, because these would form part of the non-liable earnings over the annual ceiling.

Where an employer pays NICs under class 1 in respect of an employee, and the employer also supplies the employee with a company car as part of the benefit of the employment, an employee earning more than £8,500 will, as we have seen, pay income tax on an assumed extra amount of earnings because of the car. From the tax year 1991–92, whenever an employee has to pay this charge, the employer has to pay a parallel charge at the highest level of NIC rates to the DSS on the same sum as that on which the employee is charged to income tax. In effect, this is a parasitic tax, and it borrows all the rules from income tax to calculate and impose the NIC charge. The class 1A charge is also imposed on free fuel supplied to an employee for a company car, again being imposed on the employer on the same level of assumed earnings as that on which the employee is charged income tax.

6

– TAXING BUSINESSES –

Although most of us earn our living as employees, many people are occupied in running their own businesses. For tax purposes, it is not possible to tax the self-employed in the same way as employees under an income tax, and most countries use a different set of rules. These are often the same rules as those used for companies, as is broadly the case in this country.

—— Ways of taxing a business ——

The purpose of business is to earn profit, and a successful business is one that, at the end of the year, leaves its owner with a good return either on the effort and time they have put into the business, or on the capital they have invested in it, or both. It has long been assumed that a business should pay tax on this return, and many countries have some form of profit taxes. In earlier times, businesses such as farming or importing were taxed with a levy on their production. Tax authorities have since found other ways to raise taxes.

A business can be taxed on its value at the end of, say, each year.

Alternatively, it can be taxed on profit it makes when assets, including the business itself, are sold. It can be taxed on what it uses, for example the cost of its payroll (that is, the total cost of employing its workforce or of individual members of it) or the cost of the property, including immovable property, that it uses. It can be taxed on its economic activity, that is, on the amount or value it adds to the chain of production and distribution.

All those forms of tax are now used in Europe, and several in the United Kingdom. In this chapter we concentrate on the tax which historically is the main tax used on a business, the tax on profits. Then we look at the social security tax paid by those in business. The problems of taxing companies are looked at in a later chapter. Here our focus is on the person who is conducting a business on her or his own, or together with one or more partners.

Profits taxes on business

The tax on the business profits of individuals is imposed as part of the income tax. The charging provision is, in the archaic language of that tax, set out in schedule D cases I and II. Case I imposes a tax on *trades*, and case II imposes a tax on *professions and vocations*. This suggests that there are differences between the ways a trader, for example, a shop-keeper, and a professional, say, an accountant, are taxed. In practice, there are few differences. There is also some muddle over what is a trade and what is a profession. Judges have in the past ruled that members of the oldest profession are, like stockbrokers, engaged in trade, while photographers may or may not be professionals depending on how they carry on their businesses. In this account, we talk about business, using the word to cover trades, professions and vocations without distinguishing them except where we indicate otherwise. This avoids our being trapped (as the income tax law is) in the language of the 18th century.

The case I and case II rules impose a charge to income tax on the *annual profits or gains arising or accruing . . . from any trade profession or vocation*. If the business owner is based in the United Kingdom, this charge is on the profits on a world-wide basis. If the business owner is based overseas, the charge is on the United Kingdom profits only. If the business is overseas, but the owner is in the United Kingdom, other cases of schedule D apply.

The 'annual' profits referred to in the law are *annual* in two senses: they are the revenue profits of the business, not the capital profits it makes, and they are calculated for each year. The rules make it clear that the tax is based on the *net profits*, that is, the profits left after deduction of the expenses of the business. How this is done may best be viewed by looking at the accounts of a small business.

Mow's business

Mow runs a small business from home. The business is a small advisory agency, helping other local businesses with their business planning and marketing. Mow works full time in the business, employs a part-time secretary and uses a secretarial agency locally for further help. Last year, Mow had to buy a new computer and some other equipment, and he had to undertake a lot of travelling (mainly by car) on business purposes. Mow has had a series of profitable assignments, on which there has been a good rate of return. The accounts set out below show how well Mow did last year.

Mow's story is a familiar one. The business went well, and a lot of money came in. But there were lots of bills to pay so in the end a tremendous amount of work produced only a small profit. That may be Mow's tale, and maybe Mow believes it, but it is not surprising to find out that tax inspectors are not so easily persuaded to accept the glib tale told by this, or any similar, set of accounts. Rather than take Mow's word for it, the tax inspector will insist that the accounts are reworked on a more objective basis, to comply with the income tax rules for calculating profits. Let us see what happens.

Include only business income
The first adjustment to the accounts is to the income. Mow has declared the business income, but has also added two other kinds of income: the proceeds from selling the old desk and some bank interest. Neither of these are business income.

The sale of assets does not count unless it is Mow's business to sell those assets, for example, if Mow is a second-hand furniture dealer. In Mow's case, any profit has to be taxed under capital gains tax. However, in this

MOW'S ACCOUNTS FOR LAST YEAR

Income

Cash from clients	60,000
Sale of old furniture	2,000
Bank interest	500
Total	62,500

Expenses

wages to secretary	12,000
secretary's NI	1,000
secretarial agency	4,000
purchase of computer and equipment	5,500
purchase of new furniture	3,000
repayment of loan on car	4,000
depreciation of car	3,000
travelling expenses	2,500
entertainment	600
motoring fine and expenses	1,500
office expenses in house	1,000
telephone and fax	1,200
advertisements and printing	1,000
bank charges and interest	2,200
audit charge	800
income tax	5,000
own NI	2,000
pension contributions	3,000
health insurance	500
reserve to deposit	2,000
Total expenses	55,800
Profit kept by Mow	6,700
	62,500

case there would be no charge to tax, so Mow does not have to account at all for this profit. In other cases, the line between what is income and what is capital is not so easy to define, so we shall return to it below.

The bank interest is investment income, not earned income, and gets taxed under different income tax rules (discussed in the next chapter). Under those rules, Mow is taxed on the full amount of interest, without any deduction for expenses.

These are both illustrations of the general rules that must be followed as to what should be included in the business accounts as income. It is only the income earned from the business. If Mow had more than one business, then perhaps separate accounts should be kept, although if they are both small operations, one set might do. Those accounts should not include any capital items. Nor should they include any investment income, such as share dividends, interest, stock dividends or earnings from employment. In practice, small amounts of rent earned, for example, by letting the flat above the office, can be included although again profits from property rent should be separate.

Mow left one figure out correctly. During the year a customer who had been especially satisfied with Mow's advice sent Mow a cheque for £2,000. Mow had already sent the customer a bill, which had been paid, the previous year, and Mow was not expecting to do any further business with the customer because the customer now employed a full-time staff member to do this form of work. Mow's advice had helped land a valuable contract, and the cheque was a thank you now that the contract was complete.

Gifts are not receipts from the business if they are genuine gifts. In this case, Mow had not expected the gift and had no right to it – full payment had already been made. Nor was it a payment for any future work by Mow, or any form of inducement. So Mow's surprise cheque was a tax-free present!

On this basis, the income to be included in Mow's accounts is the £60,000 from clients. Other accounts will deal with any tax due on the bank interest.

Cash or earnings?

We need to know two other things about Mow's income before we can agree with his figure of £60,000. The first is how the £60,000 was calculated? Was this the amount of bills that Mow sent out last year, or was it the amount received from the clients? The accounts suggest that it was what was received. This is what is called the *cash basis* of accounting, and is common for the smallest of businesses. As we shall see, many businesses are allowed to use it for VAT purposes. The income tax authorities are not as keen on this basis. They expect businesses to run on an *earnings basis*, including all the profits earned by the business, whether or not the customers have paid. In Mow's case, this would mean that Mow has to add up all the bills sent out, not the cash received.

A quick look through Mow's books shows that business was not as good last year as the £60,000 suggested. That figure was high partly because of a number of people paying bills late from the previous year. The actual total of last year's bills sent out was £50,000.

Work in hand
Even this adjustment does not tell the whole story. Mow had not finished all the contracts the business was working on at the end of the year. Several were part completed. Had Mow sent out bills at the end of the year for all those part completed contracts, a further £7,500 would have been due to the business. What is more, this was rather larger than the total at the beginning of the year, when work done totalled about £3,500 only. A full transfer of Mow's accounts on to an earnings basis must take these figures into account as well as the lower total of bills sent out during the year.

The full story is therefore that Mow's earnings from clients are:

Earnings from clients	50,000
Work in hand at year's close	7,500
	57,500
less	
Work in hand at year's start	3,500
Year's earnings	54,000

Stock in trade

Adjustments at the beginning and end of a year for the continuing value of a business are important for a business involving stock in trade (or inventory). At any time, a business selling goods has to carry trading stock. The business therefore has money tied up in the stock. If the stock increases or decreases, so more or less profit is tied up. In order to stop this being used to avoid tax, the trading accounts must be adjusted in the same way as with work in hand to ensure that the full profits of the business are taxed, not hidden in the stock figures.

These rules for taxing 'stock profit', or the profit hidden in the stock, work towards fairness in some cases. If there is a high level of inflation they can be most unfair. Sometimes a business can get taxed on a stock profit which is purely due to inflation, and for which it has little cash to pay. This happened to many businesses in the late 1970s.

Mow must also observe another rule about stock in trade. If a trader takes an item out of the business stock to use it personally, the value of that item must be entered into the accounts of the business as if the taxpayer had sold the item to himself. The court laid this rule down in a case where Lady Zia Wernher, a cousin to the Queen, transferred horses from her professional stables to her personal stables. The horses had to be transferred at market value for tax purposes, a considerable sum of money.

What count as business expenses?

As with income items, only those expense items should be included which relate to the business, and are expenditure from the revenue of the business. Capital items do not count. The rules are laid down by the Taxes Acts, and can be summarised as follows. Items of expenditure can only be deducted from income in calculating net profits if the items are:

(a) revenue expenditure, not capital,

(b) actually incurred,

(c) wholly and exclusively for business purposes,

(d) in the period in question,

(e) and are not expressly disallowed.

Each of these rules is important, and is best examined by reference to examples.

'Revenue, not capital'

The division between revenue items and capital items is fundamental to both income and expenditure in calculating the profits of a business. Its importance lies in the fact that capital receipts are not income of a trade or profession; they are, instead, sales of assets to be charged to capital gains tax. Capital expenditure cannot be deducted as expenses in the trading accounts. If at all, it is allowed under separate provisions known as capital allowances.

Despite this importance, the Tax Acts are almost completely silent on the issue of capital and income. Judges have, therefore, had to fill the gap, and they have done so by posing a series of tests within a general framework. The framework is that of Lord Reid in *Strick v Regent Oil*, where he said that 'the determination of what is capital and what is income must depend rather on common sense than the strict application of any single legal principle.'

The most quoted test for applying this common sense is that of Lord Cave in *Atherton v BIHC*: 'when the expenditure is made, not only once and for all, but with a view to bringing into existence an asset or advantage for the enduring benefit of a trade, I think that there is very good reason (in the absence of special circumstances . . .) for treating such an expenditure as . . . ' capital. Another leading case is *Tucker v Granada Motorway Services* where the judges sought the identity of the asset acquired for the expenditure.

As a rule of thumb, expenditure for an item or advantage that will last more than five years is likely to be treated as capital, while that for an item or advantage with a life of less than two years is likely to be revenue expenditure. Inevitably, things are not usually so clear cut. For example, if I repair a machine which was otherwise useless, but as a result it has commercial use for another three years, is that revenue or capital? It could be capital if I bought the machine in a broken-down condition and had to repair it before I could use it; but it would probably be income if I had to repair the machine because I had not bothered to maintain it properly for the last ten years, having used it in the business throughout.

Sorting out what is revenue income compared with what is capital income is not so easy, but it is, again, broadly a matter of common sense. It has caused a great many disputes because for many years tax on income was heavy, while tax on capital gains did not exist before 1962. It was worth considerable sums before that date to persuade tax officials or the courts that a sum was a capital receipt. Now that the rates of tax on both income and capital gains are the same, the division is much less important.

The key question is whether a sum is received as income of the trade or profession. For instance, if I sell a machine through my business, and make a large profit, it is not immediately obvious whether that profit is a trading profit. It will be a trading profit if I sell those machines every week (as when a car dealer sells a car). It may not be a trading profit if I have never done so before (as when a builder sells a station wagon used for his trade). The underlying question that judges ask is whether the sale takes place in the sort of way a trader would sell. Is it a commercial transaction?

A series of 'badges of trade' has been created to isolate the facts of significance in deciding what is trading income.

1 **What is the item being sold?** Shares are usually bought as investments, as are paintings, but large supplies of food are usually bought to sell again.

2 **Length of ownership**. The longer an item is held, the more likely it is to be capital.

3 **Frequency of similar transactions**. While the first time may be capital, the tenth is definitely revenue.

4 **Subsidiary work**. If I buy and sell a machine, it looks like a trading transaction if I recondition it and then sell it.

5 **Reason for the sale**. If I buy something as an investment but am forced to sell because of some personal disaster, that does not make me a trader.

6 **Motive**. Why did I buy it? Did I intend to make a profit? Did I have to borrow money to buy it?

'Actually incurred'

Expenditure cannot be put into the accounts until it has been incurred. If the accounts are drawn up on an earnings basis, the business has undertaken the liabilities for that account year rather than some future year. In the case of cash accounts, the cash must have been spent in that year.

A business cannot include general reserves in its accounts, because of this rule. For example, a business may feel that it is wise to include a reserve against a large future item of expenditure, such as the replacement of a machine, or it may wish to set a reserve in case some of its customers do not pay their bills. In both cases, the reserve cannot be included in the tax accounts – however wise it may be for commercial purposes.

'Wholly and exclusively for business purposes'

This test is laid down in one of the most fought-over sections in the Taxes Acts, section 74. It is also a famous example of that peculiar English grammatical construction, the double negative.

Income and Corporation Taxes Act 1988, section 74

Subject to the provisions of the Tax Acts, in computing the amount of profits or gains to be charged under case I or case II of schedule D, no sum shall be deducted in respect of:

(a) any disbursements or expenses, not being money wholly and exclusively laid out or expended for the purposes of the trade, profession or vocation;

(b) any disbursements or expenses for the maintenance of the parties, their families or establishments, or any sums expended for any other domestic or private purposes distinct from the purposes of the trade, profession or vocation; . . .

Section 74 goes on past the parts quoted until rule (q), but the first two are the most important. They are taken together by the Inland Revenue as preventing any personal expenditure, or expenses incurred for any other purpose than the business, from being deducted from the income in calculating profits. The rules are strict and have given rise to many disputes.

One leading case, *Mallalieu v Drummond*, involved a claim by a barrister that she could deduct the cost of the formal clothing she wore in court from her professional fees for tax purposes. The Inland Revenue agreed that she could deduct the cost of her gown and wig, but she sought the cost of cleaning and replacing her other formal clothing, and this was refused. The case was appealed to the House of Lords, who also agreed that the expenditure was not allowed as a deduction. The reason was that the barrister did not buy the clothes only for her work; she wore some to work, and she wore them at work for warmth and decency as well as to comply with court rules. They were therefore not bought 'exclusively' for work. For these reasons, the Inland Revenue routinely objected to claims for meals and refreshments at work. Food is also needed to keep taxpayers alive, not just to keep them working!

In other cases, the Inland Revenue have objected successfully to tax-payers deducting part of the cost of something. For example, a self-employed person required to spend some time in a nursing home recovering from an operation was unable to claim the extra nursing home fees that he incurred for a private room so that he could carry on his work. Similarly, the rental for a telephone used partly for work reasons and partly for private reasons is not used 'wholly' for work reasons and therefore cannot be deducted in whole or in part.

In Mow's case, several of the items in the accounts would be excluded on the basis of this rule. First, the motoring fine and expenses, if incurred by Mow personally, are unlikely to be wholly for the purposes of the business. Bad driving is not necessary for business purposes even if occasionally bad parking is. Nor is the health insurance, or income tax, although Mow is entitled to deduct half the cost of NI contributions incurred by reason of specific provision in the law. Pension contributions are also allowed by reason of specific provision if the pensions scheme is Inland Revenue approved.

The claim for 'office expenses in house' is a common one, and if reasonable is usually accepted by tax inspectors, although it often breaks the rules. This is because, in practice, a reasonable claim for expenses which could be apportioned, but have not been, will be accepted. Various of the items of expenditure on the home, for instance, electricity to heat and light the room while Mow is working in it, could be isolated. Thankfully, the ruthless logic of section 74 is not always applied to its extremes. For that reason, a reasonable proportion of telephone bills will also often be allowed.

'In the period in question'

This rule specifies that the expense must actually be incurred in the accounts year of the trade to which it relates. This is one aspect of an important assumption of the income tax rules – that profit and losses cannot be anticipated. A taxpayer can only be charged for profits actually accruing or arising, not future profits. By the same rule, a taxpayer cannot claim future expenses, only those already incurred.

'Not expressly disallowed'

It is open to Parliament to provide that particular kinds of expenditure cannot be deducted from profits. Section 74 contains a list of such items, including capital items and sums which are recoverable under an insurance contract. Most kinds of business entertainment are also disallowed, to stop people claiming a business lunch or a night out as a tax deductible expense, unless it is moderate expenditure on staff. Even this has a double edge. If the expenditure is not moderate, the members of staff will be taxed on the receipt of a benefit in kind.

Finance costs

Finance costs deserve special comment. We return to this in connection with company taxation where it is particularly important. Here we must note that Mow has claimed a deduction for repaying a loan on a car, and a further deduction for interest.

Loans and repayments of loans do not count as income or expenditure. The loan is not the property of the borrower, so is not taxable as income of the business. For the same reason, repayment of a loan does not count as a business expense. The interest may be a deductible expense if it is incurred for revenue purposes (such as a temporary overdraft funding ordinary working capital), but not if incurred on purchasing capital items (such as a new car). In Mow's case, therefore, the repayment of the loan on the car and (assuming the interest was on that loan) the interest are both not deductible (though a special allowance may be available).

───────── Capital allowances ─────────

Capital expenditure cannot be deducted against profits either at cost or in the form of depreciation. This is so, even though it would be extremely unwise of any business to calculate its profits while ignoring capital expenditure. Standard accounting practices vary, but most require some form of charge against income to compensate for the capital expenditure tied up in the business, at least where that capital expenditure is slowly wasting away, as with machinery.

Capital expenditure is left out of account in part for historical reasons. It is also because there is no clear agreement on the proper way to write off capital costs against income. As a result, commercial accounts show markedly different ways of doing this. Too much discretion on such an item would defeat one of the principles on which income tax accounts are expected to be written, namely that there is no discretion. The same rules must apply to everyone. Otherwise the position is unfair as between taxpayers. Or so the argument goes. Whether this is the best approach is considered at the end of the chapter.

Despite this ban, governments introduced deductions for capital expenditure against income, which are known as capital allowances. These only apply to certain kinds of expenditure, and under strict limits. The kinds of expenditure allowed, in whole or part, are:

(a) machinery and plant (or equipment),

(b) industrial buildings (but not offices or shops),

(c) agricultural buildings,

(d) research and development costs,

(e) specialist equipment for certain industries, such as mining and dredging.

Of these, only one category is of importance to most forms of business, the allowance for *plant and machinery*. This is a wide category of items, including for example: computers, cars, engineering equipment, tools (unless they are revenue costs), office furniture, lamps, professional reference books, movable office screening, clocks . . . everything which is equipment but not part of the structure or building. The others are all restricted to particular kinds of industry, or particular areas such as enterprise zones, and rarely apply to home-based industries (except farms).

The value of allowances

Although the law concedes the principle of deduction for the cost of capital investment, it does so currently on a restricted basis (save for research and development costs which are treated as revenue costs). There are a number of ways in which capital costs can be written off in accounts, from the **immediate write off** used in public concerns to a **straight line method** (an equal amount each year for the expected life of the asset, yielding a straight line if portrayed as a graph).

Methods used in Britain have varied depending on whether the government of the day has felt it useful to dangle tax carrots in front of business to encourage investment. At times, immediate write-off allowances (known as first-year allowances) were available. These were restricted sharply as part of the base-rate tradeoff, and the general basis for these allowances (and others) is now a 25 per cent annual allowance on a **declining balance basis**, as illustrated in the box below. If equipment has a particularly short life, for example, three years, relief can be accelerated.

CAPITAL ALLOWANCES:
ON THE DECLINING BALANCE BASIS

CA invests £100 in equipment.

In **year 1**, CA claims 25 per cent of the total expenditure: £25.

In **year 2**, CA claims 25 per cent of the outstanding balance (£100–£25) £75: £19.

In **year 3**, CA claims 25 per cent of the outstanding balance (£75–£19) £56: £14.

In **year 4**, CA claims 25 per cent of the outstanding balance (£56–£14) £42: £11.

After four years, CA gains £69 in allowances. When is £100 reached?

The post-tax cost of capital

The example on page 109 has shown how much a capital allowance is worth in terms of deduction against tax. What is it worth to the business? An entrepreneur, who wants to find out whether a particular investment is worth making, needs to find the current value of the final full cost of an investment.

If CA invest £100 now, the capital allowances give only limited relief. To make things easy, let us look at the first four years, during which £69 in allowances is released. Those allowances are not **worth** £69 to CA. They are worth only the tax they save. If CA pays tax at 40 per cent, they are worth £28 when received. Their current value must be discounted for inflation. Call that 10 per cent, again to make things easy. The tax will only be saved on the first £25 allowance between one and two years after the £100 is spent. The first part of the capital allowance is therefore only worth £10 (tax on £25) reduced by 10 per cent to 20 per cent – between £8 and £9. The second part on this basis is worth between £5 and £6 current value. The third part is worth £4 or less, and so on: perhaps £25 in total. This makes the post-tax cost about £75. The post-tax cost of equal revenue expenditure is, by comparison, about £64 on this basis. By contrast, when the tax rates were, say, 60 per cent on CA, but there were 100 per cent capital allowances, the post-tax cost (capital or revenue) of £100 expenditure was only about £55. Was that a better system?

Back to Mow's accounts

We have now examined all the tax rules applying to accounts such as Mow's, and have seen that a number of adjustments need to be made both to the income and the expenditure. The box below shows the adjusted total – slightly different from the original accounts, even though it is assumed that all the expenditure is genuine and provable.

**MOW'S ACCOUNTS FOR LAST YEAR:
CORRECTED FOR INCOME TAX**

Income

Total income (adjusted for work in hand)   54,000

Expenses

Wages to secretary	12,000
Secretary's NI	1,000
Secretarial agency	4,000
Travelling expenses	2,500
Office expenses in house	1,000
Telephone and fax	1,200
Advertising and printing	1,000
Bank charges (assuming interest was £1,700)	500
Audit charge	800
Own NI (50 per cent) (for example)	1,000
Total allowable expenses	25,000

Less: capital allowances	
First year allowance on computer and furniture	2,125
(£5,500 + £3,000) × 25 per cent	
Allowance on car (for example)	2,000
Total taxable profits of trade	20,875

Add: other taxable income	
Bank interest	500
Less: other allowances	
Pension contribution (assuming all deductible)	3,000
Total taxable income	18,375

Notes: *The £2,000 sale of old furniture was excluded because it is capital (and probably non-taxable). The following items are capital expenditure: purchase of computer and equipment (with capital allowance); purchase of furniture (with capital allowance); depreciation on car (but capital allowance). The following is not business expenditure: repayment of loan. The interest is assumed not to be allowable, although an income tax allowance may be available if it is a loan for the purchase of plant and machinery. Entertainment costs are assumed to be within the express disallowance. Motoring fines and expenses are not business expenses, nor is the health insurance. The income tax is not allowed: it is part of the profit, not an expense in earning it. Only half the NI contributions are allowed by express provision. Reserves are not allowed.*

—— What is the best form of tax? ——

In Britain, business profits for tax purposes may show sharp differences from the profits which an accountant, working on the basis of standard accounting practices, might recommend that the business adopt. Business accounts have to be produced on a prudent basis, taking account of known future liabilities. These include, for example, future taxation and major future expenses. Capital expenditure that has already been made is charged against expenditure in the way most appropriate to the business. All relevant expenditure can be deducted. Not so, however, for income tax accounts nor, as we shall see, for corporation tax accounts either. The result is that the profit figures for the two purposes are sometimes sharply different, as Mow's accounts show.

In other western European states, the accounts allowed for tax purposes are much nearer to the commercial accounts, with reserves allowed to some extent. Would that be a better approach? Should the income tax be based simply on the profit shown, provided that the accounts had been audited by a professional accountant in accordance with the statements of standard accounting practice that lay down the guidelines for the auditing profession?

There is also another route to taxing business: value added tax. We examine this in Chapter 10. In Mow's case, VAT would be collected by Mow on the supplies made (unless they are of an exempt kind), and he would claim a tax credit against that of all VAT that was paid out from the business. On the basis of the revised form of Mow's accounts, this might be a charge of VAT of 17.5 per cent of £60,000, less rebates on taxable amounts spent by Mow of perhaps £9,500 at the same rate, equalling a total of VAT payable of some £8,500 or so. This is because Mow does not have to pay VAT on staff costs or financing costs. Would this be a simpler way to tax businesses, or a more efficient way in terms of raising revenue? We shall explore that further, later in the book.

Paying the business tax

Income tax is payable on business profits at the same rate as any other income. It is paid on the profits of each year. Because no one knows what those profits are until the end of each accounts year, the rules provide that, for a continuing business, tax is paid on the accounts on what is called a **preceding year basis**. The tax is payable in a tax year on the profits not of that year, but of the accounts year that finishes in the previous tax year.

For example, assume that Mow's accounts are drawn up for a calendar year, say 1990. That accounts' year ends in the income tax year 1990–91 (ending April 5, 1991). Using the preceding year basis, Mow's business will be taxed in the income tax year 1991–92 (ending April 5, 1992). Tax from a buisness is payable as to half on 31 December in the tax year and as to the other half on 30 June of the following year, so Mow would pay tax on the 1990 profits as to half on December 31, 1991, and as to the rest on June 30, 1992. Compare that with both the tax paid by an employee (paid immediately by PAYE) and the paid tax for VAT (when the tax is paid out at the latest every three months).

The system of collecting tax from the self-employed is regarded by government as unsatisfactory and is under review. The aim is to reduce this time lag, which is seen by government as an unfair advantage to the self-employed. The self-employed view it, by contrast, as appropriate. It is particularly appropriate for a business which ends its accounting year at the end of April, as many do.

There are also complicated rules needed for the first few years of a business, and for the last few. Anyone starting a new business should be advised to seek professional help about the date for starting the business, before doing so, to use these rules to advantage (while they last). If the business started, say, on May 1, 1990, and made a loss in the first 12 months and a profit the following year, no income tax would be payable until December 1993. Certainly better than VAT! Is it better than social security contributions?

NI contributions for the self-employed

The self-employed are required to pay not one, but two, classes of NI contribution:

1 class 2 contributions, at a flat rate payable weekly;

2 class 4 contributions, at a set percentage of taxable profits.

The class 2 contribution dates back to the days when NI contributions were paid by sticking stamps in cards (they still can be, although most people pay through the bank). There was a set weekly contribution for all contributors. When the contribution system was reformed for employees in 1973, the self-employed fixed amount was kept on for all those who are ordinarily self-employed in any week (even if actually on holiday that week). This amount is payable every week unless the income of the contributor is below an annual minimum level, when the contributor can choose not to pay.

Payment ensures entitlement to contributory social security benefits, chiefly the flat-rate retirement pension at state retirement age, and the fixed amount payment is, therefore, sometimes an advantage even when the contributions are not compulsory.

Class 4 contributions are not an advantage. They are, in effect, an extra income tax levy imposed on the profits of a business as taxable for income tax under schedule D cases I and II, with a few special adjustments. They are payable at a set percentage (currently 6.3 per cent) on the amount of those profits exceeding the year's minimum level up to the year's maximum level. The contribution creates a rough balance between the earnings-related contributions of employees and the contributions payable by the better-off self-employed.

The balance is rough, because half the cost of the contributions can be set against income tax, thereby reducing the after-tax cost by 40 per cent for the better off, but only 25 per cent for the less well off. What makes it particularly rough is that class 4 contributions entitle the contributor to nothing (except a receipt, if one is asked for). Class 4 contributions are irrelevant to benefit entitlement, partly because the self-employed are only entitled to a limited range of benefits (they are excluded from unemployment benefit for example), and partly because they are entitled only to a flat-rate pension, not to the earnings-related state pension, or SERPS (State Earnings-Related Pension Scheme).

Postscript

Had Mow's profits genuinely been less than £15,000 the Inland Revenue would have accepted simpler accounts of just three lines: income, expenditure and profit.

7

TAXATION AND THE FAMILY

— The tax and social security puzzle —

Taxation and social security are muddled together as two important parts of a jigsaw puzzle from which most of us assemble our family budgets. Both tax and social security affect almost every individual, of whatever age, in the country, and they do so as part of the same process of shifting resources between citizen and state. Our taxes and our social security payments are part of the same process: a state sharing system. On one definition they can all be regarded as taxes – that is, compulsory transfer payments between individual and state. If we allow for a transfer payment to be negative as well as positive, there is a strong argument for regarding a tax I have to pay the state, and a benefit the state has to pay me as the same thing. That is my assumption in this chapter. In practice, few regard taxes and social security benefits as having anything to do with each other, beyond the fact that one finances the other, partly because of the complexity of both systems.

One reason for the incomprehensibility of the tax and social security jigsaw pieces is that there are several different systems interlocking, each having arrived with little regard to the others. Further, they are not presented officially as being part of the same overall system, partly because different government departments deal with different parts of the system, and partly because Parliament does not look at them together either. We start therefore by reviewing the different patterns involved, and we will then try and tie the parts together.

—— The state's sharing systems ——

We have seen how income tax is charged on the incomes of both the employed and the self-employed. Taxation is also charged on unearned income (usually called investment income) as we see in the next chapter. Here we need to see how much income tax families pay, and the extent, if any, to which income tax itself is a sharing system. The same point needs to be made about all our taxes. For example, do the rich pay more VAT than the poor, or the reverse?

The main sharing system appears at first view to be the contributory system: the overall scheme of contributions and the benefits financed from them. On closer view, this can be presented as not so much a sharing system as a spreading system. It spreads income from the years in which I work to those when I have retired or am unable to work through sickness.

Real sharing takes place through a series of other systems: non-means-tested social security benefits paid in cash, such as support paid to families with children, and to those with long-term disabilities; means-tested benefits, available to those with low incomes or no incomes; and state-provided services of which the most important are the national health service and local education services.

An overview

To obtain an overall view, we must examine each of the cash-saving or cash-providing systems in turn. Behind this, some families gain substantial support through the provision of benefits in kind: hospital and medical support, local social services, schools, child care arrangements and so forth. These are, cumulatively with social security benefits, the largest part of United Kingdom public expenditure. There is little that can usefully be said in this book about benefits in kind, beyond a few notes on their funding, because the pattern varies from one family to another, but they are of great importance to most families.

PUBLIC EXPENDITURE IN BRITAIN 1991–92 OUTTURN (£B)

Central government:

Social Security	62
Health	31
Ministry of Defence	23
Housing	10
Education	10
All other	14
Central government debt interest	17

Local government:

Central grants for local authority expenditure	53
Locally financed costs	11

Notes: *Based on 1991–92 Budget Statement, Supply estimates and Appropriations. Social welfare payments by central government not identified. Of local government expenditure, shares vary in local areas, but in most areas, more than half the budget goes on education, with social services and housing also being major budget items.*

Is it right to seek an overall view? The assumption of this chapter is that an overall view is the best way of seeing the context of our tax system as it applies to individuals. This is because the British system of tax and social support is indivisible in the way it operates on individuals and families, although divided in the way it is provided. British state provision can only be judged fairly as a sharing system in its entirety.

In judging it, we should note that it is possible to ensure that social benefits, such as cash benefits or health care, are provided through self-contained social security systems kept apart from the machinery of the state, and financed without involving general taxation. This happens in France and the Netherlands, and to a large extent in other western European countries. In France more than 40 per cent of the total public expenditure flows through semi-independent social security and health funds and not through central or local state budgets. Unlike in Britain, the state is not technically involved.

We might alternatively take the view that the poverty of individual members of our society is not the concern of others in society, and that consequently there need be no sharing system. That is a view that the British have never taken, although there have been – and are – some people who reject the idea of 'society' and indicate that there are only individuals. Even if we reject the idea that we are, in any meaningful sense, a community or society, few people have advocated that any individual in the United Kingdom should not have any support in cash or kind from the state – even if it is to be provided only at the most basic level. Even strong critics of the corporate state or the idea that states should be more than neutral frameworks for the individuals that live in them accept that there is at least a minimum role for help for the poor.

An undivided system?

In Britain, the state is far from neutral in the help available to individuals, and our system is a sharing system which is not divided. Each part interacts in some way with other parts. An important, though little noticed, reform in the last 15 years has increased the separation between the contributory system and the other parts of the overall system, but it has not broken the link. For example, about 15 per cent of total social security contributions are paid over to general government funds as a contribution to the national health service. It was recently estimated that this shifted the equivalent of some 1.5p from the income tax rate to NI contributions. In addition, most contributory benefits are taxable, so reducing their real value to taxpayers.

In a more general way, the system remains interlinked at the budgetary level. Increased expenditure means increased taxes. Lower taxes mean lower benefits. Any proposal which purports to increase benefits while decreasing tax is – put simply – dishonest. It may be that, through some clever sleight of hand or borrowing, benefits are increased now, while taxes are only increased later, but the link is inevitably there. Equally, the proposal that we 'cut taxes' divorced from a knowledge of which benefits we also cut is also dishonest. It cannot be done, subject to one proviso – that our systems are efficient. If they are inefficient, an efficiency gain may result in a better relationship between expenditure and taxation. Once the system is efficient (and in parts it is efficient) extra benefits mean extra taxes in one form or another. The British systems of, for example, health care are more efficient than those in other advanced states.

If you wonder why I am dwelling so long on the obvious, it is because for many people the tax and benefit link is not obvious in the British system, and it is made less obvious by the way that both the sharing systems and the budgetary machine have worked in the United Kingdom for many years. Nor is it often appreciated how much of the national budget is devoted to health, education and welfare payments. Hopefully, the new system of December budgets will help clarify this. Pending that reform, we must attempt our own clarification.

Income tax as a sharing system

One view of income tax is that, as the main direct tax affecting all individuals and families with more than minimal incomes, it is a mechanism that can be used to redistribute wealth from the better-off to those in more need. That was a general view in past years, but it is now regarded as a faulty view. Those most deserving of our support are those without any incomes, or with incomes below the minimum figure at which tax applies. They cannot therefore be helped through the income tax system, although they can be helped by it. Today's view is better in that it sees income tax as a money-collecting machine which should be neutral in its effect on people. If redistribution is to take place, it should be in the way that the income tax receipts are spent, not in the way they are collected. The only role that income tax can play in connection with the poor is in making sure they do not pay the tax on subsistence levels of income.

Reforms in the last 20 years have moved away from involving income tax as a redistribution device. For example, the calculation of the income tax liability of individuals used to take place through family units (as in France it still does). Income of children (e.g. child benefit) could be added to those of the parents (the wife's income was added to that of the husband). At the same time, allowances against income tax were available for married men and in respect of each child of a taxpayer. Other allowances gave assistance to other dependants living with the taxpayer or maintained by him.

Current personal allowances

Personal allowance:
available to everyone with additions for those over 65, and over 80.

Additional child allowance:
available to those caring for children not claiming the couple's allowance.

Married couple's allowance:
available to husband or wife.

Blind person's allowance:
available to anyone registered blind.

Most of these allowances have now been removed from the system. There is general agreement to this approach. Rather more controversial is the extent to which the rates of tax should act to redistribute, by making the rich pay more, as we noted in the chapter on the budget. Here also, the 'sharing' aspect of the tax has been reduced.

——— Taxes and marriage ———

Taxing married women

The most important recent change in personal income tax was the separation of the taxation of husband and wife in 1990. Until then, income tax had clung to the 19th-century attitude that the income of a married woman was the income of her husband (although the reverse was not true). The original approach to the income tax, dating from before the Married Women's Property Act 1882, was that on marriage the property and income of the wife transferred to the husband as a matter of law, for all purposes. It took from 1882 to 1990 to remove the rule from income taxation of married women!

Under the former rules, the husband reported all his income (including any income earned for him by his wife) to the Inland Revenue, which communicated with him, excluding his wife. The wife was forced to disclose all her income details to the husband, even though she did not see his return, and was not even aware of whether he reported what she told him correctly. This attitude came to be regarded as indefensible on privacy grounds, but survived because it was expedient.

A penalty against marriage

Just as the issue of privacy was seen as important, so another major criticism of the former system was that it was biased against marriage. A couple, both of whom worked for good incomes, would pay significantly more tax by being married than if they stayed unmarried. This difference increased for a couple with two or more children. If the couple claimed that they were single parents, each bringing up some of the children, they received twice the tax relief of a married couple bringing up the same number of children. If they made the appropriate mortgage arrangements, they could also receive twice the mortgage tax relief.

Predictably, this bias against married couples was the subject of much criticism, but it took many years for it to be removed. In 1988, after a series of government reports and suggestions, the first part of the machine creating the bias was dismantled. After that year, only one amount of mortgage interest relief was available per household, not per individual (a married couple being treated as an individual). Also, a household with a child in it could only claim one single parent's allowance.

In 1990, the main change came with the separation of the taxation of husbands and wives. This immediately meant that there were more than three million new taxpayers for the tax authorities to deal with – and this enormous administrative burden was a major reason for delays in the reform. By that time, much of the complication had been stripped out of the personal income tax system, and its administration was in a state to be handled, to a large extent, by computers. Indeed, a hidden reason for stopping the income tax system being a sharing system as such is the demand for a 'machine friendly' system – one with a minimum of detail and discretion.

Is the income tax system now neutral to marriage? No. Most of the bias has been removed, but, in 1990, a new allowance was created which biased the system in favour of marriage. This is the *married couple's allowance*, not available to unmarried couples. In 1992, this was worth about £8 a week in saved tax to most taxpaying married couples. Nearly all other forms of bias have gone from that tax, although an important one remains in the capital gains tax: if a husband and wife each own a home, only one can be tax free as their main home (see the next chapter). Unmarried couples, where each partner owns a home, can both claim tax relief. Was the former system so indefensible? Why did it reach that position? Should the current system be favourable to marriage, or should it be neutral?

The unmarried couple trap

One problem with major reforms is that people get trapped by the changes in rules – for example the Brace family. Mr Brace is a well-paid financial services adviser and his wife is a talented television actress. They own a large house and a country cottage, but they have no savings. This is partly because their children are both at boarding schools, apart from the youngest daughter who is looked after by a nanny who lives with the family. The Braces are frequently away – Mrs Brace accompanies her husband on business trips when she is 'resting' from her acting, which she has found herself doing a lot recently. At the same time, Mr Brace is not feeling quite so wealthy, as the profits of his business have been sharply reduced. As a result, they are now having financial problems. They are also, now, not getting on so well with each other.

To avoid being caught by the excessive taxation on husband and wife, Mr and Mrs Brace are not in fact married, though everyone thinks they are and, but for tax reasons, they would be. The children think they are married. The couple bought their present house in 1987 (just before the recent changes) with a large mortgage, and each claims maximum mortgage interest relief. Their incomes were never aggregated for income tax purposes, saving them both several thousand pounds before the reforms. They also both claimed to be single parents for tax and social security reasons, until this was stopped in 1988. They gained nothing from the 1990 changes. They recently considered getting married 'for the sake of the children' and to help smooth the rows, also noting that they could then claim a married couple's allowance. They were advised this was not a good idea. They would lose one lot of tax relief on the mortgage if that happened, increasing the effective cost of the mortgage by more than £1,500 a year. Further, if they were thinking of selling the country cottage at some time in the future, they might have to pay capital gains tax on it: a tax they could avoid if they stayed unmarried. The system has doomed them to stay unmarried.

——— Income tax and families ———

Compared with the British system, the French system of income tax is based on family units. The total income of the family, including all the dependent children, is added together, and then divided for the *quotient familiel*, with each adult counting as one and each child as half. For example, my wife and I have two dependent children. We therefore count as three. My own and my wife's income are added together, and the total is taxed as if our family were three individuals, in terms of allowances and rates.

The French system, therefore, reflects the sharing of income within a family, and also reflects the burden presented by the children. In the United Kingdom, a child's income is never added to that of the parent, nor can the parent share income with the child except by deliberate arrangements – most of which are ignored for income tax purposes. Similarly, husband and wife cannot share their earned income, although they can decide to be treated as each receiving half the joint investment income by putting such income in joint accounts and/or by electing to treat the income as received equally.

A self-employed spouse can engage in some income sharing, by the expedient of employing the wife or husband to assist in the business as an employee (or, more fundamentally, as a partner). Many non-working wives of professional husbands are paid incomes which are below the level of the personal allowance (and the minimum level of income to pay NI contributions, so as to avoid that burden as well), but this course of action is not open to those with income as an employee either for income tax or for NI contribution purposes.

Is the French system fairer? It reflects a policy of support to families with children through the tax system. This has now been rejected by the British system, which restricts such help to the social security systems. Is that right?

CALCULATING YOUR PERSONAL TAX BILL

1 Total all your income from every source for tax purposes. In most cases this will consist of earnings from employment for the year (which your employer will advise you at the end of the year on form P45), less any allowed expenses. There may also be bank interest or building society interest and perhaps dividends from shares. Most of these forms of income are paid subject to deduction of tax at the basic rate as shown on the tax certificates that accompany dividends). In the case of the self-employed, it will be the amount of profit in the last year's accounts, after they have been reworked for tax purposes. Ignore any income which is tax-free (such as TESSA accounts). *Let's say that is £20,000, of which £500 is interest on which tax of £125 has been deducted.*

2 Total all deductions (if any) allowed against total income. Mortgage interest is allowed if not paid through MIRAS. Personal pension contributions are also deductible if the policy is approved, plus some special savings schemes such as the BES (Business Expansion Scheme). The gross amount of covenants to charities and other charity gifts over £400 is also allowed. *Let's say that is £500 for a personal pension, plus another £100 covenanted to the local church.*

3 The net amount of 1 and 2 is the total income.

4 From this, deduct your personal allowance, plus any other allowance. *Let's say our taxpayer is a married man under 65. In 1991–2 the personal allowance was £3,295, plus £1,720 married couple's allowance.*

5 Deducting 4 from 3 produces your *taxable income.* This is subject to tax at the appropriate rates of tax for the time being. *In our example, total income is £20,000 with deductions of £600. Mortgage relief was given through the MIRAS scheme. This gives a total income of £19,400. From this deductions of £5,105 are authorised as personal deductions. Taxable income is therefore £14,295. In 1991–92 that would have been taxable at 25%, producing a tax bill of £3,573, of which £125 was paid on the interest. In practice, if the taxpayer is an employee, the rest of the tax due, taking into account these allowances, would be collected through the PAYE system, and the taxpayer would be notified of that each year by Form P3 from the Inland Revenue.*

——— The contributory system ———

The following benefits are contributory benefits in the British NI system:

- unemployment benefit (class 1 only),
- sickness benefit (class 1, class 2),
- invalidity benefit (class 1, class 2),
- maternity allowance (class 1, class 2),
- widow's benefit (class 1, class 2, class 3),
- retirement pensions (class 1, class 2, class 3).

For most employees, sickness benefit and maternity allowance are displaced by statutory sick pay (SSP) and statutory maternity pay (SMP). SSP and SMP are both paid by employers and financed out of general tax revenues. They are available only to those earning more than the level of income from which NI contributions are payable. In practice, sickness benefit and maternity benefit are, therefore, only paid to the self-employed.

Each of these benefits are, save as just mentioned, available to all who have contributed a qualifying amount of NI contributions of the class or classes mentioned in the list above, by right. They are, in effect, insurance or assurance benefits which come from the original creation of the social security system as a compulsory insurance system that all employees must join.

The main benefit of the system is the retirement pension available to women at or after the age of 60, and to men at or after the age of 65, but only if they have, during their working lives, paid sufficient contributions to allow them to qualify for benefit. It is payable in several forms. First, there is a flat-rate pension, available to anyone on the basis of contributions of classes 1, 2 or 3 (the voluntary class). In addition, for class 1 contributors only, there is an earnings-related pension, or SERPS (state earnings related pension scheme), based on the total of earnings-related contributions paid by the employee through her or his working life.

An employment may be *contracted-out* of the SERPS part of the scheme if the employer provides an approved occupational pension for the employee, or the employee has taken out an approved personal pension. If the pension is contracted-out, the employee (and the employer) have to pay a lower level of contribution to the state fund, to offset the lower benefit received. Of course, contributions to the private pension may cost considerably more than the state scheme contributions. Private contributions are deductible from earnings for income tax purposes (though not NI contributions purposes). NI contributions cannot be deducted against income tax payable by an employee. The benefits, when received, are subject to income tax. A majority of all employees now belong to contracted out employment. Because of this, the SERPS scheme is a residual or standby-by scheme, in practice.

This outline suggests that the contributory scheme is a form of pension plan with minor benefits for unemployment and sickness attached. But there is one important difference between the state scheme and private schemes. Private pension schemes are, or should be, protected by separate funds placed on trust. The state scheme is a 'pay as you go' scheme with minimal reserves. In practice, this means that private schemes are forms of saving, or income shifting, with some subsidy between contributors, but with a guarantee of future income.

The state scheme is a sharing scheme with no guarantee that those paying in today will tomorrow receive benefits equivalent to those being paid out today. In fact, there is no guarantee that any benefits will be paid later for those contributing today, if Parliament decides otherwise. For example, Parliament felt it appropriate to restrict entitlement to unemployment benefit in several ways in the last decade, even though the benefit is not financed from general taxation. In the debates about these changes, little attention was paid, by government, to the source of funds of the benefit. The contributory scheme is therefore a complicated mechanism for distribution of funds between present contributors and past contributors, from which those who have never worked are excluded.

Entitlement benefits

A second layer of state social security benefits consists of benefits
to which any qualifying individual is
entitled whether or not contributions have been paid, and regardless of the level of income or
wealth of the recipient. This layer
of benefit includes the following:

- disability living allowance (and
  attendance allowance over the
  age of 65),
- severe disablement allowance,
- pensions for the aged,
- child benefit,
- statutory sick pay,
- statutory maternity pay.

This layer of benefits is a motley
collection, all funded from general
taxation, but with differing social
objectives. These are sharing
benefits, because it is assumed
that the individual does not have to
pay towards them to claim them.
In each case, it has been decided
that it is appropriate to provide
support for the individual, whether
or not the individual has income
from any other source.

The most important is *child benefit*,
payable to the parent of guardian of
any child (all children under 16, and

**FINDING OUT
ABOUT SOCIAL
SECURITY**

There is not enough space
in this book to describe
the many social benefits
that are mentioned in any
detail. If you want to
know more, details are
available in free leaflets
from any social security
office, and you will also
find the main leaflets in
post offices, hospitals and
advice agencies such as
Citizens Advice Bureaux
or Welfare Rights
Offices. Local councils
have details of housing
and poll tax benefits.

If you want to make a
specific enquiry about
your own position, or
check up on a claim with
the Department of Social
Security, they have a free
phone enquiry service on
0800 666555.

those under 19 still at school), at a flat rate and tax-free. It is a state
subsidy for those looking after children, higher for the first child, and
higher still for a single person looking after a child, but payable in respect

of each child to its carer. It is currently the only direct cash support for most families.

The next most important benefits in practice are *SSP* and *SMP*. These are paid through the pay packet to employees in addition to, or in place of, lost pay during periods of sickness (beyond the first three days) and maternity. They are taxable, and are regarded, for contributions purposes, as part of the employee's earnings. If paid with other income, they are therefore subject to class 1 contribution laibility. They form a state guaranteed minimum sickness and maternity pay for those with income above the minimum to contribute to the contributory system, but not for those earning below that level.

The other important group is the new *disability living allowance, attendance allowance for those over 65,* and *severe disablement allowance.* These are only payable to those with some severe disability, for example individuals unable, or virtually unable, to walk, or who need regular attention to their personal physical needs (such as help with eating and drinking) or who are blind. Most of the claimants are older people, frequently older than the state-retirement age. These benefits are not taxable.

Income-related benefits

The final layer of the state sharing system consists of the benefits available only to those with no income or income below set minimum levels. The benefits in this group are:

- family credit,
- disability working allowance,
- income support,
- social fund payments,
- housing benefit,
- community charge benefit.

In each case, strict entitlement rules prevent people claiming if they, or their partners or immediate family, have any form of income above the minimum level, or if they have any savings or capital assets (other than the house they live in) above minimum levels set by regulation. This layer of benefits is divided between the benefits available to the low-paid engaged in remunerative work, and those who are not. As a dividing line, someone in paid work for more than 16 hours a week is regarded as in work.

Those in low-paid work who are responsible for younger children (those for whom child benefit is payable) can claim *family credit* if their earnings fall below a set weekly level. The family credit is payable by the Department of Social Security as a supplement to earnings. From 1992, an additional benefit called *disability working allowance* has been created. This is similar to family credit except that it is payable to a person in work, but who has a disability which puts him or her at a disadvantage in getting a job. The benefit is payable whether or not the individual is supporting a family, but it replaces family credit for those with families.

Those not in work (any work they do being less than 16 hours a week) cannot claim these benefits, but instead are entitled to *income support*. This is paid at set weekly amounts (with special additions for children, for the elderly, and for those subject to disability). In effect, this provides anyone over the age of 18 with a minimum weekly level of support. In the case of those of working age, it is subject to the condition that they should be both available for work and actively seeking work on any day of claim (unless they are not able to work through sickness or disability, or have some other good reason for not working). Entitlement to income support is backed up by *social fund payments*, which are loans or grants, made from locally administered support funds financed from state funds available to deal with exceptional expenses of those without other resources. With an important exception, income support and the two schemes to support low earnings, are not liable to income tax. Nor do they count as earnings for the purposes of contribution liability.

The important exception is that income support, payable to someone who is expected to be available to work, is taxable. The reason for this exception (and the fact that unemployment benefit is taxable) is that this means that an employee's total earnings for a year are added together with these benefits to decide the total income for the year. For example, if someone has been receiving benefit for the first two months of the year, and then finds a well-paid job, the state will in effect reclaim a proportion of the benefit as tax along with the tax on the income. There are no rules in the system to reclaim more than the tax on a benefit except in the case where damages or insurance are available to recompense the individual, and the state, for the benefits paid out.

In addition, all those on low incomes or with no income (apart from other benefits) can claim *housing benefit* in respect of rent paid for their family's housing, and *community charge benefit* (to be replaced by a council tax benefit) as a contribution towards individual poll tax liabilities. These benefits are also not taxable.

The last of these benefits is a curiosity – a state social security benefit specifically designed to pay a tax liability. The policy of the tax system, with regard to these means-tested benefits, is to ignore benefits for tax purposes except as outlined above. However, in the case of the poll tax, a deliberate decision was taken to tax those without incomes in the same way as everyone else. As a money-raising exercise this is a nonsense, as those establishing the tax knew. Their intention was to ensure that everyone paid towards the poll tax, so that everyone was aware of the levels of local taxation. But many beneficiaries did not pay the poll tax, as there was no method built into the system to ensure that someone receiving poll tax benefit actually spent it on the poll tax. If the legislation had contained provisions for direct payment of the benefit to the local authority, would the poll tax benefit have had any purpose? If it did not do that, was it fair on those receiving it?

Priorities in the sharing systems

There is a clear ranking order of benefits to stop more than one benefit being payable to the same claimant at the same time, subject only to limited exceptions. Contributory benefits take priority (and are generally at a higher level than the non-contributory benefits for those under 65), subject to the priority given to SSP and SMP already noted. Disability living allowance and child benefit are payable in addition to any other benefit entitlement, but severe disablement allowance is payable only to those not entitled to invalidity allowance.

Income-related benefits all take account of any other form of income received, including all other benefits except only the disability living allowance. So, for example, the addition to income support, because the claimant is looking after a child, will be reduced by the child benefit the claimant is receiving. A claimant who is a hospital in-patient will lose most benefit entitlement for himself or herself, but not for the family. But the level of support to the aged is such that some receiving contributory pensions are entitled to further help by way of income support or housing benefit in addition, in which case they receive a composite payment of benefit.

As a result, figures emerge as the minimum level of income that individuals and families can expect if they are, or are not, working, taking into account any family responsibilities and any disabilities. Benefits in kind such as free school education and free national health service treatment are in addition to these cash benefits.

An overview

This brief description has listed 19 benefits. It has been simplified, leaving out some minor benefits and also benefits for which no new claim can be accepted. The full list would show almost as many kinds of benefits as we have taxes in the United Kingdom. This is despite the fact that several different kinds of benefit have been abolished, or combined, in the last few years – as has happened with taxes. Why so many?

One answer lies in remembering how many people receive some sort of benefit. A form of state pension is payable to almost everyone aged over 65 either on a contributory basis or on a needs basis. Child benefit is payable for several million children. Support is payable to most of the several million unemployed, to those who are sick and to those with serious disabilities. The system has to deal with many diverse needs.

That provides a partial explanation. The parallel contributory and non-contributory systems provide another answer, for each of the contributory benefits (aside from widow's payment) is matched by a non-contributory benefit – the latter usually being less generous. If we take into account that claimants can receive a non-contributory benefit if they do not contribute, and that the non-contributory benefit can, on occasions, amount to more than the contributory benefit, we must ask why we have to contribute to receive a benefit a little bigger than that received by non-contributors, for example, because they have a disability which prevents them from competing successfully in the jobs market, and therefore prevents them from earning anything.

Why do we not abolish the contributory system, merge the different benefit entitlements so as to remove unfairness like the one just mentioned, and raise the revenues through direct taxes? This is what Australia did some years ago, and it is also, broadly, the position in Denmark. The answer is political. What politician could win votes by announcing that the basic rate of income tax was rising to 34 per cent (or, if employers' contributions were abolished, and transferred to their employees, up to 45 per cent)?

Alternatively, we could transfer the burden to other taxes. In 1992, that kind of transfer would involve, for example, doubling the rate of VAT, or some shared sharp rise in all other tax rates. Why disturb a system which causes little hassle because it is untidy, and perhaps occasionally unfair? Perhaps the psychology of tax is more important than the reality?

____ The effect of combined taxes ____ and benefits

Although a policy of combining taxes and benefits is not practical politics, different issues arise with the interaction between social security benefits and the direct taxes, particularly income tax. However, not only has there been no effort made to combine our tax and social security systems, they are not harmonised or even coordinated to any marked extent.

For example, the total of weekly earnings at which contributions and income tax become payable are not the same, nor is the upper limit for contributions related in any way to the figure on which higher rate income tax becomes payable. Nor is the personal allowance for income tax high enough in all years to prevent basic social security benefits becoming liable to tax even where the recipients have no other income.

The result is a complicated and untidy intermix of changes as the income of an individual or family rises. This intermix gives rise to two problems which are phenomena of the complexity: the *poverty trap* and the *unemployment trap*.

The poverty trap

The Smith family were delighted when Mrs Smith was given a promotion and an increase of hours at work. Mr Smith had been unemployed for some time, and the family had been relying on the money from Mrs Smith's part-time job and their income from social security and other state benefits. Because Mrs Smith was working more than 16 hours a week, the family were entitled to *family credit* to supplement her pay, as well as *child benefit* for each of their children, *housing benefit* and *community charge benefit* to offset their rent and poll tax bills, and *free NHS benefits* as well as other benefits in kind to help cut their living costs. They paid no income tax and no NI contributions because Mrs Smith's earnings were below the minimum figure at which each became payable. The family thought that they must be much better off as a result of Mrs Smith's hard work. They were wrong.

Each pound of take home pay earned cut the weekly amount of housing benefit, community charge benefit and family credit. What is more, Mrs Smith was now earning enough to bring her pay into liability for NI contributions and also income tax – though only just, because she was entitled to the married couple's allowance as well as her own personal allowance. In other words, as her earnings rose, so did both the level of deductions (9 per cent NI contributions, 25 per cent income tax on the top end of her earnings) and the total of the reduction in earnings-related benefits. In fact, when everything is taken into account she found that for each £1 extra that she was going to earn, she would only be about 5 pence better off.

The Smiths had discovered the *poverty trap*. Was it really worth Mrs Smith's while taking the added responsibility of her promotion, and the added burden of the extra hours at work when the family would see little net gain for her extra efforts. It would take significantly more than her efforts to get the family clear of this problem, and get any real increase in its net earnings – only if Mr Smith were also able to start earning, and pull the family clear of the level of earnings when the earnings-related benefits are payable.

The poverty-trap occurs because the effective marginal rate of additional net earnings of families like the Smith family is so low. Put another way, the marginal tax rate on each additional pound (£) earned, combined with the marginal loss of benefit per pound (£) earned, results in a total tax/benefit cost per pound (£) of 90 per cent or more – far higher than the marginal rates imposed on the highest earners.

Until a few years ago, when reforms to the way in which family credit took effect were carried through, the problem was even worse. At some points on the income scale, an extra pound (£) of earnings would leave the family *worse* off. This is because more than one pound (£1) was lost because of the interaction of tax and benefits because of one pound (£1) extra earnings. Why should Mrs Smith work harder if the only beneficiaries are other taxpayers?

The unemployment trap

The Jones family were particularly badly hit when the local factory closed down. John Jones and his partner Brenda Blair both lost their jobs, and there was no prospect of finding any other as they were reluctant to move because their children were happy in local schools and Brenda's elderly mother needed increasing attention because she lived at home on her own in a house nearby, and they were unable to find a hostel room for her.

John and Brenda had spent their savings, and had no income apart from state benefits. They were both registered as looking for work, and received income support, supplemented for each of their children, together with housing benefit and community charge benefit. They received child benefit, but this was taken into account in their income support calculations, so left them no better off. Because they had several younger children, all at school, they did get help with free school meals, some help towards uniforms, free prescriptions and other state and local benefits for the unwaged. This was because they lived in one of the more generous local authorities (and therefore one with higher poll taxes).

Although John had largely given up the hope of getting a job, Brenda did keep looking and one day was offered a low-paid part-time job for a few hours a week. At first, she was pleased, but, being careful, she reported the facts to her local benefit office. Their response was to inform her that her benefits would be cut to take her earnings into account, apart from the first £5. Each pound (£) more than that resulted in her benefits dropping away at nearly, or even more than, £1. In fact, she might work for 15 hours a week, and end up hardly any better off at all, because she would have to pay her fares to work by train, and get herself some tools and suitable clothes to do the job.

The Jones family were in the *unemployment trap*. The only jobs available to them would leave them no better off, perhaps even worse off, than they would be on state benefits without working. Why should they bother?

The unemployment trap is a particularly awkward problem for those keen to reduce unemployment, and also for those who regard anyone of working age on state benefit as being a 'scrounger'. Unless they ensure that the level of state benefits is minimal, the level of benefits payable to a larger family will make it not worth the adult members working (and one at least should be needed to look after the children in any event). If the level of benefits for the unemployed of working age are cut, then people like John and Brenda with large families are going to be made poor.

Are there any easy answers to this situation which for some can become a vicious circle? What changes are needed in our tax and social security systems to ensure that these problems are minimised – or do they not matter? Should we ensure that the level of benefit is right, and deal with the problems of interaction afterwards? If so, how do we finance this?

Support for housing

Nearly two thirds of all households in the United Kingdom own their own home, or are in the process of buying it with the help of mortgages or loans. Most of the others rent their homes. At some point therefore, housing costs form a part of most household budgets, particularly when the family has children. Home ownership is encouraged, and has grown rapidly until now. Part of the cause of the rapid growth of home ownership in recent years has been government support. This has involved selling public housing, at a discount to its open market price, to sitting tenants. A large part of the influence has been a combination of tax reasons plus, until 1988, a steadily rising market.

Owner-occupiers have their homes subsidised through the tax system in several ways. First, and best known, is the *mortgage interest relief*, usually now paid through *MIRAS*, the Mortgage Interest Relief At Source scheme, giving direct assistance to the cost of borrowing to buy a new home. Next, home ownership is currently not subject to any form of tax (although the new Council tax, when in effect, will reimpose a liability similar to the rates only recently repealed, and will tax homes). In addition, there is no liability to income tax or capital gains tax on any profit made in selling a main home. Further, sales of homes are exempt for VAT (though when sold by private owners there would be no VAT anyway), with sales of new homes by their builders being zero-rated (which, as we see below means they are subsidised through the tax system). The only tax directly affecting the ownership of a new home is stamp duty and even that was suspended for part of 1992.

Mortgage interest relief

Once upon a time (that is, in the first part of the 20th century), a taxpayer who paid out yearly interest or interest to a bank, could deduct that interest from his total income for tax purposes. Gradually, this relief has been reduced, and now interest relief is only available for most people for:

- purchasing your main home;
- purchasing a future home if you live in job-related accommodation;
- purchasing or improving property for rent.

There are also reliefs for interest that is used to buy into a private company or partnership, and to buy equipment for a business. The elderly can also get relief on loans to buy life annuities.

Mortgage interest relief has been tightly restricted since 1988. It is available only on interest on a loan of up to £30,000 on any house (or flat, caravan or houseboat if they form a home), however big the total loan, and however many borrowers there are. Relief is not available to any individual on more than one home (and is only available on the house which is in fact her or his main home), and it is not available for loans for repairing or improving the home.

Most borrowers receive this relief as a direct mortgage subsidy through the MIRAS scheme, in which the tax relief is deducted automatically by the lender when calculating the amount of interest payable by the borrower. The relief is paid to the lender direct by the Inland Revenue. The effect is to make mortgages cheaper – or, looked at another way, to make income tax bills higher for those without mortgages. In the present system, it pays to have a mortgage of £30,000 or so. Even if you cannot afford it, income support will pay the interest until the house can be sold – and in 1991 nearly one billion pounds was paid by the government as income support to those who could not afford to keep their mortgage payments up. That billion further increased the tax cost of our policy of encouraging owner-occupation. Is it the role of government to intervene in the housing market in this way? If so, is it being generous enough, or should the limit of £30,000 on loans be increased? If so, who should finance the increased relief?

When the property prices continued falling through 1990, 1991 and 1992 there were many appeals to help those caught in the *mortgage trap*, that is, they had mortgages of greater value than their houses. Many of these unfortunate houseowners had been tempted to buy because of the tax reliefs available to houseowners. Should they be offered further tax reliefs, as some have suggested, to help them out of the mortgage trap?

8

TAXING SAVINGS AND WEALTH

'Unto every one that hath shall be given, and he shall have abundance: but from him that hath not shall be taken away even that which he hath.' This quotation from St. Matthew's gospel is the moral of the story about receiving the rewards of one's actions. It poses a challenge that societies of all faiths and beliefs – and of none – have to answer: how far should the state look after all its citizens and strangers within its gates? It is a problem of particular importance to those determining the way we pay our taxes, as St. Matthew hints. But then Matthew was a tax collector, and in a good position to comment.

Savings and wealth defined

In this chapter, we explore taxes aimed at those regarded as wealthy, looking at the choices hidden in the taxes that we pay. We examine how our systems tax – or refrain from or fail to tax – unearned income, wealth, property left on death, and gifts. The discussion uses two terms in describing the sources to be taxed: *savings* to describe property and money accumulated by the owner himself or herself, and *wealth* to describe property and money inherited or given to the owner. This is not an official description, but it serves to draw attention to different ways in which people become wealthy, because some argue that there are differences in the treatment that each should receive.

The taxation of savings and wealth involves income tax and capital gains tax (CGT), plus inheritance tax (IHT), which is really a collection of taxes wrapped up together. We do not have a wealth tax in this country unlike, say, the Germans.

Taxing unearned income

The official term for unearned income in tax legislation is *investment income*. For many years investment income was subject to a higher rate of income tax than earned income. The policy was that those who had to work for their living had incomes which were less secure than those with savings or wealth, and should therefore be taxed less. That higher rate has now gone – the income tax rate is the same as on earnings – but the charging provisions are separate from those already noted which deal with earnings.

The main charges on investment income for income tax are:

- **schedule C** – interest on government bonds and stock;
- **schedule D case III** – interest, annuities and annual payments;
- **schedule D case VI** – other annual payments, including special anti-avoidance provisions;
- **schedule F** – distributions from United Kingdom companies.

In addition, foreign unearned income is caught, under broadly the same rules as foreign earned income, by schedule D cases IV and V (the rules of the two cases are almost identical). Capital gains are taxed under the separate CGT, at the same rate as income tax. Although there are several sets of rules under which investment income is chargeable, the effect of each set is broadly the same. Subject to rules as to timing and methods of payment, the full income is chargeable to tax as part of the total income of the individual. No deductions are allowed against investment income for costs of making or managing this income (for example, bank charges or fees for financial advice).

Were that all that the rules had to cover, they would be short and simple.

In practice, there are three major additional factors that they must also cover, and from which they gain their excessive complexity.

First, governments have sought to encourage us to save and they use the tax system as one way of doing it. As a result, there are a number of ways in which we can save money to create investment income and capital gains without paying tax.

The opposite pressure is also present. There are a number of ways in which we can reduce the tax on our savings and investment income which the government has not intended us to use – for example, trusts. There are therefore a number of anti-avoidance rules. Both these factors are explored in this chapter.

The third factor is international. If tax on savings in this country is higher than elsewhere, why should we not send our investments overseas and avoid United Kingdom income tax entirely? This we discuss later.

Tax-privileged savings

Welcome to the world of TESSA, SAYE, PEP, and BES which are tax-privileged savings schemes designed to catch your eye and your spare money. For details of any scheme mentioned here, visit your local bank or building society, or open the financial pages of the heavyweight Saturday daily newspapers. We will not pause here on the minutiae.

On a long term basis, a few forms of savings have been preferred by the British. The two most important are *homes* and *pensions*. These are given major tax privileges, not least because of the political sensitivities involved in altering them. Because they are relatively tax free, it is difficult for other forms of savings to compete. Those also have to be tax-privileged if they are to catch the eye.

Two forms of savings have been made attractive over a long period. One is *government securities*, such as National Savings. This is easy to arrange and to justify. From the government's point of view, this makes their securities more competitive. It encourages those people to save who might not otherwise do so, as there is also little risk involved. It also saves unnecessary administration in collecting back, as tax, a share of the interest paid out from the same source.

The other form of saving which used to have significant levels of tax privilege was *life assurance*. A stop was put to unrestricted tax privileges from this kind of savings some years ago. Some relief is still available on a policy taken out before the changes and on small policies taken out with friendly societies, and for payments made to a trade union, either for a lump sum payable on the death of the payer or for funeral benefits at death. For larger amounts, these provisions have been replaced by occupational and personal pensions. Other new schemes have also been created.

SAYE

One of the earliest was also one of the simplest: the contractual savings scheme or *Save As You Earn*. The saver agrees to save a set amount each month for five years (or 60 payments). A minimum and a maximum amount for each payment is set out in regulations. If the contract is successfully completed, the interest paid on the account and a bonus at the end are tax free. Further, the saver can agree to keep the savings for a further two years, to receive another tax-free bonus. The SAYE scheme has been linked with schemes run by companies to encourage their employees to save by investing in the company's shares. This and other schemes especially designed for employees are set out in the chapter on employment income.

TESSAs and tax-free interest

Since 1991, SAYE schemes have been overtaken by another version of a tax-privileged savings account, the *Tax-Exempt Special Savings Account*. A TESSA can be set up, like a SAYE scheme, with any building society or bank and is a specially certified deposit account. As long as the depositor keeps to the rules, any interest or bonus paid on the deposit is tax free for a period of five years. The main restriction, along the same lines as SAYE, is that the sums deposited into the account must be left in until the end of the five-year period.

TESSAs were established at the same time as, and in parallel with, another major change to the taxation of savings in 1991: the creation of savings accounts free of deduction of tax on interest. Until then, deposit accounts in building societies and banks were subject to a rule that the interest paid out had to be subject to tax, even if the depositor was not himself or herself subject to tax. Because of this, the rate of tax charged on the accounts was a special rate called the 'composite rate', and was lower than the main basic rate, to take account of those paying the tax who would not otherwise have done so. This has now been abolished.

From 1991, anyone who is not liable to pay income tax, such as children, married women with only small incomes and retired people with little income other than their state pensions, can open a deposit account which is not subject to deduction of tax on interest payments. If the individual becomes liable to tax, it has to be paid at that time. This reform which prevents pensioners from paying income tax by accident lacks only a snappy title. Why not call them USAs – untaxed savings accounts?

PEPs

This does have a catchy title: PEP stands for *Personal Equity Plan*. It dates from 1986. The intention is to encourage individuals to save by means of investments in stocks and shares. The scheme has evolved to allow investments at one extreme purely in the shares of one company (where it can be used to back up employee share schemes) through to more cautious investments indirectly in shares through the medium of unit trusts. The idea is to use PEPs to pursue an aim of economic policy: widening share ownership for the public. The carrot is freedom from tax both on dividends and on capital gains provided the PEP meets specific conditions, and the investment is kept in for a minimum period. The rapid take-up of PEPs shows that many think this is a carrot worth chasing.

BES

BES is the *Business Expansion Scheme*. This is a tax-privileged saving for the less faint-hearted (or, as some have found to their cost, for the gambler – some of the schemes have left their investors losing their entire investment). These were introduced in 1983, and end in 1993. A BES provides income tax relief to an individual who invests shares in a new trading company which is pursuing one of the kinds of activity set out in the rules, and subject to all the conditions in the rules. The aim was to encourage people to invest in new ventures being run by others (you cannot invest in your own company although, of course, when you do invest, it becomes your company!). The amount invested in the shares can be set off against income tax, and the tax relief is therefore the equivalent of a deduction directly against income. Shares must be kept in the company for five years for relief to be maintained.

Other forms of saving

For those taxpayers who manage to avoid putting their savings in PEPs, BESs, PPs (personal pensions), TESSAs, USAs and PPRs (principal private residences, or their homes), the tax system awaits. It treats savings income and capital gains from investments in much the same way, and levies tax at 25 per cent, or 40 per cent of the income or gain for higher rate taxpayers.

_____ Avoiding tax on savings _____ and investments

Taxpayers are understandably reluctant to lose two-fifths of their savings – even a quarter – to the tax authorities, although they are perhaps a little less reluctant to bear the present rates of tax than they were a few years ago, when the rate of income tax on investment income was 15 per cent higher than on earned income (after an initial annual allowance subject only to the earned income rate). As the income tax rate on earned income climbed to 83 per cent, so the investment income tax rate rose to 98 per cent – and in one year when a surcharge was imposed, it even rose above 100 per cent! Nor was the United Kingdom alone in having such high rates. At one time, the top tax rate in the USA was more than 90 per cent, and it was similar in other European countries. All sorts of schemes were thought up to stop income bearing these rates of tax. Even if you paid someone 50 per cent of the tax saved for some bright tax-saving idea, you were still far better off.

TURNING INCOME INTO CAPITAL

This operation bears some of the flavour of the medieval alchemist promising to turn base metals into gold, except that in this case, courtesy of the tax rules, it worked! Income tax rates of 50 per cent to 98 per cent were turned into a CGT rate of 30 per cent at most.

To achieve this trick, transactions had to be altered so that the taxpayer stopped receiving income, and instead received a capital sum.

The government itself played this trick with some Treasury bonds. They were issued bearing low rates of interest (perhaps 2 per cent), but at a discount and redeemable in full. If, say, the taxpayer bought £100 of stock at £95 and 2 per cent interest, when liable to pay income tax at 98 per cent, the result was quite good. The 5 per cent bonus was liable to tax at only 30 per cent, so was worth £3.50 to the taxpayer. The interest was worth almost nothing: 4 pence a year! To earn £3.50 after tax at those tax rates, the investor would have to earn £175 in interest, a high yield even if cumulated over several years.

Another version is to sell something which has a right to income so as to make a capital gain. This was done by selling shares just before dividends on the shares became payable. The purchaser would pay a price which took account of the right to receive the dividend (which had already been announced, so there was no gamble), while the seller received the price as a capital sum. If so minded, the investor could always buy the shares back after the dividend had been paid.

Similarly, it might be a good idea not to take income out of a profitable company in which you were a major shareholder only to see it disappear in taxes, but leave it in and in due course sell the company, realising the profits indirectly through the increase in value of the shares.

Almost anything was better than a 98 per cent tax rate (except for a 106 per cent tax rate!). It was left until 1988 for the Chancellor to wave the magic wand and cause the tricks to vanish – by making the rate of CGT the same as that for income. The same thing was done in other countries too, but was predictably unpopular with those who thereby lost, as witness the attempts for several years of US President Bush to undo a similar reform of the US federal taxes in 1986.

Tax avoidance on any large scale poses a threat of erosion to the tax base, and therefore makes tax collection less predictable and less efficient. In the present context, it makes the tax machine less successful as a mechanism for redistribution and challenges one of the assumptions of a good tax system – fairness. Is it fair if you and I have the same income, but you pay more tax than I do because I am more skilful, or persistent, or am better advised, and can reduce my overall tax burden by avoidance? There are sharp differences of opinion about the answer.

Is avoidance a bad thing?

One answer is economic. Some argue that avoidance is a good thing, because it subjects the tax system itself to ordinary economic forces, and results in the most efficient use of money. To discourage avoidance is therefore to increase inefficiency, which is not economically useful. This answer itself interacts with the efficiency of the tax system. If one tax, which is neutral but curbs avoidance, can be used in place of another tax which is also neutral but allows considerable scope for avoidance, which is the better tax? That question is posed by the use of an efficient modern tax such as VAT as compared with older taxes such as schedular income tax.

Another answer is that tax avoidance is a question of freedom. If we assume that all imposition of tax is an interference with property rights, we can argue that the individual whose property rights are subject to interference in this way does not lose any other of his property rights. He or she remains free to use property as to minimise the extent to which it is taxed. For example, if there are two ways in which you can provide funds for a business, one of which incurs substantial tax liabilities, but the other of which is subject only to low taxation, which will you choose? Should you be under a duty, legal or moral, to choose the one which increases the tax burden (and therefore the cost to you)?

> 'Every man is entitled, if he can, to order his affairs so that the tax attaching under the appropriate Acts is less than it otherwise would be. If he succeeds in ordering them so as to secure this result then, however unappreciative the Commissioners of Inland Revenue or his fellow taxpayers may be of his ingenuity, he cannot be compelled to pay an increased tax.'
>
> *Lord Tomlin in IRC v Duke of Westminster (1936)*
>
> 'No man in this country is under the smallest obligation, moral or other, so to arrange his legal relations to his business or to his property so as to enable the Inland Revenue to put the largest possible shovel into his stores.'
>
> *Lord Clyde in Ayrshire Pullman Services v IRC (1929)*

The argument that you should not be able to avoid taxes by rearranging your affairs to reduce tax – contrary to the resounding phrases of the judges quoted above – requires a more sophisticated analysis of what is happening when individuals are avoiding taxation. Their behaviour has been analysed as consisting of several kinds of behaviour. *Tax saving* consists of using provisions in the tax law which are designed by government to encourage reduction of tax bills. This might include the tax-preferred savings schemes discussed earlier in this chapter, or investing in new business equipment because of a favourable capital allowance. *Tax mitigation* means making use of the form of legislation to reduce the bill by, for example, using gaps or loopholes in the legislation about which government has no particular view – for example, in the United Kingdom there is no taxation on forestry, which is therefore regarded as a *tax shelter*, or way of preventing some asset or income being taxed.

A third kind of distinguishable activity is sometimes called *artificial tax avoidance*, although the term 'artificial' adds little but a sense of opprobrium to the general term. Here, the individual is concerned to reduce taxation by engaging in activities solely or mainly designed to reduce taxation, and which would not otherwise take place. For example, a company is established on particular terms to exploit some aspect of tax law. This category is sometimes said to be complying with the letter of the tax law but not with its spirit.

It should be noted that these labels do not have any agreed significance in British tax law. The only agreement is that *avoidance* means activity which is legal as long as *evasion* means the activity is illegal. Clearly, evasion is wrong. Is any form of avoidance wrong? Consider the following.

Saving tax with approval

Governments encourage people to save and invest. If you have savings, you should ensure that you put them in tax-efficient investments, and manage them appropriately. These are the government-favoured routes:

● *Buy your own home.* You get tax relief on the interest on the first £30,000 of the mortgage, no CGT when you sell it, no taxes (apart from council tax) on ownership, and you can derive a small income tax-free from letting a room out.

● *Save for a big pension.* You can claim a deduction (i.e. get your income tax back) for pension contributions on all your earnings up to £75,000. The nearer you are to retirement, the more you can save, as shown in the box. Once the money is in the pension fund, it is tax free (though you have to pay charges to the fund).

● *Use tax-free savings routes.* Make sure you and your family save through TESSAs, PEPs, government tax-free savings, tax-free deposit accounts and the other schemes discussed in this chapter wherever possible. If your company has special schemes, investigate them too.

PENSION LIMITS

You get full tax relief on pension contributions up to the following percentage of your first £75,000 earnings in any tax year:

Age	Limit per cent
under 36	17.5
36 – 45	20
46 – 50	25
51 – 55	30
56 – 60	35
over 60	40

The pension fund will be tax free. Your pension will be taxed like earnings, but a lump sum of up to one and a half times your final salary, or a quarter of the pension fund will be tax free.

- *Share your wealth in the family.* A self-employed person paying his wife (or her husband) can save tax and NI contributions. Gifts to the children from grandparents can save income tax (if the children do not pay any). In the longer term, spreading wealth saves the risk of high inheritance tax bills.

- *Make gifts tax free.* If you give money to charity, use a covenant or Gift Aid to get the tax back for the charity. If giving away family assets, take care to ensure maximum relief from inheritance tax, CGT and stamp duties. There are various ways of doing this. Expert advice may save you money.

- *Do not pay CGT.* The first £5,800 of capital gains of each individual are tax-free each year. Consider selling or giving any items so that you get the maximum amount tax free in any year.

All these ideas are there for you to use, and can result in a sharp reduction of total tax bills. Details on them are set out either in this chapter or elsewhere in the book. Far from there being anything 'wrong' with them, the system is expressly designed to help you save in these ways. But other methods of tax avoidance may save even more tax by non-encouraged routes. Are these also right?

Anti-avoidance legislation

The easiest way to establish that an activity of a taxpayer is 'wrong' in the sense only that it should be taxable rather than non-taxable (any other sense of wrong should mean we are talking of evasion, not avoidance) is for Parliament to say so and it frequently does. This is the reason for much of the complexity of our tax laws. The approach of the United Kingdom Parliament towards activities that it does not wish to escape from tax is a 'hole and plug' method. If it sees activity it does not like, it provides a 'plug' for the hole by means of targeted legislative provisions.

Britain has resisted an approach common in most other countries – a general anti-avoidance provision. With such a provision, the tax authorities can challenge any form of arrangement or contract by which tax would otherwise be avoided. An advantage of a provision such as this is that it makes the law simpler and it makes it fairer to those who cannot (or will not) avoid taxes. A disadvantage is that it makes the law less certain. It may be unclear, or left to the discretion of officials, as to how the general provision operates in an individual case. The British system favours certainty.

But should we have a different morality to taxation? Commentators say, for example, that the consensus system of Japan puts pressure on taxpayers to pay without seeking to avoid, and that there is little avoidance of the artificial kind. Or should we avoid anti-avoidance legislation, as some other states do, and should we not curb legitimate measures to reduce tax?

———— Taxing capital gains ————

One route to saving tax, which is not open to attack as 'artificial' in most cases, was through turning income into a capital gain. Before 1962 there was no tax on capital gains. The government introduced a *capital gains tax* in 1965 as a separate tax to income tax. Like many taxes, it started life as a simple tax. If a taxpayer made a chargeable *gain* on the *disposal* of an *asset*, CGT was paid on the gain. Real life, of course, is not that simple. The complications arise from a series of problems: what is to be done about inflation? How do we deal with companies and trusts? As it is socially undesirable to tax all disposals from assets, what do we exempt from the tax and how? Should everyone pay the full rate of tax on everything? What expenses should be allowed against the gain?

Calculating the gain

A capital gain is made whenever the proceeds of sale of an item exceed the cost of that item, together with any capital sums spent on the item, after taking into account the effect of inflation.

The sale price is taken as the actual price paid, less any incidental costs of sale (such as auctioneer's commission or legal costs). In some special cases (such as sales between relatives), the Inland Revenue may insist on the market value of the item at the time of sale instead.

From the sale price, the seller is entitled to deduct only the following four costs:

1 the purchase price, or sums spent on creating the item;

2 incidental costs of the purchase;

3 any capital sums spent on enhancing the value of the item, so that it still has some of that enhanced value at the time of sale;

4 any capital costs incurred in defending any challenge to the ownership of the item.

The seller cannot deduct as a cost anything which is, or could be, deductible for income tax purposes. In particular, interest payments and the cost of any insurance premiums cannot be deducted.

ASSETS AND DISPOSALS EXEMPTED FROM CGT:

- Principal private residences,
- Cars,
- Cash in sterling,
- Chattels worth under £6,000,
- Property left on death,
- Assets with lives under 60 years,
- Proceeds of insurance policies, if used to replace the items destroyed, lost or damaged,
- National savings certificates,
- Heritage property,
- Gifts of business assets,
- Gifts to charity,
- Debts not on a security,
- Damages for injuries.

Dealing with inflation

In order to ensure that CGT applies only to the real gain, not to any cash gain caused by inflation, each allowable deduction for the purchase price and capital expenditure is adjusted for inflation. This is done by calculating the change in inflation between each of the capital costs being incurred, and the month when the item is sold. Inflation is measured by using the headline inflation figure, the RPI, or Retail Prices Index, published officially each month. When something is sold the deductions for the cost of buying and improving it are adjusted to take account of charges in the RPI.

For example, Hilary bought a country cottage in a run down state in 1984 for £10,000 (including all the costs of purchase), and spent a further £10,000 improving it in 1986. Hilary wants to sell the cottage, which rose sharply in value until 1987, but has since gone down to the same value as it had after the improvements were finished in 1987, £30,000.

To keep the illustration simple, assume that inflation since 1984 has totalled 40 per cent, and since 1986 was 30 per cent. To find out how much Hilary will pay in tax if the cottage is sold at £30,000 (after paying estate agents' fees, lawyers' fees and other costs of the sale) we must calculate the present value of the capital expenses incurred on buying and improving the cottage. Uprated for inflation, the purchase cost is £14,000, and the improvement cost is £13,000, a total of £27,000. The taxable gain on sale would therefore be £3,000. If Hilary sold nothing else making a capital gain in that year, this is less than the annual exempt figure and the gain will therefore not be taxable.

Total of tax payable

If the total of capital expenditure is greater than the proceeds of sale, the calculation reveals a loss. That loss will be an *allowable loss* if the gain would have been taxable. Each year every taxpayer must total up all chargeable gains, deducting all allowable losses. The net sum is the *total of taxable gains* for the year. Tax is payable on that total as if it were the last part of the income of the individual or company for the year. The tax rates are therefore the same as income tax or corporation tax rates.

Tax-free disposals

Even with the adjustments for inflation, and the allowance of capital expenditure, CGT could be impossible to administer. This is because it would apply to the sale of any capital item – cars, homes, hi-fi units. It could also apply not just on sales, but every time anything changed hands – the gift of an engagement ring, the loss of a small boat in a sailing accident and so on. Not only could this be potentially unfair, it would be almost impossible to administer without vast and expensive bureaucracy.

The tax could also be harmful to businesses. If every time a business decided to change its capital investments in land or plant for business reasons it had to pay CGT, the business that tried to be flexible and keep abreast of changes in fashion would be penalised, while the unoriginal business with no strategy of change would be better off.

Similarly, if father, who had built up his own family business, had to pay CGT when he passed it on to son or daughter on retiring from the business, the business would be penalised, encouraging father not to retire. These are examples of what is known as the *locking-in effect* of CGT, that is, the discouragement from selling or transferring assets because of the tax penalty on doing so.

To avoid both harmful locking in, unfairness, and a waste of resources on attempting to tax small transactions, the charge to CGT is subject to a long series of exemptions, some of which are in the box on page 150. In all cases, of course, cash transfers cannot give rise to gains (unless the cash is some currency other than pounds sterling).

Individual exemptions

For individuals, the exemptions ensure that most people do not pay CGT. The *principal private residence* of every individual or married couple is exempt from CGT, as are all cars, all items with a predicted life at acquisition of less than 50 years (for example, a 21-year lease of a building, or a computer), all goods and chattels which, when sold, are worth less than £6,000 (for example, items of electronic equipment) and, in every case, an *exempt amount* each tax year. This is currently £5,600 a year net gains (that is, the total of all gains less all losses).

The principal private residence exemption is of significance to most families, because it allows them to invest in a family home without risk of tax. The law exempting gains on the home or main home of the taxpayer is complicated because of the need to prevent the relief being used to cover two or more homes, or for other buildings. If an individual has more than one home, he or she must choose the one that receives the exemption. (If a taxpayer does not, the inspector will!) There are also rules dealing with absences from work or other reasons, and for the overlap between selling one house and buying another. These introduce rough and ready limits, but ensure that most shorter absences from home are ignored.

In addition, the position of an individual who is required to live in job-related accommodation is covered. If, say, a club steward, is required as a condition of the job to live in a service flat, he may decide to invest in a home for retirement. CGT relief can be claimed on a house bought for this reason as if it were the home of the owner.

Exemptions for business

Other reliefs help businesses and their owners avoid the tax traps. The most important for an ongoing business is a *rollover relief on replacement of business assets*. If a business sells one of its assets (for example, a retail shop), and replaces that asset by another similar asset (for example, another retail shop somewhere else), no CGT is imposed on the sale of the first asset. Instead, the gain is 'rolled over' on to the new asset. This is done, in effect, by calculating the gain arising on the sale of the first asset, and postponing the tax charge on that gain until the second asset is sold (or the third asset, if the second is also replaced, and so on). Effectively, the tax charge occurs when the business stops owning that kind of asset, or ceases altogether.

An important relief for business owners is the so-called *retirement relief*. This applies when someone aged over 65 (or who is leaving the business at a younger age for health reasons) sells or hands over a family business. If he or she has been involved in the business for ten or more years, there is exemption from CGT completely on the first £125,000 of the value at the time of the disposal, with only half the tax payable on the next £375,000. If the owner has been in the business one, but less than ten years, and is over 55 but under 65, partial relief is given. Use of this relief deserves sensible planning. If the owner dies still owning the business, there will be no CGT. On the other hand, there will be a charge to inheritance tax.

Another relief for business owners is a freedom from CGT on gifts of business assets. This applies when the owner of a business makes a gift of the business or part of it (but not merely one of the assets of the business such as a computer) to someone else. The idea is to allow a family business to be passed on without tax penalty, but there is no requirement in law that the business be passed within a family only to claim the relief. There are conditions to avoid tax savings for transfers which are not genuine gifts.

Other gifts also used to be free of CGT, but that relief was withdrawn some years ago. The relief from CGT on transfers on death was not withdrawn, and it remains in force. As a result, a gift of an asset not covered by the specific reliefs noted will be potentially liable to CGT if made during the lifetime of the donor, but not on his or her death. This is the reverse effect of the other relevant tax, inheritance tax, which we shall see charges tax on transfers made on death but only catches lifetime gifts made within a period before the death. For tax reasons, taking the two taxes together, the worst situation is to make a significant gift of assets not long before the death of the donor, because both taxes are then payable.

—— Estate and gifts taxation ——

The chief source of wealth (rather than saving) is property left by a person on death to another, usually within the same family. The property left when someone dies has, therefore, long been seen as an appropriate base for a tax, either on the estate of the deceased or on the gifts or bequests received by the beneficiaries.

Estate taxes, or death duties as they were traditionally called, have been charged in England for more than three hundred years, and, under the name of *inheritance tax* (IHT) is still with us. Gifts taxes, or taxes on the receipt of inheritances, are common in other western European countries, but these have not been used here in recent years. IHT is also two other kinds of tax: a tax on lifetime gifts made within a set period of the death of the donor, and a tax on trusts.

The IHT charge on death is a flat-rate charge of 40 per cent of the value of the estate of a person dying, with certain exceptions and subject to a zero-rate amount of the estate. Aside from the exceptions, and a limited number of reliefs, the tax is levied on all the property left by a person when he or she dies, whether or not there is a will and regardless of to whom the property is left. Every asset forming part of the estate of a deceased person has to be valued at the market value at the date of death, and it is on this value that the IHT is imposed.

IHT on smaller estates

IHT is not meant to be a tax on smaller estates, but only to catch the property of people who leave a certain amount of wealth when they die. For this person, the tax contains important exceptions. The first is that there is a zero-rate amount of total property values before the 40 per cent rate applies. This is adjusted annually, but currently is £160,000.

There are two other exemptions which between them stop many smaller estates being taxed. First, any property left on death to the person's wife or husband is not counted for tax purposes. Even a large estate given by a husband by will to his surviving wife attracts no tax until she dies. The other exception is pension entitlements of widows and dependants. Although these can be valuable, most pension schemes prevent the value of the pension forming part of the estate of the person dying, even though they only become payable because of the death.

Small gifts are ignored for IHT purposes. Any gift of less than £100 is ignored, together with gifts of more than that amount totalling £3,000 in any tax year. Gifts to charities and similar bodies are also ignored. The result is that an individual can give away several thousand pounds a year without any tax being paid. At the same time, no tax is paid by the recipients.

Taxing larger gifts

IHT imposes tax on large gifts used to sidestep the charge on death. It works by imposing a provisional tax on any larger gift, but removing the tax partly if the individual who made the gift lives for more than three years after the gift is made. No tax is due if the person dies more than seven years after the gift was made. If, by contrast, the person makes a gift (not to a charity or to the wife or husband) shortly before death, the gift is (subject to ignoring the first £3,000) treated as part of the estate on death. Consequently, in a larger estate, the total on which the 40 per cent tax is applied is the total of both the property left on death and the taxable amount of gifts made within the previous seven years.

Problems of taxing the wealthy

Other problems arise in levying IHT, even after excluding all smaller estates and gifts. This is because a tax applying at a rate of 40 per cent may force the sale of property for the tax to be paid. If the estate includes property which is part of the national heritage, the effect of the tax may be to threaten valuable national assets. For example, if the Duke of Nowhere dies, and his estate includes his magnificent stately mansion, Nowhere Palace, with its priceless collection of antique furniture and paintings, what happens? If the Duke's estate has to pay 40 per cent, the collection will have to be broken up, and much of it might disappear overseas.

A compromise has been reached to deal with this. Tax on items of the national heritage is postponed, provided it is kept in the family and certain other conditions are observed (the main one being in many cases that the public are admitted, on an agreed basis, to see the items – which is fine provided that someone tells the public that it is entitled to access!). If the property is left on death, or by gift, to other members of the family, there is no tax. If the property is sold, tax becomes payable.

A similar issue arises with the individual whose savings and wealth are tied into the family business. This may be worth a lot, but the individual may have invested in the business so heavily that there is little free cash. From an investment standpoint, this may be valuable to the country as well as the individual. What would happen if the individual died young and the family was forced to sell the business to pay 40 per cent tax? Perhaps employees lose their jobs, and less tax ends up being paid through losses of income tax and corporation tax? Again, the answer is a compromise. In this situation, the estate will pay a lower rate of tax on business assets (usually in effect about half the tax due on other assets). Related questions arise on agriculture, where again an individual may appear wealthy on paper but have little by way of cash savings.

An avoidable tax?

The collective effect of the reliefs and exemptions already mentioned, plus others, together with the use of trusts and other mechanisms to spread the legal ownership of wealth, makes the simple idea of an estate tax in practice a tax which is complicated to work and capricious. If someone dies one year after making a gift, it is taxed (even if the death was, say, by an accident). If the gift is ten years before the death, there is no tax.

Planning can help save or pay tax. For example, a life assurance policy will help pay any tax due on death. The IHT can be reduced if the property is given away steadily. Good planning means that having to pay too much IHT can be avoided. Failure to plan can mean a high tax bill for someone who forgot to make a will and did not plan in case of, say, a fatal traffic accident. This is one area where it pays to pay for good advice in getting a will written and advice against excessive IHT.

Trusts

Trusts are potentially a good way to avoid IHT. Once property is given to a trust, it no longer belongs legally to the person who gave the property to the trust (known as the *settlor*). However, the settlor can, in the legal document setting up the trust (known as the *trust instrument*), set out the way in which the income from the property should go, or who can use the property (those entitled to the benefits of the trust are known as *beneficiaries*). But beneficiaries do not own trust property, so there can be no IHT when they die. If the settlor lives for seven years after the gift has been made, there will be no IHT when he or she dies. The people in control of the trust (the *trustees*) are not individuals in law, so cannot die.

To stop trusts being used to avoid IHT totally, IHT law contains charges on the death of beneficiaries entitled to a full interest in a trust (called a *life interest*) and also on other occasions, with the aim of stopping excessive tax avoidance through this means. CGT rules also contain specific rules about trusts, as does the income tax legislation. Trusts are useful devices (put to considerable use in connection both with charities and with pension funds and unit trusts), but they can also be effective tax avoidance vehicles. When the tax is being avoided by a charity or a pension fund, it is encouraged. When trusts are used to protect family wealth from tax, Parliament has set controls in anti-avoidance legislation.

Trusts are a British invention. You do not find them in most European Community countries, nor in North America. Trusts are a convenient and flexible device, but they add complexity to the tax system because, it is perceived that, their results can be unfair. Is it right that we should try and ignore them for tax purposes? Or should we allow those who wish to put their property into a trust to reduce tax by that means?

In an attempt to provide some answers to these issues, the tax system contains an array of anti-avoidance devices which allow some kinds of trusts to work for some purposes, but prevents others working at all. It is beyond the scope of this work to explore this difficult terrain further. Neither individuals nor companies should venture into it without expert legal or accounting advice. Mistakes can prove expensive, and the biggest mistake may be to take no advice. To show why this complexity is felt to be necessary and how the problems of avoidance are tackled, we will examine in detail one example: a deed of convenant to a charity.

Deeds of covenant

You may be familiar with the deed of covenant that charities ask you to sign to help their funds. An example is set out below so that we may look at it in detail. This covenant complies with all the legal and tax rules applying to a deed of covenant by an individual. Separate rules apply to a deed of covenant made by a company, which may need to be in different wording.

The purpose of this deed is to allow an individual to pay sums of money to a charity in such a way that the sums can be deducted by the individual from her or his income for income tax purposes. It is not obvious from the wording that this is what is going on, but, like many legal documents, there is a reason for just about everything in the wording. Again, like most legal requirements, the reasons are not themselves immediately obvious even when looking at the tax laws themselves.

I COLIN OSWALD VENABLES of East Netherton Abbey, Netherton, Trentshire, TR1 0UT, hereby COVENANT with THE ABBEY MEADOWS TRUST of 16 Trent Gardens, Badgton, East Yorkshire, HA4 6EY that for a period of four years from the eighth day of December 199* or during my life (whichever shall be the shorter period) I will pay annually to The Abbey Meadows Trust out of my taxed income such sum as will after deduction of income tax at the basic rate for the time being amount to One Hundred Pounds (£100.00)

SIGNED SEALED AND DELIVERED by me this 3rd day of November 199*

                         [signature of C O Venables]   (LS)

in the presence of : ..... (witness signature) ....

                ..... (witness address) ....

This covenant creates a valid transfer of income from Mr Venables to the Abbey Fields Trust. Venables has decided that he wants them to receive £100. To meet this requirement, Venables must comply with a rule of income tax, that gifts do not count as income. If Venables gives the Trust £100, there are no income tax consequences – not being relevant either to his income tax, nor to any income tax charge on the Trust.

Venables must, therefore, turn his gift into a form of income relevant to income tax law. He does this by turning it into an 'annual payment' within the meaning of schedule D, case III. The law says that income tax is charged on *'any interest of money, whether yearly or otherwise, or any annuity or other annual payment . . . '* (Taxes Act 1988, section 18(3)). The Act does not define what an 'other annual payment' is, but judges have done so.

Decisions of the courts lay down that a payment to another is only within this wording if it is a largely binding commitment, a recurrent payment (one that lasts for more than one year), and pure income profit (it must be a payment for which there is no consideration or price given by the recipient of the payment). For a payment to be legally binding, general law requires that it be either a contract or a gift. Because the payment must not be made for a consideration or price, it cannot in English law be made by a contract, so the covenant must be in the form of a deed. If it is not a deed, there is no legal obligation. Venables must make sure that he receives nothing back from the Trust in exchange for his gift (apart from a thank you note). He must also make payments for at least two years.

In the deed, Venables has offered to make a gift not of £100 but of *such sum as after deduction of income tax at the basic rate for the time being amount to £100*. This wording is there to avoid another legal requirement. Under section 348 of the Taxes Act 1988, if Venables pays the £100 out of his taxed income (the covenant deliberately says he is doing that), he can deduct income tax at the basic rate from the payment and keep it, and the recipient is treated as receiving the sum actually paid as one from which income tax has been deducted.

Venables' £100 is therefore treated as a sum of money from which he has already deducted income tax. If the income tax basic rate was 25 per cent when he made the payment, then he is treated as having paid the Trust £133, from which £33 is deducted. The wording is such that if the income tax rate alters, Venables will still pay the Trust £100 in each of the four years. This is important to the Trust, because it will send Venables a piece of paper (technically a form known as Form R185) asking him to certify that he has deducted £33 tax in making his payment.

The Trust wants the R185 so that it can apply to the Inland Revenue to have the £33. This is because a charity is not liable to tax on receipts of other annual payments, so it can reclaim the tax deducted from payments made to it. In due course, the Inland Revenue will pay the sum over to the Trust, which will then have received £133 in total from Venables' gift. It is so that the Trust can get this rebate that the covenant is used.

Venables is notionally entitled to deduct and keep the £33. He is not entitled to make any further deduction against the total income in computing his liability to tax at the basic rate. However, if he is liable to tax at the higher rate, he can set the £133 against his total income and claim a deduction of the difference between the basic and higher rates. In this case, Venables can therefore claim a deduction against his income tax bill of a further £20.20 if he is liable to tax at the higher rate. If so, the gift of £133 to the Trust will in the end cost him only £80.

But why a *four* year covenant, if the law only requires two payments? This is because of further complications added by anti-avoidance provisions. The requirement is that there must be a minimum of four payments unless something such as the death of the donor interrupts the period. The four years can only be interrupted by *uncertain* events, such as Venables' death or, perhaps, as long as he lives in the United Kingdom or his present home, or remains unmarried.

Nor is this the only trap that the covenant must avoid. It must also comply with requirements under which any revocable covenants or covenants under which the donor retains some interest fail to work. Our example of a covenant avoids these traps because it is an absolute and unconditional transfer of money to the Trust. It has had to weave its way through all these points to have effect, but it will work!

Conclusion

The example of the deed of covenant shows the complexity that grows into a tax system because of competing pressures between the state and those that can best resist the incursions of the state upon their property. That complexity itself finds new friends (for example, charities like four year covenants because they commit people to regular giving) who resist change. What started for one reason ends serving some entirely different interest. We saw how CGT and estate duty started. What purpose do they now serve? They raise minimal revenues (in a national sense) and do it in an arbitrary way. Should we abolish them? Or should we replace them? If we did abolish them, should we seek to tax the rich on their wealth? If so, how? Would it matter if the result were that famous works of art were sold overseas, and major landholdings were split up?

9

__ COMPANY PROFITS __
TAXES

Most bigger businesses are run as companies, as are many smaller businesses. A company is a legal person that is separate from its owners. If, therefore, a company is running a business, it is the company which makes a profit or a loss, not the owners. Consequently, the tax authorities are concerned with companies as potential taxpayers. The idea of companies as taxpayers being separate from their owners is entirely consistent with the way that advisers such as accountants or lawyers approach the use of a company. It is, in the jargon of the trade, a *vehicle* for running the trade, investment or other activity. The company has a separate legal identity, so can enter its own contracts, make its own deals and, perhaps, become insolvent without affecting the legal position of its owners.

Although legally a company is separate from its shareholders, economic reality may be different. In the case of a small company, the company is often owned by one or two people. All profits of the company are therefore profits of the owners, who may work full time in the business and have their savings in it. If the company becomes insolvent, it may force its owners into bankruptcy. Is it sensible in this case to regard the company as separate from its owners for tax purposes?

At the other extreme is the multinational corporation which is trading and investing globally. It may have a budget significantly bigger than many states. This company will, on closer analysis, usually consist of an interwoven group of many companies, with crossed shareholdings. Some companies will be *subsidiaries* owned by other companies. These may be: *trading companies*, companies engaged actively in earning money through business activities, or *investment companies*, companies the functions of which are to hold investments and not engage directly in business. The subsidiary companies will be owned by *parent companies*, which will be *holding companies* – companies holding shares in other, subsidiary, companies. The combination is usually termed a *group* of companies. This group may include some *joint ventures* run by independent companies working together, possibly in partnership or as a *consortium*. Even so, the profits of the largest company will still be held eventually by individuals.

If we accept that companies are only vehicles, a principal approach to taxation might choose to ignore the vehicle and to look at only the persons deriving profits from the vehicle – that is, the shareholders who extract or could extract profits from the company. This could be done where profits are handed on by the company to its shareholders, but it is, in practical terms, administratively impossible for larger companies which retain all or some of their profits. For that reason alone, companies are treated as separate taxpayers by every advanced tax system. Besides, if companies are taxed the tax authorities get the tax quicker, and probably get more of it!

Corporate finance

A tax law dealing with companies has to take different forms of company into account if it is to provide a system which is efficient and yet fair. It has also to take account of the way that companies are financed. In essence, a company gets its working capital from three sources:

1 its own resources, such as retained profits;

2 borrowing usually through issuing loan stock (often referred to as corporate debt);

3 issuing shares in the company to shareholders (often referred to as equity).

At basis, a company belongs to its shareholders, and so do its profits. It pays profits out to a shareholder as a *dividend*, or, more generally as a *distribution*. Because a company belongs to its shareholders, they can decide to bring the company to an end, or wind it up. If they do, the assets of the company, including any undistributed profits, are shared out in a final distribution. In the final analysis, therefore, everything the company has ends up with the shareholders. Dividends are therefore not deductible as expenses made earnings profits – they *are* the profits.

If a company raises finance by a loan, the position is different. The lender may take payment for the use of its money in a form related to the profits of the business, but usually the lender will demand to be paid *interest* for its money. Interest is defined as payment for the use of money by reference to time. The lender is not involved in the profits of the business. Any interest received is treated, like any other interest, as taxable as under the rules of Schedule D relating to investment income (Case III if the loan is in the United Kingdom). Interest is an expense incurred in making profits.

Whatever the nature of a corporate business, profits earned by a company, after paying all expenses including interest, can either be retained by the company or paid out to shareholders. If shareholders receive profits, it is as dividends or distributions, which is income – on which, in principle, they can be taxed. If profits are retained by the company, they have not received that income. Can they still be taxed?

The vast range of forms of company, combined with the problem that some pay out their full profits and others do not, raises important questions of principle for the taxation of companies. Should companies be taxed on their profits, whether distributed or not, and how should they be taxed? If a company is taxed on distributed profits, should the shareholders be taxed on those distributions too? If they are, the profits are being subject to *economic double taxation* – they are being taxed twice, in the hands of different taxpayers.

A survey of the methods of taxing companies in developed states shows no single consistent set of answers to these questions. Most states of the European Community have come up with their own distinct answers. The United Kingdom has one answer, adopted in 1972. It had a different answer before that, and a different answer again before 1965. Critics of the current British system advocate that we adopt yet another answer – we are not alone in this uncertainty. A number of other major countries have changed their corporate tax systems in recent years, for example Australia. The biggest of them all, the USA, is currently giving serious consideration to changing its system.

The two chief problems noted above are:

1 whether to take account of the fact that a company may pay tax on profits which then get taxed again when handed out as a dividend to shareholders (economic double taxation), and

2 whether to take account of the fact that a company may choose to retain its profits rather than distribute them.

Choices of corporate tax system

There are several approaches to the problems outlined above, each of which is in use somewhere. The main alternatives are:

The classical system

In this system, used by the United States Federal corporate income tax, corporation and shareholder are treated as two entirely separate persons. The corporation is taxed on its profits, whether distributed or not. If profits are distributed, shareholders pay either personal income tax or corporate income tax on the dividends received. The advantage of this scheme is simplicity. The main disadvantage is that it subjects dividends to double taxation. If a corporation makes $100, which it distributes to a shareholder, the shareholder receives $66 after corporate income tax at 34 per cent. This is subject to personal income tax at, say, 28 per cent, leaving the individual with $48. This puts a tax penalty on corporations distributing their funds, encouraging them to hold the profits in reserves. This system is also used by the Netherlands.

Funding company finance

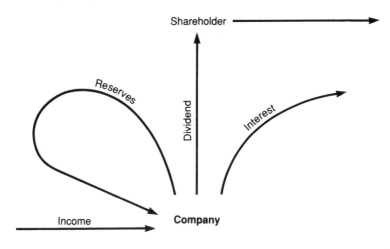

Funding company finance

The enterprise system

This is the opposite of a classical system, because it regards the company and shareholder as part of the same enterprise, with the aim of taxing the owner of the business – whether or not the company pays out the profits as dividends. For this system to work, the corporate profits have to be deemed to be paid out to the shareholders whether or not this actually happens. The idea is to put the corporate business on the same basis as the entrepreneur who conducts a business without using a corporate vehicle. This method has been used for anti-avoidance purposes on smaller companies, but it is not used generally as it is too difficult to administer on big companies. It has, however, the advantage that it entirely prevents double taxation of corporate profits, yet also prevents tax avoidance.

Dividend deduction systems

Another way of achieving an offset to double taxation is to allow the cost of dividends to be deducted in whole or in part against the company's profits, so reducing the taxable profits to reflect the amounts retained. This also deals with discrimination between interest (which is invariably deductible) and dividends, which are normally not allowed as deductions. Although this approach is adopted in Sweden, it is not widely used.

Imputation systems

These systems are compromises. The idea is to recognise that both company and shareholder are taxpayers, but that injustice or economic inefficiency (or both) result if this leads to double taxation of profits. To avoid this, tax paid by one of the two taxpayers is imputed to the other, so as to avoid excess tax. For example, if the company pays tax, it will be imputed to the shareholder who will not have to pay tax a second time.

Practical considerations make it likely that the company will be the first which can be asked to pay tax, so the imputation usually will be to the shareholder. This can be done by tax credits or reliefs. It can either be: a *full imputation system*, one where the full tax paid by the company is imputed to the shareholder; or a *partial imputation system*.

Imputation systems are increasingly popular as a way of dealing with the problem of double taxation. The United Kingdom has, since 1972, had a partial imputation system, as has Ireland. France has another variant of the partial imputation system. Australia and Italy both have imputation systems. (See the comparison on page 169 between this and the classical system.)

Split-rate systems

Another approach is to apply different rates of tax to corporate profits depending on whether they are distributed or not. If a higher rate is levied on undistributed profits, then the difference in the rates between that rate and the rate applied to distributed profits helps remove the discrimination that occurs under the classical system. Germany and Japan both have split-rate systems. For many years, the German rate on distributed profits was 20 per cent lower than that on undistributed profits. However, this system only achieves neutrality if the difference in the tax rates is the same as the individual tax rate. In practice, that is unlikely so the system only yields partial relief. It also tempts tax authorities to keep the rate of tax on undistributed dividends high.

Separate taxation of dividends

Another approach, used in Greece, is to provide tax relief by treating dividend income differently from other forms of income. In Greece, this is done by taxing distributed income at the corporate level to a zero rate of tax, while taxing the recipient. The alternative is the reverse – taxing the company and exempting the individual. For example, a system may require that the company, in paying a dividend, imposes a *final withholding tax*, that is, that the company deducts tax at a set rate on paying the dividends, but the taxpayer has to pay no further tax on that source of income. If the withholding tax rate is lower than the general rate of income tax, the net effect will again be to remove some of the double taxation. Turkey adopts this approach.

Withholding taxes

This last method noted uses, in modified form, a technique widely employed as an additional part of the tax collection procedure of many states: the withholding tax. The company paying the dividend is required, in many countries, to deduct tax at a set rate from the dividend before paying it to the shareholder. The shareholder receives the dividend net of tax, with a formal certificate or credit for the tax paid. Normally, the dividend plus tax will be regarded as part of the total income of the shareholder for income tax purposes, with a credit given for the amount of tax already collected by the deduction. As a result, the shareholder may owe more tax, or be able to claim a rebate of the tax deducted, depending on personal circumstances. A final withholding tax is one where these adjustments do not occur.

Withholding taxes are useful where dividends are payable to shareholders in another country. By imposing a withholding tax on the company paying the dividend, the country where the profits were earned can claim a share of the tax on the dividend, which would otherwise be collectable only by the country where the shareholder is based. Collection in this way is called *source country taxation* and is to be compared with taxation where the recipient is based, or resident, which is known as *residence country taxation*. International considerations are a strong influence in ensuring that much company taxation is collected by means of withholding taxes.

HOW CORPORATION AND WITHHOLDING TAX WORKS

Assume A Corpn. in State A pays a dividend to its shareholders, State A has a classical system of taxation, and its tax rate is 35 per cent on companies. It has a withholding tax on dividends of 30 per cent. B is a shareholder in A Corpn. B pays personal income tax at 40 per cent.

A has profits of 100. Company tax is 35 (35 per cent). Net profit is 65.

Net profit of 65 is paid to B. Withholding tax is 19.5 (30 per cent).

B receives 45.5 and a tax certificate for 19.5.

B's tax liability is 26 (40 per cent of 65) but B has a certificate for tax of 19.5, so only owes a further 6.5.

B keeps 39 (45.5 less 6.5). Total tax on profits is 61.

C & Co., a company in State C, pays a dividend to its shareholders. State C has a full imputation system of taxation, and its tax rate is 35 per cent on companies. B is a shareholder in A Corpn. B pays personal income tax at 40 per cent.

C has profits of 100. Company tax is 35 (35 per cent). Net profit is 65.

Net profit of 65 is paid to B.

B receives 65 and a tax certificate for 35.

B's liability is 40 (40 per cent of 100) but B has a certificate for tax of 35, so only owes a further 5.

B keeps 60 (65 less 5). Total tax on profits is 40.

_____ Corporation tax in the _____ United Kingdom

The taxation of companies in the United Kingdom has been a messy affair, the basis of which has changed several times, and none of the chosen methods have been regarded as outstandingly successful. We adopted a special tax called the corporation tax in 1965 at the behest of the new Labour government, who gave it its American-sounding name.

This may reflect the scope of the tax, which is wider than companies, because it covers 'companies' defined generally as: *any body corporate or unincorporated association but does not include a partnership, a local authority, or a local authority association.* But is corporation tax the right title, rather than company tax? The corporation tax covers bodies which are not corporations (such as local sports clubs), but does not cover bodies that used to be called corporations – local councils. Perhaps business enterprise tax might be as good a name. Whether or not its title is good, the corporation tax dovetails in neatly with the income tax. If a body is a 'company' as just defined, it is liable to pay corporation tax. If it is not, it is liable to pay income tax.

The present British system was adopted in 1972 (the law is consolidated into the Taxes Act 1988), and was called the *advance corporation tax*, or ACT for short. As part of the ACT system, a new schedule F was introduced into the income tax on individuals, operating together with the corporation tax rules. The rules apply to dividends and other distributions made by United Kingdom companies. Dividends received from foreign companies are covered by the ordinary income tax rules for foreign income. However, a company does not have to be a *British* company to be taxed under the ACT system. It is necessary only that it be resident in the United Kingdom. Any company set up under British company laws is automatically regarded as resident here. A business can trade in the United Kingdom by means of a company set up anywhere in the European Community, or in many other countries. A foreign company is a British resident if its central management and control is in this country. If its board of directors and its key management operate outside the United Kingdom, it is not within the scope of the ACT system.

ACT

The advance corporation tax works somewhat like a withholding tax, although it is *not* a withholding. A company paying a dividend must pay an advance on its corporation tax bill to the tax authorities at the same time as paying the dividend to its shareholders. The amount of the ACT payment is specifically tied by law to the level of the basic rate of income tax. When the income tax is 25 per cent, the rate of ACT is ⅓. For an example see the box. This ensures that the Inland Revenue receives, from the company, tax at the basic rate of income tax on an amount equal to the dividend plus the ACT.

ACT is paid by the company direct to the Inland Revenue, but the company also gives a certificate, called a *tax credit*, to the shareholder for the amount of the ACT. The company can set the ACT off against its own full corporation tax bill (known as the *mainstream corporation tax* bill) when this becomes due. At the same time, the shareholder can use the tax credit to set off the tax paid against her or his bill.

THE RATE OF ACT

The rate of ACT is tied to the rate of income tax. When the income tax rate is 25 per cent, the rate of ACT is 25/(100−25) or ⅓.

The ACT rate is designed so that it equals the income tax that would be deducted from a total payment consisting of both the dividend and the ACT.

If a company pays a dividend of 75, it must pay ACT of 25. The shareholder is regarded as receiving a total payment of 100, from which income tax of 25 (i.e. 25 per cent) is paid at source.

Schedule F

Individual taxpayers are liable to pay income tax under schedule F in respect of any dividend paid by a British company to them. The tax is due on the full dividend received, without any deductions. The same is true of any distribution of a compnay. 'Distribution' is defined widely and includes both capital payouts and payouts in stock or kind. It does not include the payout to shareholders when a company is liquidated.

The shareholder sets the tax credit off against the tax due on the dividend at the basic rate. This is why ACT is set at that rate. This means that the shareholder pays no further income tax at the basic rate. There will be more to pay only if the taxpayer is liable at the higher rate. Conversely the taxpayer can claim back the value of the tax credit if he or she is not liable to pay income tax.

Schedule F only applies to individuals or trusts, not companies. If a company receives a dividend from another company, it is not liable to pay income tax or corporation tax on it. However, the company can set off the value of the tax credit it receives with the dividend paid to it against any ACT it pays out, when paying dividends to its own shareholders. There are technical phrases used for these payments and receipts. The payment of a dividend by a company, together with the ACT paid in respect of it, is known as a *franked payment.* A dividend received by a shareholder, together with the tax credit received with it, is known as *franked investment income.* The law provides that a company receiving franked investment income only pays ACT on its dividends when its franked payments exceed its franked investment income.

A company that receives more dividends from other companies than it pays out will receive more franked investment income than it makes franked payments. It will therefore not be able to set off all its franked investment income against those franked payments, so it will end up with a *surplus of franked investment income.* If it does, then in most cases it cannot claim a repayment of the tax credit (unlike an individual). The system requires it to pay out the franked investment income before it can reclaim the value of the credit. The effect of this is to remove any tax charge on a company which distributes any investment income that it receives by way of dividends, but to tax it as if it were a basic rate income taxpayer for as long as it holds the investment income in the company.

The system therefore allows a dividend to pass from one company through others as many times as may be without any tax sticking to it. The tax only sticks if the companies decide not to pass the dividend on. Only when the dividend finally gets into the hands of an individual will the tax credit be usable against income tax. At the same time, the original company can use the ACT to set off against its own tax bill. How this works depends on the tax rates applying to the company.

Corporation tax rates

CORPORATION TAX RATES 1992–93

Main rate 33 per cent

Lower rate 25 per cent

Lower rate ceiling: £250,000

Main rate floor: £1,000,000

The main rate of corporation tax is shown here. This applies to all companies other than those which can claim to pay at the lower rate, or which get caught with profits above the lower-rate ceiling but below the main-rate floor. In practice, two-thirds of all companies pay at the lower rate, and only the biggest companies pay at the main rate on all their profits.

To say the lower rate applies to 'small' companies is a little misleading. It is based on the total taxable profits for a year. If profits are below the lower-rate ceiling in total, then a company pays at the lower rate. If its profits total more than the main-rate floor, it pays the main rate on all its profits. If, like many companies, its total profits are between the ceiling and the floor, it pays the lower rate on its profits up to the lower-rate ceiling and at the transitional rate on its profits above that ceiling.

Using the rates in the box, we can see how ACT, or our partial imputation system, works on both large and small companies. See below.

The result is not immediately obvious in looking at the structures of the tax, and it also depends on how we define what we see. The key question is whether ACT is regarded as company tax or individual tax. In most tables, ACT is treated as an advance payment of **income tax**, not corporation tax. If so, the corporation tax collected does not include the ACT, which instead gets added to the total of income tax paid. If we adopt that approach (which is consistent with our aim of not taxing the company if the individual also gets taxed), the examples of U plc and K Ltd reveal an interesting position. U plc pays corporation tax at 11 per cent only whereas K Ltd pays nothing. In other words, low-profit companies do not pay corporation tax. We have an enterprise system of tax!

This assumption is correct if we are able to assume, as we have so far, that companies and individuals pay tax on the **same** profits, in other words, that companies and individuals work out their taxable profits in

HOW ADVANCED CORPORATION TAX WORKS

U plc is a major British company, with shareholders B (who pays income tax at the basic rate of 25 per cent) and H (who pays at the higher rate of 40 per cent). U pays corporation tax at 33 per cent:

U earns profits of 100. Mainstream tax due 33.
U pays 67 (100 less 33) out as dividends. When it pays the dividend it pays ACT of 22 ($\frac{1}{3}$ of 67) to the Inland Revenue.

B [H] receives dividend of 67 plus tax credit of 22.
B is liable to pay tax of 22 at 25 per cent on 89 (67 plus 22).
B surrenders the tax credit and has no tax to pay.

U later has to pay 33 on its profits. It has paid 22 in ACT, so has net taxes to pay of 11 (33 less 22).

Total tax payable by U and B is 33.

H is liable to pay tax of 35 at 40 per cent on 89 (67 plus 22).
H surrenders the tax credit and has 13 to pay, so keeps 54 (67 less 13) of the dividend.

U later has to pay 33 on its profit as above, i.e. ACT plus paying 11.

Total tax payable by U and H is 46.

K Ltd is a small company paying corporation tax at 25 per cent:

K earns profits of 100. Mainstream tax due 25.
K pays 75 (100 less 25) out as dividends. When it pays the dividend it pays ACT of 25 ($\frac{1}{3}$ of 75) to the Inland Revenue.

B [H] receives dividend of 75 plus tax credit of 25.
B is liable to pay tax of 25 at 25 per cent on 100 (75 plus 25).
B surrenders the tax credit and has no tax to pay.

K later has to pay 25 on its profits. It has paid 25 in ACT, so has no net taxes to pay.

Total tax payable by K and B is 25.

H is liable to pay tax of 40 at 40 per cent on 100 (75 plus 25).
H surrenders the tax credit and has 15 to pay, so keeps 60 (75 less 15) of the dividend.

Total tax payable by K and H is 40.

the same way, and have the same tax allowances. This we must now investigate.

—— Taxable profits of companies ——

For corporation tax purposes, the profit of a company consists of its income and its gains. Section 9 of the Taxes Act 1988 lays down the fundamental rules for calculating the income: *Except as otherwise provided by the Tax Acts, the amount of any income shall for purposes of corporation tax be computed in accordance with income tax principles* . . . In other words, apart from special rules, the same rules apply to companies as to individuals.

Leaving aside rates of tax, dates of payment and the ACT system, there are only limited special rules applying to smaller companies. Most special rules deal with special kinds of companies (such as insurance companies), with groups of companies, and with changes in company structure such as mergers. The main rules, such as section 74, on what is deductible expenditure, the distinction between capital and income, the rules on capital allowances and on stock or inventory, and the rules about using accounts based on these tax principles rather than the company's audited accounts are the same for a large company as for an individual.

The rule about company accounts is important. All companies are required by the Companies Acts to produce annual accounts in standard forms and with details of the company's activities for a year, and a balance sheet. Further, all companies are required to have those accounts audited by an independent auditor. The accounts are only valid if signed by the directors, and certified by the auditors to be in accordance with legal requirements and 'a true and fair view' of the company's finances. Notwithstanding these legal safeguards and standards, company accounts usually require significant adjustment before being ready for submission to the Inland Revenue.

Among the main changes needed to change commercial accounts into tax accounts are:

• the removal of reserves except for bad debts;

- the removal of depreciation to be replaced by capital allowances;
- the removal of capital items from both income and expenses, with separate capital gains calculations;
- the removal of inter-company dividends;
- the separation of accounts for trading and non-trading income;
- the separation of accounts for subsidiaries grouped in consolidated accounts;
- special treatment of any losses.

The cumulative effect of these rules is that the company can show different levels of profit for commercial purposes and for tax purposes. It can go to its shareholders and the market with a 'healthy' profit in the same year as it persuades the Inland Revenue that it has a large loss! This should be contrasted with the position in other European countries such as Germany, where the profits declared to shareholders and the profits declared to the tax authorities are much the same. Would our tax system be better if our companies paid tax on the profits they declared to their shareholders? Would companies be as keen to declare profits? If not, what would be the effect on the companies, and on their share prices?

Two rules do allow companies generally more deductions than individuals.

(a) An investment company (holding investments, but not trading) is allowed to deduct its management expenses against its investment income. Individuals may never do this.

(b) All interest payments made by companies are deductible.

Under the general rules, only those interest payments which are genuine revenue expenditure of the business can be deducted. Individuals can claim mortgage interest relief and special reliefs which do not apply to companies. Instead, companies can claim relief for any interest as a *charge on income*, that is, they can deduct it as a charge against profits even if they cannot deduct it in calculating the profits. Technically the way this is done is different, but the result is the same.

Chargeable gains of companies

Companies (in the wide sense defined above) do not pay capital gains tax, which applies only to individuals and trusts. Instead, companies are charged corporation tax on their chargeable gains. The rules are, as with income, based on the rules of the capital gains tax subject only to necessary changes. There are special rules for groups of companies, for the rearrangement of company share structures, and for special kinds of companies, but the main rules on the calculation of gains, allowable expenses, indexation allowances and cumulation of gains and losses are the same.

Interest or dividend?

The rule allowing all interest to be deductible has an important effect on the way companies raise money for themselves. Compare a company raising capital by a loan with a company raising capital by increasing its equity, or share base. If it issues more shares, it will be expected to produce more profits, so it can pay dividends on those shares. If it borrows the money, it will be expected to pay the interest. Because interest is deductible in full, either in calculating the profits or against the profits while a dividend is not deductible at all, it is normally cheaper for a company to borrow than to issue new shares. 'Cheaper' here means that less tax is paid. This applies even though the interest payments are influenced by the level of profits being made, so that the lender is in reality taking some of the profit share. This is true, for example, where the lender is a company associated with the borrower. To stop excessive tax avoidance in this area, the Inland Revenue has general powers to treat loans of some kinds, such as these, as if they were new share capital, and therefore to apply the ACT system to any interest payments on those loans.

Dividend or capital gain?

The other choice for financing a company is to retain profits in the company for financing future capital requirements. If this is done, there is no interest or dividend to pay. Instead, shareholders receive value indirectly because the value of their shares in the company increase to reflect the increased company reserves. This also has a tax effect. A shareholder wishing to realise an investment, or to obtain income from its will, need to sell some shares. Doing so will trigger a CGT charge on the gain in the shares. However, the marginal tax rate of CGT is now the same as the marginal tax rate on income. This suggests that, aside from the dealing costs in selling the shares, it does not matter whether the income is received subject to tax under schedule F or CGT. This is oversimplified. Every individual is allowed a tax-free amount of gains each year before paying tax, and smaller sales may therefore still be subject to no CGT. In addition, the income is taxed in full, while the gain is calculated after taking account of inflation. It is the real gain, not the whole gain, that is taxed. For these and other reasons, CGT is often effectively a lighter tax than income tax.

That is not the whole answer. If a company pays out its profits as dividends, it pays over ACT which the shareholder uses to meet the tax bill on the dividend. If the company keeps the profits, it still pays the same amount of corporation tax as mainstream tax, so the accumulated profits remain taxed. When the shareholder sells the shares, no relief is available because the added value in the shares has already been taxed. Consequently, gains on sales of shares are subject to economic double taxation, although dividends largely avoid this. It is normal therefore to avoid CGT (or the corporation tax charge on chargeable gains) as far as possible, and pay tax on income instead. For example, if the owner of a small company is about to sell the company's assets, it may be better to 'strip out' all the cash from the company by a large dividend before sale, rather than hold the cash in the company and demand a higher price.

——— Other business taxes ———

Although companies are liable to pay the corporation tax on all their income and gains, this is by no means the only tax that they pay. Nor is it even the only tax on business profits. Many countries impose other direct taxes on companies, or on special kinds of companies. The United Kingdom does so, because of its oil reserves. Since the exploitation of Britain's oil and gas wealth in the North Sea, the government has sought to tax this wealth by imposing specific taxes on the oil and gas extractive industries. The United Kingdom has also in the past imposed special taxes on other groups of companies (such as a special levy on the profits of banks, and special taxes aimed at property developers) but does not currently charge such taxes.

Another form of direct taxation of companies imposed in a number of countries is a corporate wealth tax (effectively the equivalent of individual wealth or inheritance taxes). The United Kingdom has no such tax, although Germany, Luxembourg, Switzerland and Canada are among the countries which do.

Turning to indirect taxes, companies are liable to pay collected value added tax if their turnovers exceed the minimum level laid down. In practice, this means virtually every company is registered for VAT unless it is engaged, almost exclusively, in exempt supplies (see the chapter on taxing the shopping basket). Two other taxes, both major revenue earners, are paid by British companies. All companies pay the national business rate on commercial premises that they occupy. In addition, companies, as employers, pay the secondary class 1 national insurance contribution on the earnings of all employees and directors. As a company must have directors, even if it manages to get by with no employees, in practice this tax is almost unavoidable.

The final form of tax is sometimes regarded as direct, and sometimes as indirect – transaction taxes imposed on creation and transfers of company shares and other securities. Usually known in Britain as a stamp duty, this is a declining form of taxation.

Oil taxation

First imposed by the Oil Taxation Act 1975 (now a 1983 Act), the oil tax is known as *petroleum revenue tax* (PRT). It applies only to revenues derived from the British oil fields (until very recently, almost entirely from the North Sea), and is based on revenues earned by reference to the amount of oil won from the fields. However, the oil companies can set off against this their very considerable capital expenditure in exploring for and exploiting the oil, together with costs of clearing up afterwards. These capital costs are truly enormous and they meant that in 1991–92, for example, although considerable amounts of oil were brought ashore from the North Sea, no PRT was payable. This was because of the huge capital investment required in that year to maintain the integrity of the oil-winning facilities and also (in the light of Piper Alpha and other problems) further to increase safety and anti-pollution standards. In past years, governments expecting more from the North Sea than this tax produced, topped it up by an additional levy known as the supplementary oil duty. During the mid 1980s these taxes generated billions of pounds for the government. The tax revenue has never been earmarked, and it went towards producing the budget surpluses that started appearing in that period.

Alongside these taxes is one of Britain's most curious taxes, the *gas levy*. It is curious because, for most of its life (it dates back to 1981), it has had only one taxpayer, British Gas. Indirectly, most of the country has paid this tax without realising it. The gas levy is a tax (producing currently about £450 million a year) on gas brought out of the North Sea. Leaving the details aside, the aim is to impose a 'fair' level of taxation on gas so that it does not look too cheap alongside coal and other fuels. This tax is, therefore, an example of a specific tax aimed at price-rigging. It is also, as a tax, extremely efficient, partly because hardly anyone knows that they are paying it!

National business rates

Smaller non-profit-making companies frequently find that their biggest tax burden is the tax that they are required to pay to local councils in respect of all business premises which they occupy. Business taxes on land or immoveable property are common, and most European countries have them, although the burden of taxes is often noticeably lower than that on British business.

In Britain, the person occupying business premises must pay a levy each year to the local district council in whose area the premises are located. The levy is based on the *ratable value* of the premises. The ratable value, which has to be determined separately for every separate landholding or building, is a measure of the value of the land in relation to what a tenant would pay to rent the building long term. Because tenants would obviously pay considerably more for ground floor shop premises in the centre of town than they would for a small building at the back of an industrial estate several miles out, ratable values vary considerably from one property to another, and from one part of the country to another.

The levy of tax is imposed on the ratable value at a rate determined nationally each year, known as the *national rate*. This is the same throughout England (and, separately, Scotland and Wales). The levy is at a national rate because the tax is shared nationally. Although it is collected by the local council, that may be required to pass significant amounts of the tax on to other councils via central government, so that businesses in some areas subsidise activities in other areas. The business rates look like a local tax to pay for local services supplied by the councils to businesses (such as policing and refuse collection), and yet the local collection is something of a front to what is, in reality, a national tax.

Employers' national insurance contributions

It is common practice to impose a payroll tax on employers: that is, a tax paid by an employer based on the amount of the employer's payroll, or the total cost of earnings paid by that employer. In most cases the payroll tax is levied as an earmarked tax, the proceeds of which are paid over to fund social security benefits for employees. In some cases the tax is collected for general government purposes. There is now no general payroll tax in the United Kingdom (although for many years we did have such a tax), although there is an important social security payroll tax.

Employers are liable to pay both secondary class 1 national insurance contributions, and also, since 1992–93, the class 1A contribution on company cars supplied to employees. The precise amount of class 1 contribution depends on whether the employee is getting a company pension or only the state pension, but either way this contribution (which is levied at 10.4 per cent top rate), and the class 1A charge, raise significant sums.

Stamp duties

Traditionally, share transfers require a formal transfer document and the Stamp Acts require that, for the transfer to be valid, it had to be stamped with a tax based on the value of the shares transferred. One half per cent is the rate applicable in recent years in the United Kingdom.

Two problems have arisen with this tax. The first is that transfer documents are rapidly becoming out of date, as transfers 'dematerialise': that is, are conducted only by electronic means without any actual piece of paper. There is therefore nothing to stamp! The other is international competition. As it is as easy to buy shares in a major company in, say, Frankfurt as in London, competition is strong. When the Germans announced that they are abolishing this duty, Britain may be expected to follow, as it is. The United Kingdom stamp duty on share transfers is being abolished when the transfers themselves are dematerialised.

—— **Tax and the family business** ——

The owner or owners of a small business have a choice of the business vehicle they should use for the business. Should the business be put into a company, or should it be left unincorporated? In an ideal system, it can be argued that, tax should be neutral to this decision, which should be taken on broader issues such as the desirability or otherwise of incorporation, the cost of maintaining a company, the identity of the business owners and so on. On the other hand, it can also be argued that the advantage of being able to operate in corporate form should itself justify extra tax on a business, suggesting that corporate form is better but more tax expensive.

As the United Kingdom has separate forms of tax operating on companies as opposed to unincorporated businesses, and also on the self-employed, not employees, tax does have an influence on how a business should be structured, although not a straightforward one. The position is, nevertheless, much simpler than it was some years ago when companies could be used for tax avoidance, but if wrongly used could result in much higher taxes. The box below sets out the main tax factors now relevant to the decision whether or not to incorporate.

A COMPANY: YES OR NO?

● *Income tax rates*: companies pay tax at 25 per cent on profits of up to £250,000. Individuals pay 40 per cent on profits of more than about £30,000. There is little difference in the calculation of profits. The imputation system means that smaller companies, in effect, do not pay tax on smaller profits. This, therefore, makes little difference if the company pays out on its profits, rather than retains them.

- *Capital gains tax rates*: the rates are the same as for income, but there is double taxation on gains made by companies reflected in gains made by the shareholders on sales of shares. This is a tax penalty of incorporation.

- *Earnings of owners*: the self-employed pay tax direct on full profits under schedule D, plus class 2 and class 4 NI contributions. Owners of companies who also work in them pay tax (and NI contributions) as employees, or as recipients of dividends. Tax on employees (and directors) is more expensive than tax on the self-employed. But there is no NI liability on dividends.

- *Pensions and benefits*: employers can make provision for pensions for employees in a tax efficient way, while the self-employed can contribute to a personal pension. Employees are, on the other hand, entitled to the contributory benefits on an earnings-related basis, while the self-employed receive fewer state benefits, and only at a flat rate. Because setting up a company turns the self-employed into employees, account should be taken of the pension and benefit position. The self-employed are often under-provided for.

- *Timing of tax bills*: companies pay tax as ACT on dividends and then as mainstream tax nine months after the end of the year. Employees pay when they are paid. The self-employed can pay tax significantly later than that, and they gain cash-flow advantages.

- *Transferring the business*: much the same reliefs apply on transferring a business, either unincorporated or in the form of shares in the family company, for capital gains tax purposes. It is easier for inheritance tax purposes to transfer the business by shares because of the ease of planning opportunities, but currently share transfers are liable to stamp duty (minimal if the transfer is a gift). At least, once stamp duty has gone, this will argue towards incorporation.

- *Changing the business form*: this is itself a tax problem. It is relatively easy to transfer an unincorporated business into a company while avoiding a serious tax charge, but disincorporating can cause significant tax bills, so care should be taken not to take decisions to change business form lightly. Professional advice is always wise.

Taking profits from family companies

The box above shows that a major factor in choosing between companies and unincorporated businesses is the way in which the owners receive their profits. As self-employed individuals, they pay schedule D tax. This is normally advantageous, for example because of the lateness with which the tax can be paid; but employees go gain because of pension contributions made by employers being fully deductible, and also because of the perks rules, such as company cars, saving tax and cost overall where the company buys.

The other issue is whether, if there is a company, the owners should receive money as employees or as shareholders. This is not straightforward (as it was for many years – dividends as investment income were subject to a higher tax rate). If the payment is in the form of dividends, ACT must be paid. If it is in the form of salary or bonus, then income tax must be paid under the PAYE scheme. So also must NI contributions. If the employer is a high earner, he or she will pay no contributions, but the employer will, at 10.4 per cent (but deductible against corporation tax). On the first £20,000 of earnings, the employee will also have to pay a contribution, although the employer's contribution will be lower. However, the employee can set off against those earnings various deductions such as personal pension contributions which are not available against the tax on dividends.

In many cases, there is a good case for ensuring that part of the payment to the owner is by means of dividend, and not all of it is in salary form.

However, benefits in kind are tax efficient. It will often pay to calculate (or ask the company accountant to calculate) the alternatives to reach the best answer for a particular business and its owners.

10

TAXING THE SHOPPING BASKET

One of the simplest ways of imposing a tax is to levy it on expenditure, that is, to impose it on things people buy. This form of tax is usually called indirect tax. Historically these taxes have always been important, and they remain so today. We now examine the kinds of taxes on spending currently levied in Britain, concentrating on the most important: value added tax.

Taxes on spending

Expenditure, whether from an individual or a multinational company, can be tackled in a number of ways by spending taxes. The most successful way of dealing with expenditure across the board is a general *turnover tax* on total sales, or turnover, of all kinds. The turnover tax now used in the UK, and most other European countries, is VAT. Although the UK only adopted it in 1973, it has, from the point of view of the Treasury, been an enormous success and it is now our second or third most important tax (the precise position varies from year to year). Its success lies in the fact that it imposes tax, usually at the rate of 17.5 per cent, on most kinds of goods and services (including, although we do not discuss them, imports), at every stage of creation and production.

Before VAT was invented (in the 1950s), two kinds of tax on spending were widely used. First were general taxes on retail sales, wholesale sales or manufacturers' sales. These *sales taxes* are levied across the board at a level of production. One, common in North America, is a sales tax added to all local sales of goods. In Britain, there used to be one, but the sales tax was called a 'purchase tax'. And the other kind of taxes are usually called *excise duties*. These are ancient taxes, long imposed in this country and many others, on specific items.

Besides these two forms of tax, there are others which some people call taxes. Licence fees are one group: for example, the fees for licensing televisions, guns, gaming machines or anything else where the licence fee exceeds the cost of administering the licence scheme. This is also true of registration fees, and fees for issuing or dealing with any formality required by law – for example, passports. These are rarely regarded as taxes in Britain, and yet the UK government returns them as taxes to the OECD for statistical purposes because they are within the wide definition of a tax for those purposes and are often called taxes by our European neighbours.

The taxes requiring consideration in the UK are:

- value added tax,
- excise duties, especially on tobacco, petrol and alcoholic drinks,
- car taxes,
- betting taxes.

Value added tax

VAT was introduced into the UK in 1973 when we joined the European Community. We would probably have introduced it by now even if we had not joined the EC. This is because, with the exception of the USA and Switzerland (both at federal level), all the Western states of the northern hemisphere have adopted or are adopting some form of VAT or goods and services tax (as it is called in Canada, GST). The tax, in one form or another, is now found in every other part of the world. Yet, as a form of taxation in national use, it is less than 40 years old. The adoption of a VAT or GST has been the most important change in taxation this century. Why?

The secret is that VAT solves a number of tricky administrative and policy problems that bedevilled sales taxes and excises for many years. VAT does this because it allows a state to replace a whole raft of different taxes on products with one tax. Poland, for example, replaced more than 2,000 different sales taxes with one tax when, after the fall of the communist government, it adopted a Western-style VAT. The way the tax works allows all kinds of products – goods, services, land – to be taxed at every level of creation and production, but it allows this to happen in a way that does not cause distortion. By contrast, the sales taxes imposed on manufacturers, wholesalers and retailers frequently cause distortion, partly because these taxes *cascade*, that is, there is tax on tax.

CASCADING TAXES

A tax is imposed at 10 per cent on manufacturers, wholesalers and retailers of floggles. **A** manufactures floggles, and sells all floggles made to **B**. **B** wholesales them to smaller regional wholesalers, of whom **C** is one. **C** wholesales floggles to **D** who sells them to the public. **A**, **B**, **C** and **D** each make a profit of 100 on the sale.

How much tax is paid by a customer, E?

A sells to **B** at 100, plus tax at 10 per cent, charging 110.

B sells to **C** at 210 (110 plus profit) plus tax at 10 per cent, charging 231.

C sells to **D** at 331 (231 plus profit) plus tax at 10 per cent, charging 364.

D sells to **E** at 464 (364 plus profit) plus tax at 10 per cent, charging 510.

E *therefore pays 510, of which 110 is tax, an effective tax rate of 27.5 per cent.*

Cascade taxes were the usual way of taxing in Europe before the introduction of VAT. Similarly, when Canada introduced its goods and services tax (a tax basically the same as the European VAT) in 1991, it replaced three levels of tax: manufacturers', wholesalers' and retailers'. VAT avoids these cascades, and therefore avoids the distortions and the overtaxation. It does so because it taxes only what its name suggests that it taxes, the value added by the person being taxed. Unlike the sales taxes, the payer of the value added tax can set off against the tax he or she has to pay the tax that has already been paid by him or her. The next example shows how this happens. If you compare the two examples, the secret of VAT becomes apparent.

First, it is transparent: you can see what tax is being applied. The rate in the box below is 25 per cent, yet it collects less tax than the 10 per cent rate in the previous example. Why? Because the tax does not cascade.

Second, VAT is neutral to the methods of production and distribution. To test this, re-work the two examples on the assumption that **B** decides to sell direct to **D**, cutting **C** out of the supply chain, but that **B** sells the goods to **D** at the same price at which **C** would have sold them. This makes no change to the tax position in the second example, but with cascade taxes, it cuts out one layer of taxation, and therefore cuts the overall tax. This is because **B** will sell direct to **D** at 310 (110 plus profit of 200) plus 10 per cent tax, a total of 341, not the 364 that **C** charges. On that basis, **D** will buy direct from **B**, because he or she will be able to charge **E** less, and so be more competitive. In short, cascade taxes distort the market, but VAT does not, if applied evenly. Cascade taxes force vertical integration within an economy. Further, as Canada discovered the hard way, a state with cascading taxes cannot compete on even ground with a country operating a VAT. It was a main reason for Canada abandoning its old ways.

VALUE ADDED TAXATION

A value added tax is imposed at 25 per cent on all levels of production and distribution of goods and services, including floggles. As in the previous example, **A** is the manufacturer of floggles, **B** and **C** are wholesalers, and **D** is a retailer who sells to **E**. **A**, **B**, **C** and **D** each makes a profit of 100 on the sale.

How much tax is paid by the customer E?

A sells to **B** at 100, plus tax of 25 per cent, charging 125.

B sells to **C** at 200, charging tax on the value added at this stage. This is done by imposing tax on the sale to **C** at 25 per cent, producing tax of 50, but allowing **B** to deduct from that 50 the tax paid by **B** to **A**, which was 25. So **C** pays **B** 250, and **B** has collected tax of 50 of which 25 refunds the tax paid by **B** to **A**.

C then sells to **D** at 300, plus tax at 25 per cent, a total of 375. **C** uses 50 of that 75 tax to recover the 50 paid to **B**, holding only the additional 25 as tax owed to the state. This is 25 per cent of the 100 value added by **C**.

D likewise sells on to **E** at 400 plus tax at 25 per cent, a total of 500. Of the 100 tax **E** pays, again **D** keeps 75 to recover the tax paid to **C** with 25 going to the state.

E *therefore pays 500 of which 100 is tax, an effective rate, identical with the formal rate, of 25 per cent.*

This example can go one stage further. If cascade taxes were to force **C** out of the marketplace, the tax revenues would fall. What happens if **A**, in the best traditions of direct mail, sells direct to **E**? The state tax revenues start disappearing? It is a reason why direct mail sales, based in states with no sales tax, are so popular in the USA, which does not have VAT.

If the state imposed a VAT, the only difference on a direct sale to **E** by **A** would occur if **A** decided to sell the goods cheaper than through the chain of **B**, **C**, and **D**. Only if the value added were to drop would the tax drop. As the British and many other governments have discovered, VAT is a high yield tax which is hard to avoid. The United Kingdom is most unlikely to change from this form of tax, and rather more likely to increase its yield.

The British VAT

VAT law (or, rather, the UK version of the law) is now found in the Value Added Tax Act, 1983. This starts with a short, effective summary of the tax in sections 1 and 2.

Ignoring imports, VAT operates if:

- a TAXPAYER MAKES
- a TAXABLE SUPPLY of
- GOODS or SERVICES as part of
- a BUSINESS.

Business or private?

VAT is designated to catch all business transactions made by someone who is a *taxable person*, but not to catch private transactions. Most private transactions are left outside the tax because the person making them is not a taxable person (or VAT taxpayer). For example, if I sell my typewriter, and I am not a VAT taxpayer, I do not collect VAT and my buyer does not pay it. If I am a VAT taxpayer, it must be decided whether my typewriter is sold as part of my business. If it had been used as a business asset (and, probably, I claimed a VAT deduction on buying it) its sale is part of my business, but if I had used the typewriter only for private purposes, and its cost has not been part of my accounts, it would stay out of the business accounts.

> **VALUE ADDED TAX ACT 1983, SECTION 1:**
>
> A tax, to be known as value added tax, shall be charged in accordance with the provisions of this Act on the supply of goods and services in the United Kingdom (including anything treated as such a supply) and on the importation of goods into the United Kingdom.
>
> **Section 2(1):**
>
> Tax shall be charged on any supply of goods or services made in the United Kingdom where it is a taxable supply made by a taxable person in the course or furtherance of any business carried on by him.

Note that VAT applies to all business activities of a VAT taxpayer. For example, if I am registered for VAT as a writer, and I decide to make money by letting my seaside caravan, I must account for VAT on the rents received from that holiday letting as well as on my writing.

European VAT law defines 'business' very widely. It is *any economic activity whatever the purpose or results of that activity* save for the work that an employee does for her or his employer. In other words, whether it is regular or occasional and whether or not it is intended to make a profit, and whether or not it does make a profit, if it is a business-type activity rather than a hobby undertaken purely for the fun of it, then it is potentially liable for VAT.

VAT taxpayers

Two groups of persons (individuals, companies, public bodies) are included in the scope of VAT as taxpayers: those who are compelled to be taxpayers, and those who opt to be taxpayers voluntarily. In the United Kingdom, a person who is a taxpayer for VAT, or who ought to be, is known as a *registered person*. This is because he, she or it is required to register with the VAT Office if liable to be a taxpayer. To make sure the tax works efficiently, the law also provides that someone who ought to register, but who does not do so, for any reason, is treated as if he were a registered person, while also additionally liable for penalties for not registering.

REGISTERING FOR VAT

You must register for VAT if:

- your total turnover for the 12 months ending at the end of last month exceeded £36,600; or

- your expected turnover for the next 30 days is over £36,600.

A person is required to register, and apply VAT, if the total taxable transactions of that person exceed set levels of turnover. This means that if the person was registered, then all the supplies of goods and services of that person made as part of a business are added up and, if they exceed the limit, the person must register. Note that this limit is a total of turnover **not** profit. A shopkeeper may have to register for VAT even if he or she is not making a profit. Someone buying a registered business, to keep it going, will also have to register.

In addition to those required to register, a person carrying out a business with a level of turnover below the limit, or who is about to start a business, can apply to register on a voluntary basis. This may be of advantage for someone to conceal that the turnover is below the VAT level, or in order to enable the taxpayer to reclaim VAT paid out as part of the business expenses. A person who has been required to register, but whose turnover drops more than £1,000 below the compulsory level, or who registered voluntarily, can apply to be removed from the register.

While a person is registered, or is obliged to be registered but who has not done so, every supply of goods or services that the person makes which is taxable is subject to VAT. If the person does not collect VAT by adding it to the bill, VAT is deemed to be part of the price collected.

—————— Goods and services ——————

The VAT world is simple. It consists entirely of two kinds of things: goods and services. Anything which is not goods is services. The sale of equipment counts as a supply of goods, while equipment leasing is a supply of services – the use of the equipment. Land counts as goods, but a lease of land is a supply of services. However, the difference between 'goods' and 'services' is not usually important. What is important is whether the goods or services are the subject of a *taxable supply* by the registered person (or taxpayer).

Taxable supplies

There is a supply of goods whenever there is a transfer of the right to dispose of tangible property, or property treated as being tangible property. For VAT purposes, a supply of services only counts if it is a supply made *for consideration*; that is, it is made in exchange for a directly related payment in cash or kind. Any transaction which is not a supply of goods, but which is done for consideration is a supply of services, and therefore potentially liable for VAT.

It is clear from these definitions that 'supply', 'goods' and 'services' are all words given the widest of meanings, subject only to the point that there is consideration for any supply that does not consist of goods. The effect is to provide a wide tax base for the tax, with little scope for taxpayers to say that something is not caught by the tax. Just about everything is, unless it is beyond the scope of the tax, or is covered by one of the small number of exceptions provided by specific regulation to the general rule.

Supplies are beyond the scope of the tax in three broad categories of case:

1 the supply is made by someone who is not a registered person;

2 the supply is not of goods and not made for consideration;

3 the supply is not made during the course of a business.

A private sale, even if of a large item such as a house, is not within the scope of VAT even if the seller is a registered person. An example of a supply of services not made for consideration might be, for example, advice given by a tax expert to a friend free of charge. Payment of a dividend on a share in a company is also not a supply for consideration. The supply of services by an employee to the employer is not included as a supply during the course of a business, although a gift made by the employer to the employee is made during the course of business (subject to a specific exception to VAT for small gifts).

The final part of the rule that we need to know is when a supply, in this wide sense, is a taxable supply. The law's answer to that is also simple: *a taxable supply is a supply of goods or services made in the UK other than an exempt supply.*

Exempt supplies

In the purest form of VAT, all forms of supply are taxable, so that VAT is payable on all supplies within the scope of the tax. However, issues both of practicality and fairness get in the way of perfection, and a list of exceptions will always be found. In the UK, those exceptions are known as exemptions. An exempt supply is one which, by reason of a specific rule of law, is exempted from VAT. This means that someone making an exempt supply is not allowed to charge VAT on it. It also means that where someone incurs VAT in making an exempt supply, that VAT cannot be claimed back. This means that someone purchasing an exempt supply of goods or services is, in reality, still paying some VAT.

There is a long list of exemptions from VAT in the UK VAT law, detailed in schedule 6 to the VAT Act 1983, the headings of which are set up on page 195. Exemptions add a considerable complication to the administration of VAT, and they give rise to arguments about whether or not a supply is subject to VAT. For this reason, the rules about what is, and what is not, exempt have to be drawn up with care. Even then, they have in practice to be supplemented by practical guides (of which a whole series is published) and, in addition, they cause a considerable number of appeals by taxpayers from decisions by VAT officials.

EXEMPTIONS
(Value Added Tax Act 1983 – Schedule 6)

Group 1   Land
Group 2   Insurance
Group 3   Postal services
Group 4   Betting gaming and lotteries
Group 5   Finance
Group 6   Education
Group 7   Health and welfare
Group 8   Burial and cremation
Group 9   Trade unions and professional bodies
Group 10   Sports competitions
Group 11   Works of art and heritage property
Group 12   Charity fund-raising events

Why are there these exemptions? There are two broad groups.

Social exemptions

The first is social or political. One exemption, for example, is health services, exempting any supply of services by a doctor or dentist, or other medical or paramedical staff. These are socially important supplies that cannot be made to benefit a business, only an individual. They may be supplied as part of a business, but they are not received that way.

Financial exemptions

The other broad grouping is financial, and similar, supplies: finance, insurance and betting. Group 5, the finance group of exemptions, is of considerable importance. It covers most forms of transaction involving money, loans and credit, stocks and shares, financial guarantees, cheques, bank and savings accounts, saving certificates and unit trusts. It covers supplies of these services both to individuals and to business. A reason for exempting financial supplies is the difficulty of working out what the consideration should be. Is value added by the bank equal to the whole value of the interest I pay, or just the profit it makes between what I pay it, and what it pays the person from whom it borrows the money that it then lends me?

Land

Separate from both of these groups is the question of exemption of land transactions. Sales of land should not be included in a VAT because there is no added value. If I sell you an area of unimproved land, it is much the same as it was before taxation began. It is part of the environment, and no value is added by me in selling it at a profit. Of course, if I build on it, or get planning permission to build on it, then I have added something. For this reason buildings should be taxable. In practice, taxing people's homes is as sensitive an issue for VAT as for any other tax, and it may not be acceptable politically.

In some countries, an easy course out of these problems is taken by imposing a stiff level of stamp duty, and forgetting the VAT. In Britain, we have not done this. Instead, we have arranged things so that the rules about VAT on land are a complicated and expensive mess, which, however, the politicians have kept off private housing. The detail of when VAT applies to other sales and lettings, and when it does not, is complex, involving a choice of landlords, in some cases, to be or not to be taxed. It is something on which expert advice is often needed, and beyond the scope of this outline.

————————— **The rates of VAT** —————————

There are two rates of VAT, at the present time, in the United Kingdom:

THE RATES OF VAT

Standard rate	Zero rate
17.5 per cent	0 per cent

The standard rate, at 17.5 per cent, sounds awkward. It means that if you buy something in a shop to which VAT is not added separately, then for every £10 spent, £1.49 is VAT. In other words, about 15 per cent of what you have to pay is VAT – not quite as bad as it sounds. But it sounds bad enough, if we remember that the first basic rate of VAT was 8 per cent, which was then raised to 15 per cent, and then raised again. It is possible that it will rise again, or even fall, but not by much. The British government agreed in 1992 with all its European Community neighbours that there would be similar rates of VAT in all the states of the EC, with a bottom rate of 15 per cent. The member states of the EC also agreed that there would be one lower rate of VAT, somewhere in the region between 4 per cent to 9 per cent. That we do not have; instead we have the *zero rate*.

The VAT zero rate

The zero rate is exactly what it says. If goods or services are zero-rated, then the seller must charge tax on them at zero per cent. Of course, as a matter of common sense, even the VAT authorities do not expect retailers to waste their time solemnly adding £0.00 to bills, so the fact that supplies are zero-rated is left off the customers' accounts. But it is important to the retailers, who will note the zero-rated sales carefully. The reason for this is that zero-rating amounts to a tax subsidy of the activity which is zero-rated. The supplier charges its customers no tax, but claims back the tax paid out in making the supply. Consequently, it is better for something to be zero-rated than exempt. Just how much better is shown below.

PASSING THE VAT BUCK

Three suppliers have all bought items costing £100 plus VAT at 17.5 per cent (a total of £117.50) and they sell them to customers for £200, including VAT. None of the customers are themselves registered for VAT, so cannot reclaim any tax paid out. How much profit do the sellers make?

Seller **A** sells his or her item subject to VAT at the full standard rate of 17.5 per cent. This means that **A** collects £200, which is treated as being £170.20 plus VAT of £29.80. But, because the sale is at the standard rate, **A** can set off the £17.50 VAT paid out on buying the item against the £29.80 VAT collected. **A**'s profit is therefore the profit, ignoring VAT, on the sale (170.20 − 100), a total of £70.20.

Seller **B** sells his or her item at the zero rate. This means **B** collects £200, which is treated as including no VAT.

But, because the sale is technically subject to tax, **B** can still claim back the £17.50 VAT paid out (by demanding the money back from the VAT Office). So, again, **B**'s profit ignores the VAT. This time, the profit is (200 − 100) £100.

Seller **C** sells the item as an exempt supply. This means that **C** cannot add any VAT to the selling price, so, like **B**, **C** is regarded as receiving all the £200, with no VAT included. However, unlike **B**, **C** cannot claim back the £17.50 VAT paid on buying the item, so the true cost of the purchase is the full £117.50. This means the profit made by **C** is (200 − 117.50) is £72.50.

B, therefore, makes a much higher profit than **A** or **C**. This should mean that **B** sells the goods or services that are zero-rated at a cheaper rate than **A** or **C** can. Is this what really happens?

In this example, the exempt supplier earns almost as much profit as the fully taxable supplier, but the zero-rated supplier does much better. The Treasury, of course, do best out of the fully taxed supply. But they do moderately well out of the exempt supply too. This is one of the hidden paradoxes of VAT. An exempt supply, which is often assumed to be free of tax, is still taxed in many cases. But a zero-rated supply, which is said to be a taxable supply, is not taxed at all!

Not surprisingly, there is a lot of pressure for supplies to be zero-rated. Below is a list of the current groups of zero-rated items:

ZERO-RATING
(Value Added Tax Act 1983 – Schedule 5)

Group 1   Food (excluding catering)
Group 2   Sewerage and water for non-industrial purposes
Group 3   Books, newspapers
Group 4   Talking books and radios for the blind
—
—
Group 7   Fuel and power for domestic and charity use
Group 8   Construction of dwellings and charity buildings
Group 8A   Alterations of listed buildings
Group 9   International services
Group 10   Transport
Group 11   Caravans and houseboats
Group 12   Gold supplied to central banks
Group 13   Bank notes
Group 14   Drugs and aids for the handicapped
Group 15   Imports and exports
Group 16   Supplies to and by charities
Group 17   Clothing and footwear for children and for protection.

The absence of groups 5 and 6 from the list is deliberate as they were removed some years ago. Nearly all the other groups have been cut down in scope in recent years, too. The exemption of food now covers only some kinds of food supplied cold. Catering supplies, and supplies of hot takeaway foods are subject to VAT, as are sales of chocolate and other 'luxuries'. Since VAT was introduced, it has been extended to many more kinds of supply.

——— **Paying VAT to the supplier** ———

In deciding how much VAT there is to pay, liability to pay VAT should be checked in the following order:

(a) is the supply within the scope of VAT?
(b) if it is, is it zero-rated?
(c) if it is not, is it exempt?
(d) if it is not, it must be liable to pay VAT at the standard rate at the time of supply.

Supplies are within the scope of VAT if they fit within the charge of the tax outlined in this chapter, and they are exempt, or zero-rated, only if covered in either Schedule 6 or Schedule 5 of the VAT Act, 1983. For the rest, these are supplies liable to some of the £30 plus billion VAT collected each year by the Treasury.

If a supply is subject to VAT at the standard rate, the tax must be collected at that rate on the supply. Sometimes the supplier will mark prices saying 'VAT excluded', or 'ex VAT'. In those cases, the supplier is entitled to add 17.5 per cent tax to the bill. In other cases, if VAT is not mentioned, the supplier is not entitled to add it later, unless this is the custom of the trade. For example, a hotel quotes its room rate at £60 per night, and does not mention VAT. If that is so, the hotel must not add VAT to the bill. If it does so and is a VAT taxpayer, then you can refuse to pay. If it is not a VAT taxpayer, it may be breaking the criminal law in adding the tax.

The reason why VAT cannot be added (unless the supplier tells the customer) is not a matter of VAT law, but of customer protection law. Under the trades description laws, suppliers must not mislead on the subject of price. Because VAT is always included in a price, whether the seller says so or not, by reason of the Value Added Tax Act 1983, section 10, the buyer is entitled to assume that the seller has included the VAT unless he says otherwise.

Tax invoices

If VAT is paid, the seller must give the buyer a special receipt, called a *tax invoice*. The receipt must show the details of the supplier, including the VAT number. In the case of supplies costing more than £100, more details must be shown including the amount of VAT and full details about the kind of supply made, and the person to whom the supply was made.

These tax invoices are vital to the customer if he or she wishes to reclaim the VAT on a purchase, because in most cases no reclaim will be allowed for the tax on the purchase unless the receipt can be produced. This allows the VAT office to cross-check that they have collected the VAT from the supplier.

Keeping VAT accounts

VAT has been described as a 'paper-pusher's paradise', as the rule on tax invoices illustrates. It is a tax which sounds simple to operate, but in practice it depends on detailed records of every transaction made by a business, both purchase and sale. It is obvious that the VAT Office will be concerned that all taxable sales are included in the records in some way, whether or not VAT is collected on them. Equally, unless the taxpayer has good records and keeps all invoices of tax paid out, the VAT office may not allow a deduction, so the taxpayer will pay too much VAT.

Taxpoints

When is the transaction treated as taking place for VAT purposes? The time when the tax is applied to the transaction is known, in jargon, as the *taxpoint*. The general rule is that a supply of goods takes place at the earliest of any of the following dates:

(a) when the goods are delivered or the services rendered,
(b) when the customer pays for the supply,
(c) when the tax invoice is issued.

VAT is thus imposed at the first formal stage of the transaction. In practice, this rule is overridden by a more practical one. The taxpoint is the date on the tax invoice, provided that the tax invoice is issued not more than 14 days after the delivery of goods or the rendering of services. In either case, the date of payment does not matter, unless it comes before any other stage. The consequence of this is that VAT can become due on a supply even though the customer has not paid.

All registered persons must make a tax return to the VAT Office on the set tax return form within 14 days after the end of a return period, setting out all supplies made by them for which the taxpoint is in the return period, and offsetting any input tax incurred during the period for which they claim a deduction. The balance of output tax less input tax is the tax due, and that has to be paid at that time. In the case of those making annual returns, they will have agreed with the VAT Office to make ten monthly instalments of the tax at an estimated level, instead of the payments with the return.

Bad debts

If a customer has not paid VAT on a supply at the time that a return is made, the supplier still accounts for the VAT to the VAT Office. This causes problems because, in effect, the supplier lends VAT to the government until the customer has paid. If the customer becomes a bad debtor, and the supplier is never paid, why should the government still get the tax? There is a good answer to this available at option to smaller VAT taxpayers: the *cash accounting scheme*. Under this scheme the registered person puts in the accounts all sums which are actually received, rather than supplies made. If a sum has not been received, it is not subject to tax. This only applies to taxpayers with a turnover of less than £250,000 who reach an agreement with the VAT Office. In other cases, relief for VAT payments which are not paid by the customer can only be claimed as a bad debt. This is allowed only after the debt has been outstanding for a year.

——————— Other sales taxes ———————

There are several other sales taxes of importance, particularly excise duties. These apply in the United Kingdom to an odd group explicable as the remnants of a long former list of specific sales taxes. Those still on the list are:

- tobacco duties,
- duties on alcoholic liquors,
- hydrocarbon oil duty (or petrol tax),
- car tax and vehicle excise duties,
- taxes on betting, gaming and lotteries.

The taxes on alcohol and tobacco are sometimes called *sin taxes*. Whether this is an accurate description is another matter. They were originally imposed when many items were taxed, not because of any moral approach, but, because they represented items that could easily be taxed and, often, which were owned by wealthier people and not by poor people. Let us ignore the history and ask why we should now be imposing heavy taxes on smokers and drinkers. Most of our European neighbours also tax smoking and at least some forms of drinking with heavy taxes. That gives the subject an additional dimension, and complication: the European aspect. This we will explore later. It also suggest that this kind of tax is regarded by governments as a good idea.

Perhaps the answer is that these taxes are regarded as useful because they make both political and economic sense. At the political level, it is convenient to regard them as 'sin taxes', particularly in a nation which has regular twinges of puritanism, and perhaps likes to feel that it is being punished when it enjoys itself! It is much easier for a Chancellor to stand up and announce an increase on cigarettes than on, say, televisions. TV is, to most of us, a necessity, while smoking is an unhealthy luxury. We can be told that smoking is bad for us.

Tobacco and alcohol taxes also make more economic sense compared with most specific sales taxes. The reason for this lies in the way a heavy tax will affect the behaviour of potential customers. If the price of my favourite luxury is suddenly doubled, I can do several things: I can pay twice as much; or I can compromise, and buy a little less; or I can consume half as much for the same money; or I can change my behaviour and find some other favourite luxury. How I react will vary from product to product.

Some products have elastic demand: that is, if the price goes up for any reason, sales drop away fast. If the reason for the price increase is a tax, the tax may end up destroying the product on which it is based, as well as raising no revenue. That is the aim with some customs duties. If the product is inelastic, with sales responding only a little to price levels, then a sharp price rise because of taxation will cause only a small drop-off in sales, and there will be a significant tax revenue. If we put a high tax on jigsaw puzzles we are likely to find sales dropping fast. Experience shows that smokers do not give up that easily.

There is another aspect to elasticity. A further way in which I could react would be to go on buying the product, but doing so illegally, avoiding (or, rather, evading) the tax – or, alternatively, making it ourselves. Smuggling and illegal stills are, after all, part of British history! The tax authorities also want taxes they can enforce efficiently. In modern conditions, with a limited number of manufacturers and importers of products which are difficult to make at home in any quantity, and an effective Customs and Excise Department, this can be done for products like tobacco and spirits.

The economic arguments for these taxes, and the high levels of revenue generated by them, may pose a different dilemma to the government. It has been argued that if the real reason for tobacco taxes is to reduce smoking, some of the vast resources generated by the tax should be diverted towards prevention. Do you agree, or is it enough that smokers have to pay a price for their behaviour?

Licence fees

Is the fee charged for a television licence a tax or a charge? Because it is compulsory, and applies whether or not the licence holder watches BBC Television, it is a tax. This is so even though the money, or most of it, goes to a specific earmarked purpose. Is a gun licence also a tax? Again, the answer is: yes.

One trend in recent years, in trying to cut back the level of taxes, has been to impose fees and charges for publicly provided services, rather than taxes. The argument is that instead of financing the service out of general taxation, we should find its cost and make those who want the service pay for it. This has been done in Britain on a number of services, such as applications for planning permission. Perhaps one of the most controversial charges is the prescription charge. Here the benefit approach to taxation gives way in part to the ability to pay argument with exemptions for children, social security recipients and older people. Although this example is controversial, few other charges have encountered much criticism. On the contrary, part of the advice given to many Third World states looking to reform their systems is to replace tax revenues with fees and charges even if – in reality – the fees and charges are merely specific, earmarked taxes.

11

——— A DUTY-FREE ———
EUROPE?

1 January 1993 will be remembered as the day the Single European Market finally took shape and the frontiers between the states of the European Community finally started being taken down. It is a crucial date in the evolution of tax laws of all member states, including the United Kingdom. In this chapter we explore the European dimension to our tax laws and policies. The coming of the Single European Market brings to a head the issues of the sovereignty of the member states on tax matters for, in major areas of fiscal competence, sovereignty no longer lies with member states acting alone. Rather, it lies with member states acting together.

——— Tax and the Single Market ———

The Single Market and the economic aspects of the European Union, taking form under the Treaty of Maastricht at the end of 1991, are both aimed at achieving the **four freedoms** between member states: the freedoms of movement of goods, services, labour and capital. At the same time, member states are committed to giving equal treatment with their own nationals to nationals of the other member states. Each of these principles has consequences on the traditional approach to taxation of member states.

The age-old method of discriminating against foreign goods is by means of customs duties. Complete removal of discrimination against goods from other member states means complete removal of customs duties, and of any other taxes or charges having the same effect as customs duties whether applied at the frontier or internally. Full freedom of movement demands in addition that there be no frontier for tax purposes – that any way of discriminating between local and imported goods should not exist. What are termed *fiscal frontiers* cannot be part of a Union which is a genuine economic entity in Europe any more than in North America.

A central theme of the achievement of the Single Market in 1993 has therefore been the removal of fiscal frontiers and other tax barriers between member states. The nature of those barriers varies, but they have their most obvious manifestation in the customs houses that have for centuries been part of every British port with pretensions to foreign trade. Are they relevant now?

The customs union

The first step of the Common Market towards freedom of movement was the creation, between the original six members (Belgium, France, West Germany, Italy, Luxembourg, Netherlands), of a customs union. The Economic Treaty (or Treaty of Rome) of 1957 laid this down in detail in Articles 9 to 30.

TREATY ESTABLISHING THE EUROPEAN ECONOMIC COMMUNITY, 1957

Article 9.1:

The Community shall be based upon a customs union which shall cover all trade in goods and which shall involve the prohibition between member states of customs duties on imports and of all charges having equivalent effect, and the adoption of a common customs tariff in their relations with third countries.

The customs union is now, in effect, between all 12 member states (besides the original members: there is the United Kingdom, Denmark and Ireland who joined in 1973; Greece, Portugal and Spain who have joined since, and East Germany who was absorbed after the fall of the Berlin Wall). It is being expanded to include for most purposes the seven members of EFTA (the European Free Trade Association of Austria, Liechtenstein, Finland, Iceland, Norway, Sweden, and Switzerland). These 19 states now share what is called the *European Economic Space*, within which free movement of goods, and increasingly of other economic activities, will operate.

As the United Kingdom is a member of the customs union, it cannot impose customs duties on goods being imported from any other member state of the Community. Nor may the UK impose charges at the frontier in place of those duties. Conversely, British goods can be exported freely to any other member state, and we can insist that no duties or charges be placed on them at those frontiers. For example, if the Italians try to impose duties or charges the European Commission, and in addition any firm or individual directly affected, can challenge that duty or charge before the national courts and, ultimately, before the Court of Justice of the European Communities.

The majority of British foreign trade is with other states of the European Community. It follows that most of our trade now takes place free of any customs regime. However, British customs officers can and do charge customs duty at the frontiers on goods coming in from other states such as the USA. They do so as agents of the Community, and the customs tariffs they impose are the same as those imposed if the Americans were to import the same goods into any other state of the Community. The customs law of the Community is one law. You will not find it in the British statutes, nor has much of it been passed into law by the United Kingdom Parliament. This is because it is a law of the European Community taking direct effect through Community regulations by reason of the obligations on member states in the Economic Treaty.

This is not as big a loss of British sovereignty as it might seem, because even the European Community is not really free to do what it will in imposing customs duty. The Community, as a whole, is itself a member of the GATT (the General Agreement on Tariffs and Trade) to which nearly every state in the world belongs. Membership of GATT imposes standard rules for dealing with many aspects of customs duty. It also imposes internationally agreed limits on the freedom of states to impose customs duties as they will. No state may discriminate against specific other states unless it believes that that other state is itself discriminating, or it is satisfied that particular firms are dumping products (selling them at a deliberately low price).

Standard valuation rules and customs procedures are applied by all members. Clear rules exist to stop discrimination, and to restrict the scope for imposing fiscal limits on imports. There are rules for dealing with the contentious question of where goods are produced, and there is a well-tried disputes procedure through panels of experts which deals with arguments about application of the GATT rules. The formalities of customs law are coordinated by a body called the Customs Cooperation Council. Precisely because it is so effective at its job of coordination, we hear little of it.

Border tax adjustments

Customs duties are only one of the forms of taxation that operate at the frontiers of a self-contained state tax system. All indirect taxes have to be adjusted at the frontier as well. These adjustments are known as *border tax adjustments*, adjustments of internal taxes made at the borders of a state in order to ensure that the taxes work fairly internally. For example, if a state decides to impose a high level of tax on all motor cars manufactured in the state, it will have to impose a similar tax on all imports. If it does not, it will be cheaper to import cars than it will be to manufacture them locally, and the only effect of the tax will be to damage the competitive position of local car makers. Two kinds of tax, apart from customs duties, require national adjustments within the European Community: value added tax and excise duties.

Value added tax required adjustment because, under the general principles of VAT applying throughout Europe (including most non-member states), VAT is levied as a *destination-based tax*: that is, supplies of goods and services are taxed where they are received, not where they are made. If goods are exported from Ireland to France, they leave Ireland without any VAT imposed on them, but are taxed to VAT as they arrive in France. There is an adjustment at the border by both Ireland and

France. Ireland provides a credit to the exporter for all VAT so far paid. France charges the importer on the value at the frontier. The effect is that goods imported into France pay the same tax rate as goods made in France.

Different issues arise with the excise duties. For example, the British impose an excise duty on wine. The Germans do not. If the British were to impose duty only on English wine, and not on German wine, there would be serious problems for the English wine-growing business. If the British impose wine duties on wines which the English vineries try to export to Germany, they will again be at a disadvantage. To deal with these problems, goods liable to excise duties are also subject to border tax adjustments, so that imports are treated in the same way as local products. This is particularly important in connection with goods such as tobacco and spirits which are subject to high levels of tax. This is because of the high risk of smuggling. It is also because of the huge revenues derived through the operation of so-called 'duty free' systems.

Community VAT law

We saw in the last chapter why VAT was adopted, and why it has become the standard tax of the Community. What was also important was that all the Community states had the same form of taxation of goods and services. Only by adopting a common form of general tax on supplies could the Community ensure that distortion from trade in goods and services between member states could be removed. Once the Community chose the VAT as the common form (with hindsight, probably unavoidably once VAT had been invented), it had to be imposed on all members, including all new members. That, of itself, made one aspect of removing fiscal barriers simpler. The former mess of different indirect taxes between member states was potentially a formidable barrier to cross-border trading.

Agreeing to adopt a common method of taxing was not, in the view of most of those involved, sufficient. The aim was to introduce a tax which operated in a non-discriminatory way in each of the states. In part, this was achieved by providing for the destination-based method of taxing.

Destination or origin basis?

Assume goods are exported to Ireland from France, and vice versa, of value 100 ecu. France has a VAT rate of 10 per cent and Ireland of 20 per cent. Assume also that local producers can produce the same goods for sale to the importers, also at 100 ecu.

Destination-based tax

Ireland exports goods to France valued at 100 ecu free of local tax
Value on import to France: 100 ecu. French VAT: 10 per cent
French price of imported goods: 110 ecu.

French local goods produced at value 100 ecu free of local tax
Value on sale in France: 100 ecu. French tax: 10 per cent
French price of local goods: 110 ecu

(The same will be true of sales in Ireland, except the price of both local and imported goods will be 120 ecu.)

Origin-based tax

Ireland exports goods to France valued at 100 ecu before tax
Value on export to France: 100 ecu. Irish tax: 20 per cent
French price of imported goods: 120 ecu

French local goods produced at value 100 ecu before tax
Value on sale in France: 100 ecu. French tax: 10 per cent
French price of local goods: 110 ecu.

The imported goods will therefore be at a disadvantage compared with the local goods. But the same is not true in reverse:

France exports goods to Ireland valued at 100 ecu before tax
Value on export to Ireland: 100 ecu. French tax: 10 per cent
Irish price of imported goods: 110 ecu

Irish local goods produced at value 100 ecu before tax
Value on sale in Ireland: 100 ecu. Irish tax: 20 per cent
Irish price of local goods: 120 ecu.

In this case, it is the local goods which are at a disadvantage. In other words, the French goods are always at an advantage, because the Irish VAT rate is higher, if an origin basis of tax is adopted.

The alternative approach to the destination basis of taxation is the *origin basis*. Under this basis, goods are taxed where they are made, not where they are consumed. The box, on page 211, shows what would happen if goods were taxed on the two bases on exports between Ireland and France if we assume that Ireland imposes a 20 per cent rate of tax on the times, and France a 10 per cent rate. As we shall see below, there are serious problems in applying the origin basis.

There are also major problems with the destination basis of VAT within the Community. The most important, as we have seen, is that it requires a double border adjustment to every cross-border supply. Community states agreed in 1967 and again in 1977 to a form of VAT which involved border tax adjustments because they were a more acceptable solution to the problem of cross-border VAT than the answers then available to the problems with the origin basis of tax. The formal solution adopted was for all states to agree that VAT should be imposed on all supplies that amounted to imports, and should exempt exports **with credit**. The 'with credit' rider meant that the state from which the supplies were exported should rebate or credit the exporter with all VAT paid on the supplies up to the time of export, so that there was no VAT hidden in the export price. This is the system now worked by all member states.

The destination basis of VAT is not the form of taxation the European Commission wants, because of the continuing need for border tax adjustments. In the Commission's view, VAT should be on an origin basis, but the chief problems of discrimination between states should be removed by the member states agreeing to have similar rates of VAT. And this, with minimum publicity, is what member states are working towards. It has been agreed at political level by the member states that the minimum main rate of VAT imposed will be 15 per cent. If you look at a table of rates of VAT in the Community, you will see that they have been moving steadily towards this rate for some years. Even if rate discrimination is neutralised for individual transactions, a further level of neutralisation may also be needed. This arises because some states will export much more than other states, which will be net importers. On the origin basis of tax, the exporters will collect proportionately more tax than the importers, even if the rates of VAT are the same and no discrimination arises. These problems have not yet been solved.

Common rates of VAT

Adopting common rates of VAT is not just a matter of setting a band of main rates. In recent years, member states have had as many as six different rates of VAT from zero per cent (in the UK and Ireland) to 36 per cent (luxury rate in France). Even if a similar main rate were adopted by countries, agreement also has to be reached about the higher and lower rates. In addition, if one state exempts a supply, which is taxed in another state, discrimination will also exist.

The Community reached a considerable measure of agreement on one aspect of common rates in 1977 when it adopted the Sixth VAT Directive. The Directive provides for a common list of exemptions in all states. More recently, states have been negotiating towards common agreement on the application of rates other than the main rate of VAT. It has been agreed that there should be no higher rates. It has also been agreed at political level that there should be one lower rate of VAT, in the region of between 4 per cent and 9 per cent, but with the UK and Ireland being allowed to maintain their zero per cent, or zero rate on agreed groups of items.

Even this level of coordination is not enough to avoid hidden discrimination. There must also be common rules on valuing supplies for the purpose of imposing the tax, for deciding when and where a supply occurs (to stop double taxation on cross-border supplies), for deciding who shall pay the tax, and what kinds of activities are covered by the scope of the tax. In short, there must be a common definition of the tax base of the tax.

Rules for all these matters are now laid down as standard for the entire Community in the VAT Directives, and in particular in the Sixth VAT directive, as amended by a number of subsequent directives. The Sixth Directive does not impose common answers to all questions. It leaves a substantial number of detailed issues (such as taxation of second-hand goods, and taxation of farmers) only partly covered, and it allows a number of derogations to individual states. But it provides a core for a common Community VAT on a basis which member states cannot ignore. Further, because of the dynamic nature of Community law with its own court, the steady flow of cases to the Court in Luxembourg has ensured that the scope for creating national differences through different interpretations of the common rules is kept under control.

The Sixth Directive removes important differences, but it does not remove border tax adjustments. This proved a significant embarrassment in connection with the adoption of the Single Market in 1993. The Single European Act amended the Economic Community Treaty to remove the right for member states to have border tax posts. How do you run a Europen VAT if you are unable to impose border tax adjustments?

Under recently agreed measures, from 1993 border tax posts are removed completely, and no checks of any kind can take place purely for tax reasons at a frontier. This means that border tax adjustments can no longer take place at the border. They still have to take place, so that they are, instead, imposed at the point of first destination in the receiving state. Because of the heightened risk of fraud, and also because of potential delay in payment of VAT as there is no physical control over goods until surety for payment is established, the Community also agreed to a strict regime of mutual assistance and exchange of information between the member states.

Even though some problems remain unanswered, the intermeshing of VAT rules in member states now gives individual states little room for originality or political manoeuvre. In practice, the United Kingdom has already used most of its room to manoeuvre to minimise the impact of VAT. For example, our registration level is far higher than in several other states, and our zero-rating more generous. It is hard for the UK to be more generous than it is at present, though quite easy for it to decide to impose VAT at the full rate where it does not now do so. But as it does so, it loses the right to reverse the decision, and further moves the British form of VAT to the common Community form.

A Community VAT

VAT also forms one of the resources of the Community. Member states are obliged to pay over to the Community budget a set percentage of the total VAT collected nationally each year. The figure is currently 1.4 per cent. That may seem a small figure, but throughout the Community it is a significant sum.

As member states rely more heavily on the VAT, so the pressures for uniformity of approach in the EC grow, and so also does the Community's own VAT proceeds. These pressures, linked with the ban in customs duties between member states, and the requirement that the only general sales tax allowed in the Community is VAT, mean that member states have largely lost the power of independent action, and a Community VAT, which individual member states can do only a limited amount to alter locally, is largely already in being. The extent to which, post 1993, the process of harmonisation and approximation of national VAT laws has happened already, leads some to view VAT as being a federal tax already. If the transfer from destination basis to origin basis is completed, the metamorphosis from national tax to federal tax will have happened.

Excise duties

The abolition of border posts, and the inability to check cross-border transfers of goods subject to excise duties, is potentially of greater significance to individual transactions than the loss of customs control over movements of supplies subject to VAT. This is partly because of the risk of smuggling and illegal movement of goods before duty is paid: it is also because a major industry has developed out of the high level of excise duties in most Western European states, and because industry risks losing its privileged position if the wrong changes are made to excise duties.

The business at risk is duty-free shopping at ports and airports. 'Duty-free' traditionally means free of all customs duties, excise duties and VAT. Where there are major price differentials, the added bonus of being able to haul one's holiday goods back home free of tax is valuable. But it is as nothing in terms of volume of trade to the cheap alcoholic drinks and cigarettes bought on the ship or at the airport on the way to a holiday, and on the way back. So high is the duty in this country on these products, that there is a profit of many hundreds of per cent per bottle or box to be made from travellers as they rush in their thousands on their way out and back again. It is not surprising that these profits have been underwriting the profitability of ferries, airlines and airports.

DUTY FREE ALLOWANCES

Travellers between the United Kingdom and other member states may bring in the following free of VAT and excise duties at the frontier (there are no customs duties), provided that they buy them in those other countries (not in other duty free shops):

- 1.5 litres of spirits,
- 4 bottles of wine,
- 200 cigarettes,
- £425 worth of other goods.

Travellers between the United Kingdom and non-member states may bring in the following only, free of VAT and excise duties, and any relevant customs duties:

- 1 litre of spirits,
- 2 bottles of wine,
- 200 cigarettes,
- £32 of other goods.

Unfortunately for the business, 'free movement of goods' means that duty-free facilities should go, except on journeys to and from states outside the Community. The Commission proposed total abolition of restrictions, and consequently total abolition of 'duty-free allowances', from 1993. Heavy lobbying by transport interests persuaded some, including the British government, that there was too much at stake in the duty-free market to suddenly abolish the allowances. The market is, therefore, being phased out. But who loses from its abolition? And who subsidises whom during the phase-out period which lasts until 1999?

The in-fighting over duty-free privileges is only one of the battles taking place between the member states over excises. When the Single Market was first proposed, Lord Cockfield argued strongly that it involved total harmonisation of excise taxes throughout the Community. There were to be Community-wide excises on three product groups: tobacco, alcoholic drinks and oil products – with a ban on any other excise of international significance. Further, the rates of excise were to be the same in each member state, as were the other rules. This plan proved overambitious. States such as the United Kingdom, which rely heavily on excises as revenue earners were not prepared to risk losing the revenue. At the other end, there were states which had no intention of raising excises. Germany, for example, has no excise on wine, and does not intend to introduce one.

Agreement has now been reached to deal with the problem of ending border tax adjustments. This involved agreement on minimum rates of tax for each of the excises. The agreed minimum rate for wine was zero per cent! That was, however, the exception. A degree of harmonisation has been obtained on the excises – not least in the formal position that the only excises that states will raise are the three groups noted above. Most action is occurring in connection with the oil product taxes, of which there is more in the next chapter. But here again we see that the independent powers of the separate member states are limited.

— Non-discrimination in tax matters —

Another limit applying to all states in the Community is the cumulative effect of a series of prohibitions which have the effect of preventing a state from using its taxes to discriminate against the nationals or products of other member states. Articles 7 and 58 of the Economic Treaty impose a blanket ban on discrimination against individuals or companies based on nationality (in the case of companies, their place of registration). Article 48 bans discrimination preventing free movement of workers, and article 52 prevents freedom of establishment on equal terms with the locals. Once the regime of free movement is fully established, other articles will prevent discrimination against free movement of capital.

The most effective ban is Article 95, on the use of taxation to stop the free movement of goods. The text, set out in the box below, is derived from Article III of the GATT, and applies in weaker form to most countries. In the Community it is enforceable directly against governments at the instance of either the European Commission or of individuals affected by a breach of the ban.

> ## EEC TREATY ARTICLE 95
>
> No member state shall impose on the products of other member states any internal taxation of any kind in excess of that imposed directly or indirectly on similar domestic products.
>
> Furthermore, no member state shall impose on the products of other member states any internal taxation of such a nature as to afford indirect protection to other products.

The article has been used in a series of actions by the Commission to prevent member states using excise duties to discriminate between different kinds of alcoholic drink. In cases before it, the European court has ruled that spirits such as whisky, brandy and similar strong spirits must be treated as similar products, and are, therefore, subject to similar taxes. In a more controversial judgment, the Court even went as far as ruling that beer and cheap table wine were similar products, so that states could not use excise duties to discriminate in favour of one against the other.

Cumulatively, the effect of article 95 and the Court judgments on it have further restricted the way that member states can use VAT and excise duties – and any other indirect taxes, such as those on motor cars – to favour domestic production. Article 95 (and the underlying GATT obligation) does not, however, affect direct taxes. Community tax law now does.

Direct taxes in the Community

Until recently, Community law had little effect on direct taxes of the member states. This was because the member states made sure that this was so. They can do so because, under the voting rules of the Community, measures adopted dealing with taxation (other than customs duties) require unanimity. Unlike most Community questions, each state has a veto on proposed action affecting taxes. From 1969, when the European Commission first made proposals for common action by member states in the field of direct taxation, until 1990 one or other state applied the veto to every proposal made, with the sole exception of proposals to ensure mutual assistance between the tax authorities of member states.

There were at least two reasons for these vetoes. One was of course the national interest of individual member states. In different ways, the tax systems of member states allow them to compete on the world services markets. At the same time, the vetoes allowed member states to follow social policies and priorities that other states did not accept.

A second reason was that states saw another route for dealing with their common problems relating to direct taxes. This is through the use of bilateral double taxation agreements negotiated under the aegis of the model adopted by the OECD. As the 12 member states are all members of the OECD, a body based in Paris, there was good reason to consider that their problems had an adequate forum for solution elsewhere. This is particularly so as such treaties allow the states to reach desirable solutions untrammelled by the restrictions of Community law. Or so it was thought until recently.

Until 1990, the Commission's own priorities lay with the indirect taxes. If there was a view of the direct taxes, it was perhaps that they were a safety valve for members while they agreed to align their customs duties and indirect taxes. In 1990, longstanding antagonisms towards two 1969 proposals disappeared in the face of the need to take action to avoid distortions in the Single Market. The Council adopted two new direc-tives. One, called the Parent-Subsidiary Directive, restricts taxation on the flows of dividends from the subsidiary to the parent company. The other, the Merger Directive, is aimed at preventing double taxation on mergers, divisions, transfers of assets and exchanges of shares between associated companies to the effect that businesses are transferred. Both were cautious measures. The texts present the national government with problems, and offer more than member states have felt able to deliver in terms of tax relief. But they were adopted, and with them the Community signalled its interst in direct taxation.

A third directive had also been negotiated with the two adopted, on the effect of disagreements between member states when they determined that a multinational enterprise had been transfer-pricing between com-panies based in two member states, thereby avoiding tax in one or more of the states. When transfer-pricing is discovered, the action taken by a state to stop adverse effects on its own tax collection may result in the multinational group being subject to double taxation. The Commission had argued, since 1976, that this was not acceptable in the Community. In 1990, the member states agreed, but significantly they did not agree that the Community was the appropriate route for their agreement. Instead, they turned the directive into an international treaty which does not take effect until all 12 member states have accepted it. To date only some have done so, although the two directives are already in effect.

At the same time, the Commission took the lead from these directives to direct its own attention to the issues of restrictions on freedom of movement arising from direct taxation. Similarly, the European Court has been asked to rule on questions of discrimination in direct taxes.

So far, little has occurred to limit the freedom of individual states to deal with individual and corporate income taxes as they wish, save for actions involving taxation between the member companies of multinational corporate groups within the Community. However, the remorseless logic of the Single European Market and the European Union is that all forms of discrimination should go. If they do, it will have a major effect on the direct taxes of most member states.

Logic, to date, has had little effect, but the existence of tax competition between states has had effect. What has been evident for a few years is the extent to which an adverse tax system can penalise the service industries of a state. For example, if a company can borrow money for its activities in any one of the member states, or can deposit its spare money in any state to earn interest, it is likely to borrow or lend the money where it gets the best return. If one state taxes those deposits at a higher rate than another, the other will be the beneficiary.

The challenge of the Single Market is that it is steadily lifting the barriers preventing the flow of capital between member states. Events have already shown that as those barriers are opened, so tax systems have to accept the competitive pressure that their opening releases. When the UCITS Directive (Directive on Undertakings for Collective Investment in Transferable Securities – or Unit Trusts as they are called in the UK) took effect, British unit trusts found that they could sell some of their products throughout the Community. But they also discovered that the competition was tough because companies in Luxembourg could also do so – and the tax regime in Luxembourg was considerably more friendly to unit trusts than that in the UK. The result, until a swift change of the UK tax rules, was the start of a mass migration of British unit trusts to Luxembourg. Were the British to choose to tax unit trusts more heavily again, the migration would no doubt start again – and there is nothing in the Single Market that the British government could do to stop it.

Unless member states choose to cooperate to prevent the downward pressure on taxes, tax competition could prove to be a fearsome pressure, in years to come, on the more mobile aspects of our economy, such as bank deposits.

Social security and taxes

The biggest difference between the national patterns of taxation of the Community member states lies in social security. France and the Netherlands fund all their social security payments through separate schemes involving little general taxation (to the extent that more than four francs in every ten collected by public authorities in taxation in France is by way of contributions to French social security funds). At the other extreme, social security funds receive minimal amounts by way of compulsory contributions in Denmark, as with other Nordic states. Britain is somewhere in the middle, with about half the cost of its social security, health and welfare budgets being drawn from specific contributions. Of what concern is this to the Community?

Social security benefits, and therefore contributions, are affected by Community law in a number of ways. The first and most fundamental way is that all aspects of social security schemes are subject to the non-discrimination provisions of the Economic Treaty. Another Community aspect of social security contributions, and benefits, imposed in the Economic Treaty is Regulation 1408/71. This prevents an individual being required to contribute to the social security schemes of more than one state at the same time. It also ensures that a person who contributes to a social security scheme in one state, and then moves, as a worker, to another member state, must be given the benefit in the second state of the contributions made in the first state. It is for the two scheme administrations to sort out between themselves how much money the first state should refund to the second state because of this. The effect of the 1971 measure is an important degree of coordination between all Community social security schemes.

Here again the individual member states of the Community are required to ensure that their tax systems take full account of Community obligations and, to that extent, that their joint will as the Community Council, and as parties to the Economic Treaty, prevails over their individual views.

Agricultural taxes

The final specific tax of importance in the Community is that of agricultural taxation. This is, along with customs duty, an area of community tax rather than national tax. The taxes in question are the agricultural levies imposed on Community farmers as part of the price adjustment procedure called the Common Agricultural Policy (or CAP). The CAP is imposed by Treaty and Community Regulation, so has direct effect on all Community farmers without featuring in the national legislation.

Agricultural levies are imposed when a farmer sells farm goods at more than a set price. They are taxes because the levies are compulsory. If a farmer or food supplier does not pay the levies, they can be enforced in the same way as a non-paid tax such as VAT. However, they form part of a system which uses the levies to pay out subsidies, so that a farmer may find himself or herself paying levies on some other kind of produce or activity. The total throughput of funds in the Community is heavy, and it forms the larger part of the total Community budget in any year. The money collected is payable to the Community and not to national tax authorities, although national officials act as agents in collecting the levies. There has been much pressure in Britain for reform of the CAP, and of the levy and subsidy system. Notwithstanding this, and reforms achieved under British pressure so far, the interests of the Community as a whole again outweigh the national interests of individual member states. Unanimity is not required for the adoption of CAP measures by the European Council, limiting the significance of reform proposals put forward by one state but not supported by a number of others.

The Community budget

In this chapter we have noted three sources of finance of the European Community itself, all tax-based. First, was the net proceeds of customs duties, after allowing a rebate towards national collection costs. Second, was the 1.4 per cent levy on national VAT collections; and the third, just noted, is the proceeds of agricultural levies. The community also levies an income tax on its own staff members. Full-time employees of the Community are exempt from national taxation, but they are subject to a relatively light form of income tax imposed by the

> **The Community's own taxes**
>
> The EC is funded direct by its own resources, the most important of which are:
>
> - All customs duties,
> - 1.4 per cent national VATs,
> - All agricultural levies,
> - A levy on states based on their GDPs (national output).

Community itself. This does not deal with more than a minor element of the cost of Community officials, let alone meet the other demands on the budget.

Taken together, the three sources of tax revenue (ignoring the income tax) meet much, but not all, the Community budget. Beyond those proceeds, the Community does not enjoy further taxing power. Instead, it is entitled to an agreed annual levy of all member states for the so-called fourth resource – a sort of poll tax of member states! Under an agreed formula, each member state contributes a further share to the total sum, until the amount necessary is collected. Like many other aspects of the Community, this is at present an untidy compromise. In the view of the Commission, the Community budget must be expanded over the next few years to meet the commitments entered into by its members (for example, towards redeveloping the eastern half of Europe). If it is to do that, it will need, directly or indirectly, extra tax revenues. How should it receive them? Would a further share of VAT revenues be a sensible approach? Or a similar levy based on some other tax?

The sovereignty question

By way of summary, we can see that the European Community has much unfinished business in connection with taxation. Even at this stage, it is possible, without exaggeration, to note the emergence of a federal tax system, and one where the freedom of the individual member states is subject to important limits.

At the same time, those limits derive from the negative force of tax competition, as well as from the positive force of deliberate harmonisation and approximation. This is important in viewing the total picture. Member states have retained – and do not hesitate to use – an individual veto power over positive initiatives to reform community taxes. There is no veto available from the effects of tax competition. The downward pressures of competition may, of themselves, force states to take positive action to prevent harmful levels of competition. Either way, no British Chancellor or Parliament can ignore the Community when making tax decisions.

12

TAXES AND THE ENVIRONMENT

'Taxes can be the most effective means of tackling environmental problems, and so merit serious examination. However, their use raises wider economic, social, and industrial consequences which need to be weighed in the balance . . . Environmental taxes can be used to encourage as well as to discourage. Taxes can be levied at different rates to reflect the fact that one course of action is less environmentally damaging than another.'

With these words, the British government, in its White Paper *This Common Heritage: Britain's environmental strategy* placed taxes and the environment on the British political agenda. In this chapter we examine arguments for and against taxes as environmental aids and we look at specific aspects of 'green' taxation in Britain. The scope of this 'green' taxation is wide because we cannot, to borrow Anthony Newley's words, 'stop the world, I want to get off.' It is concerned with pollution, that is, with activities which contaminate our surroundings. It is also concerned with other kinds of damage to our environment, such as the potential damage caused to future generations by the use of exhaustible non-renewable resources.

—— Environmentally friendly taxes ——

Taxation is a powerful tool in changing people's behaviour. It is the oft-quoted reason for high taxes on tobacco. The example of tobacco makes another point. Taxation is just one way of influencing behaviour.

It is one of several ways in which tobacco consumption is limited. Some limits are private, when people ban smoking in their homes and offices. Some are persuasive, through health warnings and bans on cigarette advertising. Some are regulatory, by requiring licences to make or sell tobacco products, and banning smoking, for example, where food is being prepared. Some transfer costs, for example, allowing a claim for compensation or industrial injuries benefit for a non-smoker acquiring lung cancer at work from fellow workers who are smokers. Some are proscriptive – using the criminal law to stop shopkeepers selling cigarettes to those under age. And some are fiscal.

Compare the way that the British authorities handle drugs such as cannibis. Fiscal measures are inappropriate in a direct sense and instead the criminal law is used. But, among other measures, there are powers to seize and forfeit all drug dealers' profits. A sort of 100 per cent income tax? Which methods are best?

In the broad context of 'the environment', taxes have several uses:

- making polluters pay;
- encouraging environmentally friendly activities;
- offsetting the use of non-renewable resources.

The polluter pays principle

The general approach of developed states to pollution is the 'polluter pays' principle. This has been accepted by the United Kingdom and other OECD members. It is official policy of the European Community. The principle is an economic one, that the full cost of pollution by a product should be identified and added to the cost of the product, by taxation if necessary. The converse is also valid, that government should not subsidise activities where this leads to pollution without counter-measures.

In economic terms, pollution causes *externalities*, that is, it imposes on the world costs which are not paid for by either the supplier or the person supplied. If, for example, I sell you a battery made with cadmium, you pay me a price, and after you have used it, you probably discard it. Neither of us pay for removing the cadmium from the battery nor for disposing safely of a highly toxic poison – unless, that is, either the law makes us, or you demand a better product and I, or someone else, produces it. It is fair to note that since attention was drawn to this problem, there has been much lower use of this pollutant because of this last solution.

Similarly, until recently we have been happy to let coal-fired power stations produce cheap electricity in the British Isles, while omitting to be concerned about forests in Norway and Germany dying as a direct result of the acid rain caused by those same power stations. This example shows another problem with pollution questions – they cannot be solved within one state's borders. To that extent, by definition, national taxation is not a sufficient solution.

The argument for pollution taxes is that they can be used to increase the price of products to pay for pollution prevention. The assumption is that a compulsory government levy is the most direct and manageable method of altering prices. That alteration can be achieved by a number of techniques. The most successful to date in the United Kingdom is the price penalty on leaded petrol. It was achieved by a certain sleight of hand – by reducing the cost of unleaded petrol as compared with leaded petrol, and then increasing both! Over a few years, use of unleaded petrol grew from a habit of a few 'freaks' to the most important form of car fuel. This was partly because the petrol companies were anxious to increase the lead-free fuels, but they did not want, individually, to have to take the market risks of being first. They were happy to have the new tax regime imposed on them.

The price alteration can be imposed as an additional levy. This can be voluntary. One problem, highlighted by the White Paper, was the cost of disposing of car tyres. Since then the tyre industry has imposed a small 'voluntary' levy on the sale of each new tyre to pay for the cost of disposing of the previous one. The government preferred this approach (which in practice is compulsory to the customer) to imposing a special tax. But it might have done so.

The advantage of the tyre levy is that it is likely that the tax will be used to deal with the pollution. That can be guaranteed only if taxation is used with other legal techniques. An example of this is the additional charge placed recently on companies applying to the government for pesticide licences. The charge was raised to pay for the government scientists who monitor the new forms of pesticide. Their job is to ensure that no undue environmental harm is caused. Pesticide manufacturers must hold a licence to sell any particular pesticide. They, therefore, pay for the cost of ensuring environmental protection in the licence fee. This will be passed on to customers along with development costs. It may be arguable whether this is a charge or a tax, but either way the potential polluter pays to prevent the pollution.

Earmarked taxes are, however, the exception. There is a strong temptation to use these taxes just to raise money. People will pay because they 'feel good' about it. This will have part of the desired effect, in making people less likely to use polluting products. But it does not cure the pollution as such. If they are really meant to stop us polluting, then why are the tax proceeds not used for that purpose? One answer is that it does not matter. If the result of the price increase on the product is a satisfactory diminution in the level of pollution, that will, of itself, achieve the desired objective. The surplus tax produced is free for use on other social objectives.

A compromise route for pollution taxes is a levy paid to a fund to deal with pollution. For example, a levy on all oil shipments can be paid to a special reserve fund. If and when oil spillages occur, the fund finances the clean-up operation. The levy is an earmarked tax, spreading the cost of pollution control over all the risky activities. In other words, it is a form of compulsory insurance for an activity which those insured might not otherwise undertake.

What is needed is a coherent approach to ensure that, whether by taxes or charges causing price rises, or by the diversion of resources received from those taxes or charges, the pollution is tackled at an appropriate stage. We shall explore at the end of the chapter whether such coherence can be found in our tax system.

Encouraging environmentally friendly activities

Taxation can play a part in several different strategies for encouraging desirable behaviour. It can:

- finance government expenditure from general non-earmarked taxes,
- use general non-earmarked taxes to finance grants to private persons for favoured activities,
- impose earmarked taxes for these results,
- allow taxpayers direct deductions from their taxes for favoured activities.

These techniques are, to a considerable extent, the reverse of those we have just noted for pollution control through taxation. As the example of the tax on lead-free petrol shows, it may sometimes be a matter of doubt whether a particular fiscal measure is making a polluter pay or encouraging desirable consumption. What is presented as one may in fact be the other! One is the stick and the other the carrot.

'Carrots' may be most useful in dealing with particular targeted problems in a broad context. The Water Act 1989, which regulates the water industry and British fresh waters, illustrates this. One problem confronting the industry is an excess level of nitrate in some water catchment areas. These require action because of European Community standards to protect health. The chosen route is to designate areas as nitrate sensitive areas, and to empower the government to reach agreements with local landowners, especially farmers, to ensure appropriate use of land in these areas. The legislation authorises payments in respect of such agreements, subject to repayment under conditions to be specified.

Tax deductions also have a role to play. A number of countries have toyed with tax privileges for environmentally friendly expenditure, or for bodies for protection of the environment. In Britain, examples include tax allowances for payments made for restoring waste disposal sites and to the oil industry for costs of making good abandoned drilling sites in the North Sea. Such provisions are needed because of the narrowness of the general rules for deduction of expenses. Unless it is wholly and exclusively for the purposes of the trade, it does not count. If pollution is an externality, then abating it is not an expense for the purposes of the trade, unless legislation makes it so!

— Use of non-renewable resources —

The prime, but not the only, example of this kind of question is that of fossil fuels: coal, oil, gas. The challenge is to establish the relevance of a tax system, if any, to the problems occurring with the use of non-renewable resources. Essentially there are two: the first is to ensure that the resource is not squandered, and that responsible use now conserves supplies for the future. The other is to look ahead to the time when the money flow to a state's economy from the non-renewable resource runs out.

The monetary aspect is easier to tackle. It can be done along the lines of the fund established for the benefit of the Shetland Islands by the oil companies. Payment of a small royalty on each barrel now is used to provide a large capital fund which will provide an income flow once the oil has run dry. Similar funds, sometimes imposed by law and sometimes as part of local agreements, are found in Alaska. This is a slightly unusual use of taxation. Normally that is assumed to be funding current expenditure, as the British petroleum revenue tax does. But where the local economy has no alternatives to the oil, this is a sort of state or locality pension fund. Why not?

Broader questions arise when the use of taxation is designated to ensure that the resource is not squandered. In this case, a tax burden on the product itself achieves the desired object if the right level of taxation is determined, and the destination of the revenues generated is less relevant. An interesting example of this is the tax imposed in the USA on CFCs. The CFC products, used widely in refrigeration, are blamed by many for the thinning of the ozone layer and the increase of damaging sunshine and also for the greenhouse effect or global warming. Many states, including the USA and the UK, have decided to phase out CFCs as soon as possible, and find suitable replacements. Meanwhile existing CFC stocks were there for the taking – except that a significant tax was imposed upon the products, so making CFCs instantly more expensive to consumers, and replacements instantly more worth finding. Perhaps the best example of this technique is the Italian tax on plastic bags. Once the tax was imposed on each bag, Italians reduced by half their consumption of such bags. Perhaps the British ought to do that with plastic bottles?

The most significant, and complicated, area of use of this form of tax is on fossil fuels. The dilemma affects everyone. Our advanced societies use ever-greater amounts of energy. We are, in particular, gas (or petrol) guzzlers. We have renewable energy sources readily available to us with wind, waves and sunshine and also nuclear fuels (although the latter raises other pollution questions). But non-renewable energy sources such as coal, gas, oil and peat – even wood – are much cheaper. The common element to all these fuels is carbon. Should we impose taxes on these fuels in order to make our economies more resource sensitive? Is a carbon tax a good idea?

The carbon tax

The European Community has been investigating for a little time now the benefits and costs of adopting a general regime for taxing carbon fuels. The idea is to adopt a Europe-wide approach to the tax. It is not sufficient that one state decides to adopt this form of taxation, because it will merely damage its own economy with little net gain to the world's resources. Such an approach has to have as wide a base as possible. A similar approach taken by 12, perhaps twice that number, European states has strong attractions. But will it work? Unlike most taxes, these taxes are means to ends which are other than raising money, and they may therefore fail more obviously.

What has been agreed so far is that it is right for the member states to pursue a policy of increasing, in real terms, the excise duties on hydro-carbon oils. This the British government has been doing, in common with others, for several years past. But British policy is not that clear. Indeed, it is not at all clear that the British have a policy on non-renewable resources, though one may be emerging now that the government has finished its privatisation of the gas and electricity industries and of the part of the oil industry which it owned.

Current tax strategy for our fuels suggests that one prime aim has been money raising; and another prime aim (perhaps now past) was ensuring the successful privatisation of the previously state-owned industries. It does not suggest a coherent approach to the carbon tax. We have, as already noted, a Gas Levy – though its aim was essentially to earn revenue. We also have, as again noted, excise taxes on fuel. Again, these are primarily revenue earners.

Less obviously, we have a basic form of the carbon tax, a *fossil fuel levy*, created in the Electricity Act 1989. It is payable by the electricity generating companies on electricity generated from fossil fuels – coal and oil). Its destination is that part of our power-generating system which runs on non-fossil fuels (i.e. nuclear fuel). This is because nuclear power stations cost more to run than cheap gas-fired stations. The cheap stations are therefore required to subsidise the nuclear power stations.

A full picture of the government financing of our energy business would need to include the heavy sudsidies paid to the coal industry, for many years, out of general tax revenue. This directly contradicts the policy of a fossil fuel tax. If we mean to impose a fossil fuel tax or carbon tax (rather than just an oil tax) we should presumably be pleased to see our coal industry coming to an end. Perhaps that is what is happening. The South Wales coalpits employed some 250,000 people in 1900. In 2000 there may not be any!

Taxing the motor car

If our taxes on fossil fuels seem to lack coherence, this is as nothing to the approach taken to the car. It may be instructive to finish this chapter by looking in detail at how in Britain we approach the question of taxing cars, including the fuel on which they run and the roads they use.

As to the cars themselves, we both tax them and relieve them of tax in an oddly muddled way. In the European context, it is well known that cars cost more in Britain than in some other Community countries, and the tax is part of the reason for this. At the same time, we do not have any taxes in Britain aimed at particular kinds of car, such as 'gas guzzlers' (as they have in the United States, with Jaguar as one of the chief cars penalised), or aimed at encouraging small cars rather than big cars (France and Denmark have both tried this, the latter with some success).

Indirect taxes on cars and car use

The main tax that we impose directly on cars is the *car tax*. This is not, as many people think, the payment for the excise disc on the windscreen. It is a separate tax, imposed at 5 per cent of the wholesale value (10 per cent until 1992), on the price of any new car, locally made or imported. Both directly and indirectly it increases the price of British cars. There is also a small charge for the registration of the car but, like the charge for a driving test and driving licence, no systematic use is made of this as an opportunity for monopoly pricing or of imposing a tax. The only profit element present in the pricing structure is for so-called 'cherished numbers' both on first registration and on transfer.

The tax disc represents payment for the *vehicle excise duty* of £100 a year. It is flat rate on cars, though steeply progressive and expensive when applied to lorries or trucks. The cost for keeping a car on the road has been declining steadily in real terms, because a deliberate decision was taken some years ago to shift the burden from this tax to the oil duties. This can be done without affecting inflation, but it is advantageous because of the high level of evasion of the vehicle excise duty (VED), while oil duties are extremely difficult to avoid. Implicit in this is therefore a real increase in the cost of running expenses. Originally the VED was imposed as a 'road fund tax', with proceeds going to a special road fund to pay for new roads. The earmarking failed politically and ended, although the VED did not.

The next tax on cars is *value added tax*. This applies to cars, as to most other manufactured products, at the standard rate. The VAT levy is based on the price of the car plus car tax, so effectively converts the tax burden to a total of 23.25 per cent (with the tax on tax effect) for those who have to pay the VAT and cannot reclaim it. In addition, the usual rules of VAT have been altered so as to reduce VAT relief on cars. Manufacturers who use their own cars are, for VAT purposes, treated as selling the cars to themselves so a 'self-supply' charge is imposed. Also, the VAT charge on a new car is not recoverable (except by car dealers), so it has to be paid by all purchasers, whether private or not. The cumulative effect of these charges on a business is to add a significant business cost, especially now that VAT has been raised to 17.5 per cent.

Hydrocarbon oil duty applies to petrol (leaded or otherwise) at a level which has increased in real terms over recent years. The increase is partly due to the transfer to this tax from VED of the burden of the 'road tax'. VAT is charged on the fuel and on the duty, so, again, there is a 'tax on tax' effect, which has increased as VAT has increased. The amount of tax on petrol is disguised by price movements although about half the pump price paid by the private motorist is tax.

At present, little use is made of taxes for road use as such. The regime of parking meters imposes what is realistically a tax for on-street parking. In one sense, it could be argued that this is not a tax, but, given that public funds provide the roads and public authorities restrict alternative parking locations, it is difficult to describe the right to park as a 'service'. *Road tolls* are rare for public facilities. They require special legislation and have only been used for some bridges and tunnels. By comparison, rail travellers using British Rail's services are required to contribute, each time they travel, towards the cost of maintaining the rail lines, signals and other parts of its permanent way. Is that fair?

Although the combined effect of these indirect taxes is to impose significant taxes on cars and their use of the historical effect of the direct taxes has been to make them significantly cheaper. This arises through the rules of income tax and NI contributions and, to a minor extent, those of capital gains tax. But some direct tax rules, especially those on capital expenditure, work the other way.

Income tax on cars and fuel

We noted in the chapter on earnings that many cars are provided to employees by their employers as 'part of the job'. Or it did, until recently. How far are cars still tax efficient (or, environmentalists might say, tax subsidised)? This depends on car size, use, value, and age, among other things, so it is hard to generalise. The Automobile Association publishes annual figures for the average mileage costs of different cars. These are full-cost figures covering the hidden advantages (no need to pay interest on loans) as well as open costs such as depreciation. On the basis of figures such as these, there is usually felt to be limited advantage now in having a company car unless it gets significant business use. The income tax rules also apply to charge employees on the provision of free fuel, on a different and lower tariff.

Incidental advantages of company cars have been treated as being part of the car. For example, if the employee is provided with a top of the range car including special extras (fitted child seats, high grade sound systems), this does not increase the income tax charge for the car as compared with the basic model of the same range of engine size. One effect of this is that British cars tend to have more 'extras' fitted as standard than do cars in countries where there are fewer business purchasers. This, the Chancellor has announced, is to be changed with the tax charge based on the car's value. Extras which cannot become part of the car are already subject to additional charges, for example the services of a chauffeur for private occasions. The additional tax charges for added car-based perks also covered the advantage of a job-related car-parking space, until special rules were introduced to cancel the potential tax charge.

Social security contribution liability

Until 1991, contribution liability did not apply in any way to benefits in kind, so that cars, free fuel and the incidental benefits supplied with cars were free from any social security contribution levy unless they could be said to be cash payments. However, new class 1A contributions were then introduced. These deliberately parallel the income tax rules, but impose the charge on employers rather than employees. This has the effect both of ensuring that the cost applies to all cars supplied while many employees receiving such benefits are above the social security contribution cut-off level), and of highlighting the burden of car costs. There is also a charge to employers on free fuel, again based on the income tax charges. The combined effect of this levy with the income tax levy (and the VAT levy as well) is to make the cost of providing a car by an employer significantly higher, while cutting its advantage to the employee. On a given tariff, the combined marginal rate is 35 per cent for those paying basic rate tax and 50 per cent for the higher rate payers.

Taxing employers on cars

An employer making a profit may be less concerned with the cost of providing cars – and paying the social security car levy – because the costs can be written off against its own corporation tax bill. This discounts the rates. However, as the rates of corporation tax drop, the level of discount also drops, exposing a higher post-tax rate. Employers are also exposed to higher post-tax rates because of limitations in the income tax and corporation tax rules applying to deductions for the capital cost of cars. As with VAT, there are special rules preventing the deduction of the capital cost of a car in the same way as most similar expenditure (in this case, plant and machinery).

The cost of capital expenditure on plant and machinery can usually be written off on a 25 per cent declining balance basis, that is, each year 25 per cent of the cost incurred that year, or carried over unrelieved from the previous year, is allowed. By contrast, the allowance for cars is subject to a cut-off at a capital cost of £12,000. In other words, the maximum annual capital allowances is £3,000 however much the car costs. The limit is also applied to car leases, so as to prevent the limit being avoided by alternative methods of instalment purchase or rental. Although in theory the full cost of the car will be allowed in due course, the net effect is to make the purchase of a car more expensive than the purchase of a similar quantity of other machinery at the same time in post-tax terms.

Taxing sale proceeds and disposals

The final possible application of direct tax to cars is on any profit generated on the proceeds of sale. Realistically, given the rapid rate at which cars deteriorate, such gains rarely surface except on such cars as vintage cars and the most expensive cars (where large profits have been made). The capital gains tax rule (for individuals and companies) is that the proceeds of sale of a car are exempt from the tax charge. Consequently the profits on vintage cars are not taxable, but equally the losses on, say, stolen cars or cars involved in traffic accidents are not allowable. This rule contributes to administrative simplicity of the tax.

After a car has been scrapped, it continues to be a hazard to the environment. In particular, disposing of old tyres and batteries is necessary to stop undue pollution. The cost of disposal of both these elements of cars was highlighted in 1990 in the government's White Paper. It was indicated that (as in other countries) the answer should be on the polluter pays principle. The user of the tyre or battery should pay extra, through a tax if necessary, to ensure disposal. Since then arrangements already noted in this chapter have operated to achieve the intended result without resort to a tax imposed by law.

UK TAXES ON CARS AND THEIR RUNNING COSTS

Cars are made **more** expensive by:

- Car tax at 5 per cent,
- VAT on the car price,
- Vehicle excise duty,
- Excise duty on petrol,
- Absence of any relief on capital losses on disposals.

Cars are made **less** expensive by:

- Absence of road use taxes or tolls,
- Absence on charges on any gains made on sales,
- Absence of driver registration taxes.

Company cars are made **more** expensive by:

- Preventing deduction of the VAT on the car,
- Limitation on capital allowances for capital cost,
- Social security class 1A levy on employer.

Company cars are made **less** expensive by:

- Discounts on income tax charge on employees as against true costs saved.

Taxing the driver

The final element in the story is whether or not drivers should be taxed. Although they need licences, we have already seen that this opportunity to tax is not used. Drivers are, however, effectively subject to a different form of compulsory payment to avoid another kind of environmental hazard – the traffic accident. The compulsory insurance of all drivers, backed by the criminal law, ensures that drivers are, or should be, taxed against third party risks. Is the compulsory insurance premium a tax? Many people would not think so because rates are competitive and subject to no set maximum or minimum. It fails the 'tax' test technically because payments to the insurance companies are not payments to government. But what if we introduce a state-controlled insurance system? Where is the line drawn? Does it matter, if our principle is that the polluter (or person who presents the risk which may cause the injury) pays and is compelled to pay? It might finally be noted that the insurance premiums are not themselves subject to further tax, as they are not liable to VAT. Nor is there any tax on the receipt by a private individual of insurance money for a car.

Conclusion

The box above summarises the complexity of the picture we have seen. Cars can be targeted for taxes simply because they exist, or because they are kept available for use on a public road, or because they are used on a public road (or at all), or because the driver is able to use them on a public road. They can be relieved of tax by not targeting any of those aspects of the car/driver relationship.

As the consensus slowly grows that cars are to be discouraged, not encouraged, so we shall see the targets shifting. Insofar as the main complaint is pollution caused by car exhaust, this is being addressed through taxes already. Insofar as it is caused by the problem of over-crowding on our roads, the use of taxation becomes more appropriate, as well as the removal of any hidden subsidy of the car owner or user. Insofar as our worry about the non-responsible use of non-renewable resources (oil), the taxes on that product will be felt to be appropriate. Interaction suggests that higher fuel costs are on the way as well as a removal of the tax subsidy hidden in the company car. A start has been made to both processes. Is that a proper use of tax? Are there other ways in which we should be attempting to achieve these aims, or should we not be attempting them at all?

— FURTHER READING —

The study of taxation can be approached from many angles. This introduction has tried to give something on several aspects: a general description; compliance and planning by taxpayers and their advisers; the economics of public finances; the use of taxes for social engineering; the underlying philosophical questions of fairness; the political importance of taxation; the relationships between the taxpayer and the state; relationships between member states of the European Community; history. Each aspect has a literature of its own. This note is designed for the reader who wants to take matters further.

The law

Updated and annotated texts of the laws are published annually in *Butterworths Yellow Tax Handbook* (income, corporation and capital gains taxes) and *Orange Tax Handbook* (inheritance tax, NI contributions, stamp duties and VAT), and *CCH British Tax Legislation*.

Commentary on individual provisions is provided in annual *Moores Rowlands Orange and Yellow Tax Guides*. General accounts of the law are contained in the annual *Butterworths UK Tax Guide* and *CCH British Tax Guide*. These are all aimed at practitioners.

General practice introductions to UK tax law include the annual *Daily Mail Tax Guide* and *Which?* guide to income tax (aimed at helping you fill in your annual returns and claim your allowances), and the *Allied Dunbar Tax Guide* (a more detailed summary of all relevant UK taxes). The Allied Dunbar series contains several other guides including my introductory *Tax for the Self-Employed* (published by Longmans). A companion volume to this in the Teach Yourself series, *VAT: A Practical Handbook*, by David Lee is a sound introduction to VAT, and this book avoids duplicating the detail in that text.

The Inland Revenue and Customs and Excise both also publish free guides to their taxes. Leaflets about the direct taxes are available through local offices of Inspectors of Taxes. They produce a separate leaflet listing all the other leaflets, and this is worth obtaining, as are many of the leaflets. A particularly good one is the guide to capital gains tax. H. M. Customs produce a major series of Notices and guides to VAT. The key is *VAT Notice 700, The VAT Guide*, which can be obtained from any local VAT Office.

The Benefits Agency produces a detailed free guide to NI contributions for employers, leaflet NI 269, plus many other leaflets on other aspects of the scheme. The Benefits Agency produces similar leaflets on social security benefits. All are available through local social security offices, and some through Post Offices.

Major accounting and law firms also produce their own guides to areas of taxation for clients, and sometimes the general public, again as useful introductions pointing out the difficult areas.

Additional notes on specific topics:
The poll tax disaster

The definitions of tax is based on that used by the OECD (Organisation for Economic Cooperation and Development, Paris) in its annual volume *Revenue Statistics* which is also the source of many of the statistics used in this book. For other general comparisons and approaches see the annual *World Development Report* of the World Bank. These bodies, together with the International Monetary Fund, are responsible for international comments and comparisons on tax matters.

The law imposing the poll tax in England and Wales is found in the Local Government Finance Act 1989. The rates were imposed by the General Rate Act 1967, which was repealed in part by the 1989 Act.

The council tax was introduced by the Local Government Finance Act 1992. General summaries of these taxes are produced by district councils, which are responsible for their administration. The account of the problems of the poll tax is based on contemporary press reporting and comments.

Good and bad taxes

The passage quoted in Chapter 2 comes from Adam Smith, *The Wealth of Nations*, Chapter V. For a detailed recent analysis of 'good' taxes in the United Kingdom, see the Meade Committee Report 1977 (Allen and Unwin). Two members of that committee summarised their views on its main arguments in *The British Tax System* (OUP). The work has also been continued through the research of the Institute for Fiscal Studies whose journal (*Fiscal Studies*) and regular publications provide analyses that are often original and always professional across the whole range of public finance. A full commentary on the economic issues is presented in James and Nobes, *The Economics of Taxation*.

Taxes and taxpayers

The account of the history of taxation included here draws heavily on an excellent general summary of fiscal history: C. Webber and A. Wildavsky, *A History of Taxation and Expenditure in the Western World* (1986), Simon and Schuster, New York. The comments on European history also rely on F. H. M. Grapperhaus, *Taxes, Liberty and Property 511–1787* (1989), Meijburg & Co, Netherlands. The events of the so-called glorious revolution are covered in more detail in my '300 Years on: Are our tax bills right yet' (1989), British Tax Review. *The British Tax Review* also contains other articles on various aspects of our fiscal history, particularly by Sabine and by Ferrier. The best history of income tax is B. E. V. Sabine, *A Short History of Income Tax*.

Taxpayers' rights in connection with the direct taxes are covered in UK law in the Taxes Management Act 1970. Rights in connection with the indirect taxes are now partly a matter of European Community Law (see Chapters 10 and 11). The Inland Revenue and Customs and Excise have both issued Taxpayers' Charters, which are available free from them, and the Contributions Agency has issued a Contributors' Charter.

In this year's budget

The new budget process from 1994 is set out in the government White Paper *Budgetary Reform* (1992) Cm. 1867. The details of each year's budget speech are published in full in Hansard (the Official Journal of the House of Commons), but this is issued, along with considerable extra detail, in a series of Press Releases by the Treasury, the Inland Revenue and Customs and Excise on Budget Day. These are normally printed in full the next day in the serious newspapers, especially the *Financial Times*. The Treasury also publishes an annual *Financial Statement and Budget Report* (known as the Red Book, and sold by HMSO) on the same day. This contains details of taxes collected and anticipated. Annual volumes are also published of *Inland Revenue Statistics*, and these list UK tax expenditures. The concept of tax expenditures was first described by Stanley Surrey in *Tax Expenditures*.

The politics of taxation is discussed in C. T. Sandford, and J. Hills, *Changing Tax*, Child Poverty Action Group, 1988.

Taxing the workers

The key provision, Schedule E of the income tax, is laid down by Income and Corporation Taxes Act 1988, and the NI contributions law by the Social Security Contributions and Benefits Act 1992. For this and the other specific topics, see the legal and practical accounts at the top of this note.

Taxing businesses

The income tax law is contained in Schedule D, Cases I and II of the 1988 Taxes Act, and the associated caselaw.

An account of taxation aimed at the business administrator is Sprackly and Pointon, *Principles of Business Taxation*, Oxford University Press. The *Allied Dunbar Tax and Business Guide* is a useful detailed description of the key issues. Particular topics are dealt with in full detail in books in the Tolley's Taxation series.

Taxation and the family
Taxing savings and wealth

The relevant law is in the Income and Corporation Taxes Act 1988, together with the Taxation of Chargeable Gains Act 1992 (capital gains tax), Inheritance Tax Act 1984 (inheritance tax), and the annual Finance Acts. Detailed guidance on many of the provisions is published by the Inland Revenue.

These are topics addressed at length in the personal finance pages of the Saturday and Sunday papers, all of which contain useful guidance. Banks, building societies, life assurance companies and others produce their own guides to the preferred kinds of saving scheme.

The government discussion papers on reforms of family taxation are:

The policy of taxing savings and wealth has been received in a series of studies by the Institute for Fiscal Studies, including *Neutrality in the Taxation of Savings* (IFS Commentary 17, 1989).

Company profits taxes

The government's own explanation for corporation tax was published as a Green paper, *Corporation Tax*, Cmnd 8456, in 1982. Detailed arguments for reform have been published by many groups, including the CBI's tax department. A recent authoritative critique of the British system is *Equity for Companies: A Corporation Tax for the 1990s* (IFS Commentary 26, 1991).

Taxing the shopping basket

This is covered in much greater detail in David Lee's *VAT: A Practical Handbook*, also published in the Teach Yourself series.

The law is contained both in the Value Added Tax Act 1983, as (heavily) amended, and in the EC VAT Directives. The texts of both UK and EC law are contained in the Butterworth's Orange Tax Guide or the CCH British Tax Legislation, vol. 2.

A duty-free Europe?

Much of the detail of this fast-moving area is drawn from press coverage and press releases. Community Law is contained in the Official Journal of the European Communities and the judgments of the Court of Justice of the European Communities, both operating under the terms of the Treaty Establishing the European Economic Community (1957), as amended, particularly by the Single European Act (1987). These are brought into British law by the European Communities Act 1972, also as amended. European Commission proposals are published in the 'Com. Doc.' series by the Commission. The EC produces a short general guide, *Tax in the Single Market*, which describes current issues. Useful critical studies have been prepared by the CBI and the IFS.

Taxes and the environment

'Green taxation' is another issue regularly discussed in the newspapers. The key economic discussion was by Professor David Pearce, who has published a number of books and papers on the issue. A series of comparative studies of the law is published as *Taxation and Environmental Protection*, ed. R. Westin, Quorum Publishing, USA, 1991.

BASIC ACCOUNTING
J. RANDALL STOTT

A complete, step-by-step course in elementary accounting, with clear and concise explanations of accounting principles and practice.

This introductory text assumes no prior knowledge of book-keeping or accounting. Clear explanations and diagrams, worked examples and summaries of key points enable the student to master the basic principles in easy stages, and then to apply them to assignment problems. Separate revision exercises are provided to test progress, and more than 150 examination-style questions are included for further practice, self-testing and revision.

The book covers the examination requirements of all first-level courses.

BOOK-KEEPING
A. G. PIPER

A straightforward introduction to the principles of book-keeping and the practical skills of recording transactions, posting the ledgers and preparing final accounts.

This book explains the purpose and use of books of original entry as the basis of the double-entry system, and describes the processes of recording purchases, sales and cash transactions. It then shows how these records are used to prepare the final accounts – the manufacturing, trading and profit and loss accounts, and the balance sheet – to provide accurate financial statements. Other topics covered include petty cash, depreciation, partnership, updated sections on relevant company law and an additional chapter on business documents. Revised and enlarged in line with RSA and LCCI examination requirements, this edition provides worked examples throughout, together with a wide range of carefully graded questions and examination papers with sample answers.

SETTING UP A BUSINESS
VERA HUGHES AND DAVID WELLER

This book is an invaluable guide to setting up and running your own business. It helps you identify your product or service, consider the marketing and financing required, and suggests where to go for further advice.

Starting your own business can be a daunting prospect. In addition to helping with the everyday aspects of running a small business, the authors give guidance on specialised areas such as legal requirements, time management, opening a shop, starting an office-based business, staff selection and basic import/export terms. There is also a section on the particular problems faced by women in business. 'Key facts' boxes in each chapter give a checklist of important points at each stage.

The authors have been running their own business for several years, and so have an abundance of tips and useful information for the new entrepreneur.

'Brief and sensible, the advice here makes a good starting point for would-be entrepreneurs.'

Daily Telegraph

VAT: A PRACTICAL HANDBOOK
DAVID LEE

This book is for everyone who has to deal with VAT. Whether you are self-employed or involved in a small business, it shows you when to register, how to fill in your returns and what to do if, and when, the rules are broken.

Most self-employed people worry about VAT. What is it? How does it work? What happens if I get it wrong? The complex set of rules is one of the first hurdles to confront the new business. In recent years, the introduction of the Keith Penalties – interest and penalty for any mistakes – has added greatly to the confusion, particularly as simple errors can now be very costly.

The author explains how to get it right in clear, straightforward language. For those who may have got it wrong already, the procedures for minimising the damage are covered with a realistic look at penalties and the right of appeal. Finally, a section on problem areas and a glossary help the reader to unravel the jargon and make a success of this complicated tax.

OTHER TITLES AVAILABLE
IN TEACH YOURSELF

All these books are available at your local bookshop or newsagent, or can be ordered direct from the publisher. Just tick the titles you want and fill in the form below.

Prices and availability subject to change without notice.

HODDER AND STOUGHTON PAPERBACKS, P.O. Box 11, Falmouth, Cornwall.

Please send cheque or postal order for the value of the book, and add the following for postage and packing:

UK including BFPO – £1.00 for one book, plus 50p for the second book, and 30p for each additional book ordered up to a £3.00 maximum.

OVERSEAS, INCLUDING EIRE – £2.00 for the first book, plus £1.00 for the second book, and 50p for each additional book ordered.

OR Please debit this amount from my Access/Visa Card (delete as appropriate).

CARD NUMBER ☐☐☐☐☐☐☐☐☐☐☐☐☐☐☐☐

AMOUNT £ . . . .

EXPIRY DATE . . . .

SIGNED . . . .

NAME . . . .

ADDRESS . . . .

. . . .